THE UNITED NATIONS
AND U.S. FOREIGN POLICY

Revised Edition

A study from the
Center for International Studies
Massachusetts Institute of Technology

The United Nations and U.S. Foreign Policy

A New Look at the National Interest

REVISED EDITION

LINCOLN P. BLOOMFIELD

Little, Brown and Company
Boston

LIBRARY OF CONGRESS CATALOG CARD NO. 67-18883

FIRST PRINTING

Published simultaneously in Canada by Little, Brown and Company (Canada) Limited

PRINTED IN THE UNITED STATES OF AMERICA

For: Pamela
Lincoln, Jr.
Diana

who will inherit
the world we make.

Preface to the Revised Edition

Plus ça change plus c'est la même chose is not a bad motto for history, and U.S. participation in the United Nations is no exception. The fundamental problem of how to think about global diplomatic organization has changed little since 1960, and theory formulated then about how the United Nations relates to national interests can stand unamended now.

I would thus not change in any significant way the philosophy underlying this book, as it was first written. Nations still act out of a sense of where their interests lie. The highest task of statecraft is still to interpret those interests in ways that will benefit not only one's immediate clientele but the cause of world peace and welfare as well.

But the world has not stood still since 1960. On every global front, from Southeast Asia to the Caribbean, from strategic deterrence to peacekeeping, from foreign aid to population explosions, the picture has shifted in ways that call, at a minimum, for a reappraisal of United States policies. Actors have come and gone, power has shifted to new hands, coalitions have been formed and reformed. In short, the details of international life have, even in a few years, undergone alteration in virtually all phases.

The uses to which this book has been put, both inside and outside the Government, have suggested that there might be value in the continued attempt to spell out the interconnections between U.S. national purposes and U.N. capabilities. In the process of revision, virtually every sentence has been rewritten. Much that had become dated has been deleted. A significant portion of this revised edition consists of material written since 1960.

Again, as before, I am indebted to Richard W. Hatch for his unparalleled editorial skill. As I did not do before, I now record my continued high regard for Donald R. Hammonds of Little, Brown, who gambled on the first edition and prompted the second. But a very special debt is owed to Irirangi Coates Bloomfield, who by refurbishing her earlier professional talents became in this period my closest collaborator on all my efforts in this field. Only her modesty prevents me from adding her name to the title page of the present book.

The author is grateful to a number of publishers for permission to adapt for present purposes the following articles: "The U.N. and National Security" and "Peacekeeping and Peacemaking," both of which appeared in *Foreign Affairs* (in July 1958 and July 1966, respectively) and both copyrighted by the Council on Foreign Relations; "American Worldviews and the United Nations" from *World Politics* of January 1966; "Outer Space and International Cooperation" from *International Organization*, Summer 1965; "The United Nations in Crisis" from *Daedalus*, Fall 1962, published by the American Academy of Arts and Sciences; "The U.N. at Twenty and After," *Headline Series* No. 173, 1965, published by the Foreign Policy Association; and "The New Diplomacy in the United Nations" from *The United States and The United Nations*, edited by Wilcox and Haviland and published by The Johns Hopkins Press in 1961.

LINCOLN P. BLOOMFIELD

Cohasset, Massachusetts
February, 1967

Preface to the First Edition

The postwar years effectively dissipated many of the extravagant and utopian ideas which the American people and some of their leaders earlier entertained about the United Nations. But the process of disillusionment, as so often happens, left a void. So long as the earlier notions were not replaced with more serviceable attitudes, the American view of the United Nations in the succeeding years has tended to become increasingly mechanical. We have gone through the motions of pledging support, making speeches, and voting on resolutions. At crucial moments – Korea, Suez, the Congo – the United Nations suddenly seemed to dominate American policy making. The remainder of the time it existed in a backwater of policy. But in neither case did American performance reflect an entirely rational view of the place of international political organization in world affairs. The reason for this, I believe, is that we have not as a matter of national concern comprehensively reappraised the United States national interest in the United Nations, nor have we figured the real cost of sustaining that interest. In a period when the Soviet Union has begun to grasp eagerly at the opportunities offered by the United Nations' world-wide forum, the United States has devoted little or no official attention to reviewing systematically the connections that exist – or should exist – between the United Nations and other, better understood sources of national strategy.

The relative isolation of the U.N. sector of American foreign policy is, however, intelligible only as part of a far greater problem. I refer to the difficulty the United States has in identifying its general political goals and objectives, and acting upon them. The relationship between the two problems was brought home to me strikingly from a position of modest official responsibility for policy planning in regard to American U.N. participation during eleven years of postwar service in the State Department. It became increasingly clear that until the United States acquired a better over-all strategic doctrine in the political realm, until its broad and sometimes vague goals were made more explicit and backed by a more purposeful program of action, this country could not have the assurance that it was employing such instruments of diplomatic and political action as the United Nations with maximum effectiveness to achieve desirable ends. In the absence of a more meaningful over-all program of national strategy, the United Nations – both as a symbol and as a place of business – has appeared to many Americans a baffling mixture of ward politics and high morality – stepchild of foreign policy one day and prodigal son the next.

The conviction grew upon me that there was only one logical way in which to examine afresh the strategic uses of the United Nations for American policy over the next decade. That was to spell out systematically the foreign policy objectives of the United States, across the board, and to relate them to the capabilities and limitations of the United Nations as best those could be estimated from the available evidence.

The Center for International Studies at the Massachusetts Institute of Technology offered an opportunity for just such an assessment at a crucial juncture in the history of the United Nations. It had just been sorely tested by the Suez and Hungarian crises of 1956. And within the U.S. national security community the ordeal of planning and policy-making in the late fall of that year revealed once again the lack of adequate bridges between multilateral diplomacy and the other vital elements of strategic planning and action.

The Center's United Nations project made it possible to commission a number of inquiries in this general field of study. As director of the project, I sought to answer the question: What is the American national interest with respect to the United Nations as we go into the 1960's? This book thus concentrates on the larger political aspects of U.N. policy rather than on its technical or administrative aspects. Its focus is on strategic issues of policy rather than on the tactics of face-to-face, day-to-day diplomacy. (The organization of American participation is discussed in the Appendix.) Its underlying thesis is that a better understanding of the general strategic connection between U.S. policy imperatives and U.N. potentialities – and limitations – is the indispensable basis for reconsidering what relevant uses this important world instrumentality may have for American and free world interests in the period ahead.

My gratitude must be first of all to the Center, and above all to its inspiring Director, Max F. Millikan, for affording me the opportunity to apply scholarship to experience in a uniquely satisfying environment. Max Millikan, Norman J. Padelford, and Walt W. Rostow offered invaluable substantive advice and encouragement in the present enterprise, while Donald L. M. Blackmer and Arthur L. Singer, Jr. smoothed the administrative ways throughout. Elizabeth Park Hoban and Joan Narcus shared patiently and loyally the burden of seeing both the author and his work through the always painful stages of production.

I join a goodly company in reserving a very special acknowledgment for the Center's Editor-in-Chief, Richard W. Hatch. His talents can, I believe, be fully appreciated only by those who have enjoyed his friendly editorial whiplash and seen him evoke form and clarity out of the most disorderly raw materials. My own debt to him is literally unpayable.

L. P. B.

Cambridge, Massachusetts
September, 1960

Table of Contents

II *The United Nations and National Security*

III *The United Nations and the Superpowers*

PART I The United Nations and the National Interest

CHAPTER ONE

The Place of the United Nations in National Strategy

CHAPTER TWO

The Basis for Planning

CHAPTER THREE

Strategic Doctrine and National Interest — A Guide for Planning

CHAPTER ONE

The Place of the United Nations in National Strategy

The United States has been a member of the United Nations since its founding in 1945. During that time the leaders of both political parties in this country have proclaimed American fidelity to the purposes and principles of the U.N. Charter. The Congress of the United States has consistently appropriated funds for U.S. participation in the United Nations, which have averaged about one-third of the world organization's total budget. It has affirmed through other legislation the nation's basic decision to play a leading role in the organization. American public opinion, however fickle through alternating national crises of overconfidence and disillusionment, registers general approbation of the United Nations and faith in its prospects. Citizens' organizations throughout the country publicize the United Nations and its family of specialized agencies on a scale unparalleled elsewhere. There can be no question that of all the great powers the United States has been the prime supporter of the United Nations from its founding to the present.

Americans have sensed – rightly, in the author's opinion – that an important mutuality of interests exists between the United States and the United Nations. They are aware that the U.N. Charter spells out what are, in effect, American aspirations about relationships among nations. They have generally felt that the prospects of the Western world and of mankind itself are tied in vital ways to the prospects for world organization.[1] This has been true despite exaggerated and unrealistic statements about the United Nations from American leadership of both parties. More surprisingly, it has persisted in the face of the harsh realities that have forced a reappraisal of the impact of the United Nations on American interests.

The process of reappraisal began as early as 1945, when the first frigid winds from Moscow, conveying resumed Soviet hostility, hit the United Nations. With the conflict over Soviet troops in Iran, the Communist-sponsored Greek civil war, the Berlin blockade of 1948, the Czech coup and, finally, the overt use of force by a Communist puppet state in North Korea, it became evident that the shape of the postwar world organization, at least in its political and security aspects, was not being determined by a blueprint that had, in the short run, clearly been overoptimistic. While it is true that the planners of the Charter expected conflict to take place, it is also true that they assumed such conflict would take conventional and recognizable forms and could then be suppressed by a concert of the great powers acting in unison to preserve the peace — a pair of related assumptions that proved false. Reality for the United Nations was given its shape by national and ideological forces in conflict and armed with increasingly destructive weapons; by processes of technological revolution; by change and growth in the underdeveloped countries that was at times convulsive; and by old-fashioned nationalism — all these coexisting with the optimistic aspirations and ideals about the future of world order.

The seedling that was the United Nations in 1945 was, in the process of becoming full-formed, bent and shaken to the point of deformity by the gales of cold war. It was profoundly shaped by

[1] Illustrating early postwar expectations, according to a *Newsweek* poll in October 1946, 52 percent favored scrapping national armed forces, 54 percent believed the United Nations could easily be made into a world government, and 63 percent wanted the U.N. to create immediately a representative world congress empowered to "solve all international problems." At the beginning of 1966 7 out of 10 Americans polled still believed that the United States should cooperate fully with the United Nations. See Alfred O. Hero, "The American Public and the U.N.," *Journal of Conflict Resolution,* Dec., 1966.

explosive forces generated by the breakup of the old colonial empires put together by white Europeans over the last four centuries. And its development was increasingly influenced by the states that were heirs to that process — the nonwhite, non-European, and passionately anticolonial "emerging countries," driven by resentment of past injustices and aspiring to all the benefits of affluence and influence so long the monopoly of the white man.

In January 1961, in the pervasive spirit of ebullience and optimism of the incoming Kennedy Administration, the American approach to the United Nations shared in the general hopefulness that new and more satisfactory bilateral relationships could be developed by a judicious application of both power and diplomacy. The omens were good for important changes. The Secretary of State was a former head of the U.N. affairs office in the State Department. The U.S. Representative to the United Nations, as a former candidate for the presidency, was in at least as good a position as his predecessor to link Washington and New York at a high and serious level of policy-making. Perhaps most importantly at the tactical level, Adlai Stevenson reestablished a rapport in New York with representatives of the new nations, generating new hope for a reversal of the growing resentment of the United States on the part of this proliferating politically neutralist majority.

But there were shadings in this picture. The possibility of moving toward far-reaching understandings with the Soviets based on their more realistic reappraisal of the objective situation met chilling and persistent setbacks, commencing with the Vienna Summit of June 1961. The Berlin Wall and its accompanying crisis followed in the summer of 1961. The Soviet risk taking in the Cuban missile crisis of the fall of 1962 shook the world. And in the United Nations the Soviets reacted savagely to the evidence that their beachhead in Central Africa was being spoiled by the evenhandedness of the United Nations' Congo operation.

The potential of the United Nations, in terms of what it could do in the next crisis, was being sharply limited by the insistence of the Russians — their worst fears having been confirmed by the Congo operation — on a narrow construction of the organization's peacekeeping powers. This clash of purposes brought the United Nations to its most severe internal crisis in twenty years of existence, culminating in 1964–1965 with a 19th General Assembly that could not act and a budget in near-bankruptcy. The crisis was tragically punctuated by the death of the American representative who had done so much to give larger acceptability to the stern and energetic measures Washington felt forced to take in Cuba in 1962, in Stanleyville in 1964, in the Dominican Republic in 1965, and in Vietnam throughout.

The crisis over financing was made worse by other unfavorable factors. The intransigence of de Gaulle's France toward *any* form of international organization and the radicalism of some Africans and Asians were symptoms of a more general defection from certain American positions. The defecting nations added up to a majority that, in the end, could not be counted on to enforce the Charter against the dozen-odd countries refusing to pay their assessed share of peacekeeping operations in Gaza or the Congo.

The central factor throughout the constitutional-financial crisis was the Moscow-Washington relationship, which acted as both cause and moderating factor. There had been limited arms-control agreements in 1963–1964, and Khrushchev's successors appeared constrained by the same forces that had moved him toward a degree of détente with the West.[2] Even in the financial crisis, with the United States blinking this time as the two superpowers tried to stare each other down, the Soviets showed a notable indisposition to wreck the organization.

The United States for its part was unwilling to sacrifice the machinery of international cooperation for a principle that could not be enforced by a voluntary association of sovereign states. Nor was it certain that the United States was itself willing to abide by all the implications of a taxing power in the hands of an organization whose majority will, while still consistent with deeper American interests, could, at least theoretically, act in defiance of those interests.

The firm United States stand thus eventually dissolved in the acids of uncertain moral grounds, premature assumptions about international sovereignty, a Soviet Union that played the game of

[2] See Lincoln P. Bloomfield, Walter Clemens, Jr., and Franklyn Griffiths, *Khrushchev and the Arms Race: Soviet Interests in Arms Control and Disarmament, 1954–1964* (Cambridge: M.I.T. Press, 1966).

chicken unblinkingly, and a host of unconvinced fellow members of the United Nations who, whether through conviction, fear, cowardice, or realism, preferred not to see the organization fractured on the rock of an abstract principle. Ambassador Arthur J. Goldberg's formal act of surrender on the principle of collective financial responsibility (Article 19) on behalf of the United States, in August of 1965, merely confirmed an intractable fact of international political life.

There were other evidences of evolution in Soviet attitudes, all within the larger framework of "struggle." During the mid-1960s Moscow took some surprisingly judicious positions on the need for the pacific settlement of international disputes. The Soviets abandoned their classic precondition of Chinese Communist seating in the Security Council and, instead, became the first to ratify the U.N. Charter amendments increasing the size of the Security and Economic and Social Councils. In the space negotiations they dropped their hampering criticisms of United States reconnaissance satellites and of the private nature of the U.S. Communication Satellite Corporation, and they made it possible to agree to a treaty in 1966 on such functional questions as the nationality, legal ownership, liability, and return of spaceships and their crews, as well as the limitation of arms in space.

If one had to sum up the U.S. and Soviet relationship to the United Nations in the first two-thirds of the 1960s, three things could be said. Perhaps more than at any time since 1945, U.S. policy was seeking to be rational and realistic about the uses of the organization in furthering American and common interests. Second, the general environment in which U.S.–U.N. policy operated, which was created by the emerging trends of Soviet policy, was in many ways more promising than before. But third, that same Soviet policy was unbendingly hostile to the aspirations of the liberal West toward genuinely supranational organization. Moreover, it was capable of occasional peace-shattering gambits such as Cuba in 1962 – and who knew what other subterfuges, secretly planned assaults, and other maneuvers so logical to the operational code of communism. Rather like a bather who prematurely moves his beach gear closer to the water's edge because he is convinced the tide is going out, the United States in these years all too frequently found itself drenched as the waves returned, temporarily obscuring — if never quite washing away — the deep-seated belief that a larger, more favorable trend was still at work.

In the face of all this, American policy-makers continued to seek to live with both realities: the longer-term tidal movement of Russian communism, perhaps toward something approaching alliance in the distant future (or at least a workable understanding that Chinese and other grossly destabilizing movements must in the common interest be checked); and a solid sophistication about the shorter-term tactics of the Kremlin strategists. In official utterances American doctrine combined in about the same proportions as before the national ideology of problem-solving through world order and unblinking recognition of the battle between competing systems. In action it took its cue largely from the unpredictably shifting scenery of the times to try constantly to move onto new operational ground.

At certain critical junctures — such as Korea in 1950, Suez in 1956, and the Congo in 1960 — the United Nations suddenly and for a brief time acquired overwhelming importance in the minds of those at the highest levels. Even while believing that the basic policies followed in these instances were the correct ones, one can ponder the fact that three American Presidents at times in those crises acted as though the United Nations were somehow a substitute for responsible national decision-making and for the American diplomacy and power without which the United Nations is an empty abstraction.

When the United Nations failed to act to counter the Soviet tanks that smashed the Hungarian revolution in 1956, it was because no U.S. support was made available. The Cuban missile crisis of 1962 demonstrated how the many diplomatic instruments available — including the United Nations — can be orchestrated to achieve a vital purpose. But in the absence of a sound concept of the interrelationships of these instruments on the part of leadership and public alike, all these events were subject to misinterpretation, contradictory criticisms, and the drawing of erroneous conclusions for the future.

A sharp division between ideal and reality, between official platitude and official policy, has thus characterized the American relationship to the United Nations. This in turn reflects a well-recognized paradox in the historic American style — a style that favors the pragmatic and the seemingly expedient, that rejects planning from abstract or theoretical premises, but that is invariably accompanied by top-level assertions about the moral nature of international politics and the American vision of a more perfect world. It is with respect to the United Nations that this duality has reached its most extraordinary level; that the most abstract sentiments and loftiest goals have been voiced and the profoundest human aspirations evoked; and that, as a consequence, the contrast between hopes and results has been the most acute.

The downgrading of the United Nations has of course been a worldwide phenomenon. But the most dedicated — and least sophisticated — proponents of world organization and order have been found principally among Americans, and their own government has often been the target of their frustration. A common criticism of American policy has been that it "bypassed" the United Nations. Sometimes this accusation has been justified. But at other times it has been doctrinaire and unhelpful, urging multilateral action for the sake of internationalism, regardless, so it has seemed, of the merits of the particular case. And, of course, equally unbalanced have been the right-wing criticisms of the Government for "turning its policy over to the United Nations."

The key to understanding U.S. policy toward the United Nations can be found only in the violently shifting world environment in which both must function. Profound changes have taken place in the equations of world power and in the atmospherics of the international climate. It is precisely because things have not stood still there is an urgent need for reappraisals of strategies and policies which have served us reasonably well under different circumstances.

The postwar years have already given way to a different era. Not only are external power relationships altering; significant changes are also visible within both the Soviet and Western societies. Space exploration and other technological developments in what has been called the "Age of Acceleration" are outmoding recently perfected military weapons systems. We are facing certain strategic choices of policy goals and actions that are crucial in a sense that never fully applied before. The shape that has been assumed by the East-West conflict and the nationalist movements in Asia, Africa, the Middle East, and Latin America, demands new decisions, new directions of policy, and new styles of thinking and planning from the richest and still most powerful nation in the world.

In the United Nations itself problems of staggering proportions must be faced. For the United States the crucial questions must be reexamined: the premises of democratic diplomacy and majoritarianism; the role of the great powers; the uses of the U.N. Assembly and Security Council; proposals regarding weighted voting and the composition of U.N. organs; future capacities for peacekeeping and for financing it; Charter revision and Chinese representation; bilateral versus multilateral aid; the liquidation of the remaining Portuguese colonies in Africa; and the growing determination of the Afro-Asian bloc in the United Nations to bring about the downfall of South Africa unless it abandons its policies of *apartheid*.

These momentous issues can be approached satisfactorily only in a much wider context of the U.S. national interest and national strategy.

The role of the United Nations in peacekeeping is valid only when it is formulated in accordance with existing realities: the setting of great-power military systems, the dangers of escalation, and the United States' concern with regional institutional growth. The desirability of channeling development assistance through United Nations agencies can be gauged only in the light of overall U.S. economic and political purposes measured against the capabilities and limitations of the organization.

American votes on racial issues become rational only when seen as one manifestation of the complex pressures and aims governing United States policy in Africa, toward China, in Western Europe — and at home. Defusing the monumental time bomb in southern Africa, if it can be done at all, must be handled in the context of trade relationships and the achievement of goals of stability and of welfare, and not only by condemnatory resolutions. No less true, the history of the postwar years has amply demonstrated that strategic decision-making at the highest level must take consistent account of interests represented in the worldwide forums of diplomacy and negotiation if the United States is truly to thrive in a complex and pluralistic world.

CHAPTER TWO

The Basis for Planning

THE OBSTACLES TO PLANNING

The difficulties in formulating national strategy with respect to the United Nations are striking.

One major difficulty arises from the image held by some Americans of the United Nations as an interesting and hopeful experiment that exists apart from the mainstream of strategy and diplomacy. This image is an unhelpful one, for it leads to two common errors. One is the neglect of useful possibilities for action; the other is the occasional departure from the strategic moorings that anchor policy makers in other areas.

Another major difficulty in focusing on the United Nations as an instrument of U.S. policy arises not so much from conflicting ideas and ideals in the minds of men as from trends in the changing international scene, faithfully reflected and sometimes magnified within the United Nations. In the early days of the cold war it was not uncommon for the vote in the U.N. General Assembly to be 55 to 5 on a whole range of issues. The lines were sharply drawn; the balance of power was so rigid and bipolar in structure that little flexibility for maneuver was left within the United Nations (or, for that matter, outside). In such a setting the presence of Soviets and Americans under one roof posed a novel problem for Western diplomacy. At a time when we were struggling to organize a worldwide defensive coalition against the Communist threat we had to meet and negotiate with our allies in the presence of the enemy. Each issue and each vote thus came to represent a separate test of free-world unity, and often it was more important in this sense than because of the actual question involved. As time went on, the unity of the non-Communist states was put under increasing strain by the growing split between the poles of what might be called North and South, primarily on issues arising in the colonial field. But the overall alliance held together, albeit with difficulty.

After Stalin's death in 1953, the tone and mode of Soviet diplomacy both in and out of the United Nations began to alter. The political effect of the change was acute, coming at a time when the bipolar political world was itself beginning to splinter. With the development of something like a military standoff between the United States and the Soviet Union, forces within the two coalitions began to assert their freedom of maneuver and to move toward positions relatively independent of the two leader states. Britain, France, India, Yugoslavia, Poland, Egypt, Japan, China, and Germany began to emerge as actual or potential foci of new independent action and even of leadership. "Automatic majorities" and "automatic leadership" in the United Nations, if they had ever really existed, became things of the past. The world was changing, and the United Nations was changing with it.

With the growing strength of the uncommitted countries, the success of the West in gathering support through the United Nations has become increasingly dependent on the stands which Western nations take on issues of primary importance to the peoples of those areas. These have not been such issues as capitalism versus communism, or German unification, or the liberation of the East European satellites; but rather such issues as colonialism, "self-determination," economic development, and racial discrimination. More than half the present membership for one reason or another see these as the crucial issues and put the United States to the test in regard to them with increasing frequency. The issue often is purely symbolic; it may reflect an accumulated heritage of resentment or be designed to play off the East against the West. But in the United Nations these issues take concrete shape in resolutions and action programs in which Soviet and American (and perhaps soon Chinese) performance is constantly made the measure for a host of other attitudes.

The way in which the United States has taken the lead in restructuring the United Nations itself has added to the American dilemma. The United States urged a greater role for the General Assembly (where all nations, whatever their size, have equal votes) in order to offset the importance of the Security Council when, in the light of the Korean experience, it appeared essential to remobilize the capacity of the United Nations for collective military action. The United Nations in June 1950 had been able to respond to the march of North Korean troops into South Korea only because the Soviet Union was boycotting the Security Council at the time. The boycott ended very soon indeed after the Security Council had authorized United Nations support for South Korea.

American action since then has discouraged military risk-taking by the Communists, and the Assembly's real role in this field is still not measurable. But the Uniting for Peace Resolution of 1950 which enables the Assembly to initiate action if the Council cannot or will not, has upgraded the importance of the Assembly. During the same period the Assembly has become a prime political forum for the nations that remain outside the East-West camps and pursue their own goals of political independence, economic improvement, and racial dignity.[1] In this situation the "North-South" conflict cuts across East-West issues and makes its own powerful demands on American diplomacy, at the same time offering frequent opportunities for the Soviets to seize the political initiative.

THE CHANGING ARITHMETIC

The United Nations started out with fifty-one members, shortly to stabilize at around sixty. One-third were Latin American allies of the United States. There were only two states from Black Africa (Ethiopia and Liberia). The dais was presided over by the elected President – as often as not a Westerner; the Secretary General –

[1] As Yugoslav President Tito put it, where colonialism and related issues were concerned the so-called third world "can be neither non-aligned nor uncommitted." Quoted in *New York Times*, May 16, 1966.

first a Norwegian and then a Swede; and his executive assistant — Andrew Cordier, an American.

In 1966 the dais was presided over by an Afghan in the president's chair, a Burmese Secretary General, and a Deputy Secretary General from India. Thirty-three independent African states south of the Sahara, combined with fifteen from Asia and another fifteen from the Middle East (including North Africa) make up over half the membership. The Western states (plus Israel and Nationalist China) now constitute less than 40 percent of the whole. Thus the Afro-Asian bloc could at least stop any other group in the Assembly from having its way, or if it voted with the Soviet bloc it could theoretically command about 61 percent of the votes — close to the two-thirds required for important questions.

Put differently, there is a theoretical possibility that states with only 5 percent of the world's resources and 11 percent of its population could, if they ever voted together, command a two-thirds majority; states paying only 2 percent of the total U.N. assessments could, in theory, make up a "blocking third" to majority action on important issues.

Unquestionably, the effects of the new arithmetic have been profoundly felt in the voting. Without attaching undue importance to numerical headcounts as such, it is obvious that they do represent tests of political strength. Resolutions condemning South Africa, Portugal, and Rhodesia in the last few years have begun to gain majorities of 80 or 90 votes, going as high as 106 to 1 on one South African vote, and 114 on South-West Africa.

Sometimes the United States has had the unfamiliar experience of being in opposition to the majority. This took place, for example, when an oil embargo on South Africa was voted on in 1963 and when the same Assembly called for a ban on nuclear weapons. In 1966 84 voted against Washington (and London) for shorter-term U.N. employment. Earlier, in the 1965 session Washington was on the losing end of resolutions refusing to accept the credentials of the South African delegation, calling for a diplomatic break with Portugal, and calling for dismantlement of military bases in colonial territories; and worse yet, the last one by a simple majority rather than the constitutional two-thirds required for important questions. As might be imagined, the United States has often been outvoted in the Special Committee on Colonialism: in the Committee's ordering an investigation of conditions in the British Crown Colony of Aden; its voting in late 1964 to accept a report on South West Africa; and again in 1965, its deciding to meet in Africa. In 1966 the U.S. position in the Committee was overridden on the questions of Basutoland, Bechuanaland, and Swaziland; of the Portuguese African territories; and of the implementation in colonial territories of the 1960 Declaration on the Granting of Independence to Colonial Countries and Peoples. Basutoland and Bechuanaland became members in 1966.

Sometimes the United States has abstained from voting. It did this in 1963 on a measure which received ninety affirmative votes calling on Britain not to transfer power to Rhodesia; on a Security Council vote along the same lines vetoed by Britain; on a committee resolution approved by ninety-six members to investigate British Oman; and on a resolution favored by ninety-six states to expand the Security Council to fifteen (which the Soviet Union voted against but which both powers have now accepted). In 1964 the United States abstained on a Council resolution deploring British air attacks on Yemen (for which the French voted). In 1966 Washington abstained on strongly-carried resolutions on economic policy and sanctions against South Africa.

Other statistics can be adduced to support a pessimistic view. To take just one, while it has frequently been pointed out, accurately enough, that the United States was on the winning side on 71 percent of the votes in the three years prior to the 1965 Assembly, the fact is that only sixteen countries were outvoted as often as the United States, and ten of them were in the Soviet bloc.

The other side of the numbers story is equally persuasive. The Afro-Asian countries seldom vote as a bloc. At the 16th, 17th, and 18th Assemblies, for instance, "the votes of nearly half of the Afro-Asians coincided as often or more often with the vote of the United States than with the vote of the Soviet Union" (and the final outcome of those votes was in fact much more favorable than that to Washington because of the votes of European and Latin American states).[2] Even with the recent increase in the size of the

[2] Testimony of Ambassador Adlai E. Stevenson before Senate Committee on Foreign Relations on United Nations Charter Amendments, April 28 and 29, 1965, Washington, D.C., p. 60.

Security Council to fifteen, according to Secretary of State Rusk,

> on some of the key issues . . . we would need only one African-Asian vote in order to make up the majority of nine . . . [and] no Asian-African vote will be needed to prevent the Council from taking action . . . if we have the West Europeans and at least one Latin American with us.[3]

There have been encouraging signs of at least some maturity on the part of certain of the newer states and of their growing divergence from the hotheads. When the Soviet Union vetoed the Security Council resolution on Malaysia in September 1964, the Ivory Coast and Morocco – its two African members – voted with the seven other non-Communist states (Czechoslovakia joined Moscow in voting in opposition). In the virulent debates in late 1964 over the Congo rescue mission at Stanleyville the Nigerian representative wisely – and courageously – criticized the radicals for "inconsistency," saying: "One of the qualities that we expect from independent states anywhere in the world is the observance of what we now know to be civilized conduct in relation to fellow human beings and various societies. And Africans are not going to be different if they are going to be members of the United Nations or of any organization worthy of the name." He pointedly warned his fellow Africans that "subversion of the Congo may ultimately mean their own subversion." In May of 1966 the African call for the use of force in Rhodesia was defeated in the Security Council.

The Communists themselves have contributed to the increased sophistication of African and Asian states. After China's attack on India in 1962 President Radhakrishnan sounded a warning when he said: "What has happened to India may happen to anyone tomorrow." The new states certainly do not accept the established order in detail; but it is true that no new state can be said to have failed to comply with a formally rendered decision of the International Court of Justice although the refusal of the Court to deal with the South-West African case on its merits in 1966 after taking testimony for four years may leave the Africans so disillusioned that they will not lightly turn to the Court again for redress. (They led the successful 1966 drive for U.N. "take-over.")

As for the Assembly votes on matters of political and security

[3] *Ibid.*, p. 19.

importance to the United States, in 1963, for example, a majority of seventy-six favored the continued financing of the Congo peace force, with only eleven Communist nations opposing it. The United States–Soviet agreement to refrain from orbiting nuclear weapons passed unanimously. The United States, as part of its policy of isolating mainland China, succeeded in blocking a Soviet move to open League of Nations treaties to non-U.N. members, 79 to 0. The Commission on Unification and Rehabilitation of Korea was continued, 65 to 11. The United States Secretary of State has said that "we have never been confronted with a situation that was vital enough to our interests to require the veto. . . ." [4] U.S. Korean policy was again supported in 1966 (63-24).

It should also be added that the United States position has itself come around in some instances. Washington voted in 1965 with the great majority to bring to an end the breakaway of Rhodesia's white minority government. It supported a World Disarmament Conference to which Communist China would be invited. And it supported sanctions against Rhodesia in 1966.

Two related points need be made about the arithmetic. The first is that on some issues, as indicated, the United States and the Soviet Union have been able to reach at least a tacit understanding. Thus, for example, the Cyprus peacekeeping operation was launched and continued without Soviet opposition even when, as in the August 1964 call for a cease-fire, Moscow abstained. Even more spectacular was the success of combined Soviet and American pressure in the United Nations in the fall of 1965 to end the renewed fighting between India and Pakistan.

The second point relates to the concern some Americans, notably Senator J. W. Fulbright and Senator Henry M. Jackson, shared a few years ago, particularly after Suez, as to the apparently corrosive effect the United Nations was having on our NATO relationships. This concern has had much justification in the past, and it is true currently that United States support of a majority highly censorious of Portuguese colonial policy has certainly not endeared Washington to Lisbon, to the possible jeopardy of the naval base in the Azores. But the fact also stands out that in the 1961–1963 Assemblies the majority of NATO countries voted with

[4] *Ibid.*, p. 41.

the United States on 37 out of 40 colonial issues and that the farther Western Europe travels from its colonial past, the freer it appears to be to act on both political and moral grounds that are shared with the United States.

But there can be no complacency about the future. Many thoughtful people in the West believe that, despite the success of the United States in having its way on most truly vital political issues, a membership approaching 130 will, by its predominantly non-Western complexion, jeopardize important Western diplomatic positions.

The failure of the United Nations to affect significantly the present degree of world stability and well-being, combined with the projected trends, has led a number of observers to the conclusion that the United Nations represents essentially an obstacle – merely embarrassing or actually menacing – to Western security. Such descriptions have been applied in recent times by some professional American diplomats and European political leaders in their private assessments of the situation. Even apart from certain overriding crises when, in a manner of speaking, all signals were off, a case could be made that the fulsome and seemingly wholehearted statements by American leaders that participation in the United Nations is in our national interest have been contradicted by the facts.

NEW DIRECTIONS FOR PLANNING

Given the deadlocks, the frustrations, and the intractable facts of life in and out of the United Nations, can anything genuinely new be added to the common estimate of its actual worth? Given all these obstacles to creative planning about the uses of the United Nations, including the obstacles found in the planning process itself, is it really worthwhile to try to spell out afresh the framework for our U.N. policy?

It is not entirely certain that we have always been asking the right questions about the United Nations. Like the issue of numerical majorities, the questions commonly asked about the potential of the United Nations imply assumptions which are not necessarily valid. Can the United Nations prevent nuclear war? Can it bring about harmony between the Communist Chinese and ourselves? Can it replace governmental action in the financing of all development programs? Or, the ultimate deception, can it replace governments themselves? The answer to all of these questions for our times is and must be "No."

But are these indeed the vital operational questions? The crucial questions about the United Nations are those which proceed from the real rather than the supposed requirements of national strategy. Military strategy has largely revised its earlier premises about the probability of all-out war as compared with limited war. Yet the traditional test for United Nations value has been either whether it can achieve a United States–Soviet military combination – absurd from any present standpoint – or whether it can by itself somehow eliminate the threat of aggressive war. Because national strategy depended for some years on the notion that war with the Soviet Union must by definition be all-out, only that which was responsive to such a contingency had military value. Today, for familiar military and technical reasons, all-out war seems less likely than other more limited forms of military engagement. The questions to pose about the United Nations' security capabilities must consequently address themselves to the organization's capacity and limitations with respect not to the least likely, but to the most likely contingencies: insurgency situations abetted by, but not necessarily caused by, the Communists; border clashes between new states with ill-defined territories; explosive vacuums left by eventual Portuguese withdrawal from Africa; neo-imperialism by new states; and – most sinister of all – internal civil wars between men of different-colored skins.

Similarly, if the question about United Nations' capabilities assumes that the only choice is between world government or no world order at all, the cards are stacked very badly indeed against constructive action. A strategic doctrine for the United Nations that so ignored realities would be no better than one that continued to underestimate its capabilities.

The temptation is always strong to wipe the slate clean and imagine into existence a different kind of world, one in which international relations would partake of the qualities making for stability and mutual confidence in domestic societies. In response to the frustrations of the world we know, many proposals have been advanced that would utterly transform the nature of the

United Nations by abandoning national sovereignty, drastically revising the Charter, and so forth. These suggestions are, at best, premature (although at the end of this book, I have offered a few far more modest proposals). At worst, they are fantasies for evading the exigent problems that confront us. Of course a global war could bring about a world government overnight. A series of trips to the brink might profoundly shake the rooted values and habit systems that place national sovereignty above virtually all else in today's world. But our experience with such trips so far (i.e., Berlin, Korea, Cuba, and Vietnam) suggest instead an astonishing tenacity of present forms. These contingencies thus cannot furnish a reliable base for planning.

What follows does not assume that nation-states as we presently know them are in their terminal state. It does, however, assume that there is a contemporary historical trend toward integration and limited forms of supranationalism, running parallel with a countertrend to ultranationalism and fragmentation of international society. This trend toward integration does not for the present era connote a tendency toward world government but rather suggests a possible historical middle way between a world unified by force — the only presently available means — and a continuation of the international anarchy of the past. The alternatives of world government or of substantially reducing the present authority of the United Nations are thus not exhaustive.

Other relevant policy questions have to do with the building of political, economic, cultural, and technical bases for new sectors of the world community and with ways of fulfilling the promise contained in existing movements for federation and integration. Here the uses of the United Nations should be tested against its capacity to open up a middle ground between true supranationalism and the sort of unfettered national sovereignty that today is pursued only by the more adolescent new states, the paranoidal extremists of left and right, and — in the late 1960s — the nostalgic de Gaulle. New and more acceptable forms of international concern for inexperienced new countries are needed to take the place of the imperial tutelage that lies in the past but without being open to the charge of "neocolonialism." We need an open mind toward possibly drastic changes in the concept of foreign aid and also toward population curves that are rising even faster than living standards. In posing questions about any of these situations, we require to know if action programs are possible – now, not in some unspecified utopia – that neither depend upon assent by the Communists nor close the door to their eventual participation.

The question remains whether any given step toward the solution of these problems can better be taken inside or outside the United Nations. Put another way, how can the United States make the most effective use of the United Nations in achieving its paramount objectives in the years immediately ahead?

The working assumption is that there will be no all-out global, thermonuclear war in the period ahead. But the collateral assumption is that nonetheless we are not at peace but in a conflict whose stakes are the attitudes of mankind and the design of the political world. We would do well, in reformulating our national strategic doctrine with respect to the United Nations, to obey the advice Demosthenes gave to the Athenians in 351 B.C.: "In war one must not allow oneself to be at the command of events. One must forestall them."

CHAPTER THREE

Strategic Doctrine and National Interest — A Guide for Planning

Given a rational basis for planning national strategy with respect to the United Nations, we must be guided in the planning itself by a realistic evaluation of the uses of the United Nations over the next few years from the standpoint of American national interests. In other words, the potentialities and limitations of the United Nations must be intimately connected to the national goals, objectives, and strategies that, independent of the ideals of the U.N. Charter and the aspirations of the individual citizen, provide the real substance of U.S. foreign policy.

The ensemble of goals and resources, of purpose and power, can be summed up in the phrase "strategic doctrine."

> Strategic doctrine translates power into policy. Whether the goals of a state are offensive or defensive, whether it seeks to achieve or prevent a change, its strategic doctrine must be able to define what objectives are worth contending for and to develop the appropriate force for achieving them. By establishing a pattern *in advance* of crisis situations, strategic doctrine permits a Power to act purposefully in the face of challenges. In its absence a Power will constantly be surprised by events. An adequate

strategic doctrine is therefore the basic requirement of American security.[1]

To develop a comparable doctrine that focuses on the possible uses of the United Nations, a more modest analytical effort is called for. It is an effort, nonetheless, that borrows from the larger picture some of its coordinates and that seeks to place the United Nations in the perspective of the broad national enterprise. For either task – grand or, in this case, specialized – the starting point must be located in relation to the determinative forces in the political world.

THE HISTORICAL SETTING

The contemporary international scene is dominated by three major forces that have the capacity to reshape the world. One is the force of the several Communist movements which, though fragmented, dispose of the power of one-third of the globe. The second is the force of nationalism powering the dynamic political and economic movements in Asia, Africa, the Middle East, and Latin America. The third is the force of Western civilization centered in Western Europe and North America and in outposts such as Australasia.

Remarkable changes have taken place in world communism as the Sino-Soviet split has grown during the 1960s. Although events could bring together again these two giants of communism, their differences in relative development seem to dominate their external policies. In its mediation between India and Pakistan at Tashkent in the fall of 1965, as well as in its policy of relative restraint in Vietnam, Moscow has shown a growing concern about violence that could involve the increasingly bourgeois Soviet Union. Peking, while cautious in becoming physically committed to violence, preaches an uncompromisingly hostile, interventionist line. Both compete for influence among Communist parties and radical nationalist movements the world over. And both retain in varying degrees some special benefits derived from the discipline of organization, doctrine, and fanatical belief.

It is thus not necessarily overrating the future of either wing of

[1] Henry A. Kissinger, "Strategy and Organization," *35 Foreign Affairs* (1957), p. 380.

the Communist movement to acknowledge its skill and the inner power conferred by such a revolutionary and imperialistic frame of mind. John Stuart Mill perceived the enormous advantage of ideology over non-ideology when he said, "One person with a belief is a social power equal to ninety-nine who have only interests." A contemporary writer elaborated this theme:

> All too naturally, by identifying himself with the *antithesis* of the Dialectic, that is, by professing a religious faith, the Marxist put himself into the state of mind of a man going upstairs on an escalator.[2]

Even while the Soviets wrestle with deep inner conflicts between doctrine and consumer demands and the Chinese encounter failures in external adventures, they keep two particular advantages. One is an unparalleled organizing capacity through which small and dedicated forces can apply immense leverage, by a sort of political judo, to overcome large, disorganized, and relatively inert masses of superior weight. The other advantage is the planning faculty summed up by Nathan Leites:

> The superior ability of the Party in diagnosis and prognosis is a major factor making for its victory. All appraisals must in principle be made on a world scale and with a long perspective. All details of the Party's policy must be part of an over-all plan. The Party must not permit itself to be dominated by the appearances of the moment, but rather derive all actions from a long-range plan based on long-run forecasts.[3]

To be sure, our own pragmatic approach to politics has given us a resiliency which the Communist approach lacks, and in the long run the dogmatism of communism will surely be among the internal contradictions causing its own downfall. But for the period ahead the United States and the West as a whole are still disadvantaged both by their failure to look sufficiently ahead and by their preference for improvised and essentially defensive reactions to crises that have mounted to the point where they cannot be ignored. The more our society is believed to be incapable of developing dynamic political, economic, and social doctrines over

[2] Edmund Wilson, *To the Finland Station* (New York: Harcourt, Brace, 1956), p. 196.

[3] Nathan Leites. *A Study of Bolshevism* (Glencoe: Free Press, 1953), p. 185.

a protracted period, the greater the success that can attend Communist strategy and the greater its opportunity to carry off its pose of the future incarnate.

The second prime contemporary force – nationalism in the world of nonwhite, economically underdeveloped, anticolonial, and politically neutralist countries and territories – also has a strategic doctrine, although a far less monolithic and coherent one than that of the Communists. The astounding strength of the newly energized nationalist movement does not arise from the clarity of its detailed program or from the possession of conventional attributes of national power. But the purposes of the nationalist movement are sufficiently explicit and potent in their appeal to have placed the Western powers on the defensive; and the Western powers have yielded up one territorial, economic, or political position after another while remaining unable to substitute another image of themselves for the already obsolete "neo-colonialist-imperialist-racist" image that continues to serve the revolutionaries as a target.

The third force – that represented by Western civilization – still counts for much in the balance scale of world power and influence. In comparison with the explosive growth of the other two it seemed for a while to have become a latent rather than a dynamic force. Historically, the society which represents social and property values subject to massive assault by new revolutionary forces labors under a handicap. Its paramount ideology is by definition a conservative one, representing an established position to be defended, a fixed terrain to be held. In the present age the Western world has been in such a position.

In recent years vigorous economic growth, technological and military expansion, and inventive techniques for social change have reversed the trend in the West's favor. In the all-important realm of ideology, secular Western ideas of freedom, human dignity, and high living standards have retained their intrinsic value and have indeed been borrowed at will by other movements. But the West in recent times has not always been able to derive satisfactory political profit as the evangelical force behind these ideas. They have become common property; their source of inspiration is virtually no more than a historical footnote. Where the West aids others in achieving these goals it is often regarded as recompense for past wrongs. Thus Western Europe has not fully developed a doctrine to take the place of three centuries of empire, or even to account to itself for the harassed and often ignominious way in which European colonialism has all but ended. Caught between outgoing Continental power and incoming hostility from the world to the South as well as from that to the East, Europe has appeared suspended between two ages. Meanwhile, basic American strategy, whether expressed in political, economic, or military terms, has been reactive in nature and vulnerable to transient domestic and international pressures. As a result, short-term goals have tended to dictate American policy, while long-term goals have remained unrealistic or unformulated. The war in Vietnam was taken up because of a generally correct appraisal of the long-term consequences of permitting a Communist take-over attempt through terrorism. But the successive events that led to growing American involvement all illustrate the capacity of unplanned tactical moves to form a chain of policy with a life of its own.

All of these truths have been sensed over and over again by Americans as the facts of life in the postwar world were pressed home to them. Yet the grounds for determined strategic actions have been insufficient, perhaps because the alternatives never could be portrayed in black and white as they can in a fighting war. The alternatives are rarely those of total destruction of the United States and its civilization, on the one hand, and the victory of the American Ideal in all the world, on the other. Defeat for America, if it ever came, would likely be slow and corrosive until the moment when, with the nation politically and spiritually isolated, the issue would at last be resolved in the one way doomed to fail — by force. A peaceful victory, however it might be defined — as the spread of democratic institutions, the achievement of greater international stability, or the establishment of a more predictable world order — would be unspectacular and perhaps imperceptible as all the components of the world equation — including ourselves — changed in the process. Because success and failure in this kind of process can hardly be conceived in sharp or simple terms, between them lies the tempting zone of indifference and inadequacy.

THE NATIONAL INTEREST

All attempts to formulate a suitable strategic political doctrine lead inexorably back to the same starting point: the identification of national goals, purposes, and objectives. National strategy is without meaning unless it points toward the accomplishment of a nation's larger purposes. And unless those purposes are sufficiently defined there can be no end to improvisation, to the dominance of military over political objectives, and to the application of tactical rather than strategic principles to the use of instrumentalities such as the United Nations.

Thus, the inescapable precondition to a rational reexamination of the uses of the United Nations is the identification of the goals and objectives of American external policy. Without spelling them out we have nothing tangible against which to estimate the extent to which the use of U.N. machinery may advance or retard our cause. The utility of the United Nations, then, is tested in the light of what in political shorthand has come to be called the "national interest." We have not always failed to recognize this interconnection, but we have found it uncommonly difficult to define precisely what our objectives actually are and what we really mean by national interest.

Two classic definitions of national interest are clear and unambiguous. One – perhaps the only one not capable of a depressing number of alternatives – is the primordial interest of self-preservation, that which William Pitt once called "the first law of nature" for a sovereign state. The nation has a primary duty of preserving itself.

Much past analysis of the problem of national interest has also centered around geographical factors, an approach which was summed up by Napoleon when he stated: "The foreign policy of a country is determined by its geography." National interest as an expression of a country's physical location and topography is an obvious element of strategy. The British government was for several centuries explicit that its primary national interest was to prevent the creation of a preponderant combination of power on the European Continent. Every detail of policy, from intrigues with France and Spain to the barrier policy favoring Belgian neutrality, flowed from the grand strategy defined by the national interest. The United States was also able for a time to define its prime national interest in geographical terms centering around its role as a dominant hemispheric power. Today this interest remains, but only as one of a host of other more complex and diffuse interests.

Beyond the definition of self-preservation and the definition determined by geography, the national interest becomes elusive. An analysis the author once had made of the assertions of American Presidents and Secretaries of State during the postwar period concludes that the U.S. national interest has invariably been defined in the highly generalized terms of "Peace," "Security," "Freedom," "Justice," "Well-Being," and "Prosperity." [4] As thus defined it does not tell us how we should act toward the Soviet Union or China in a given set of circumstances, nor whether disarmament poses greater dangers to our security than rearmament, nor what kind of objectives we should be striving for in our relationships with Asia and Africa. Above all, it does not tell us anything tangible about the uses of such diplomatic institutions as the United Nations.

One profound difficulty lies in deciding what we mean by the United States. The British anthropologist Geoffrey Gorer has questioned whether the United States is a territorial state on the old European pattern, or a political organ dedicated, like the USSR, to an idea. The conviction that the essential meaning of this country is embodied in a unique metaphysical idea has a long and honorable history. This tradition, running back to our beginnings as a nation, has persistently translated our enthusiasm for our own continental experiment into a missionary attitude toward the world at large. In 1813 John Adams wrote to Thomas Jefferson that "our pure, virtuous, public-spirited, federative republic, will last forever, govern the globe, and introduce the perfection of man." Woodrow Wilson said, "The idea of America is to serve humanity." This theme remains as a potent counterpoint to the hardheaded calculations of national advantage which otherwise

[4] Michael Brower, *The U.S. National Interest — Assertions and Definitions* (Cambridge: Center for International Studies, Massachusetts Institute of Technology, 1959), mimeographed.

govern strategic thinking. Undoubtedly, either one is neglected only at the nation's peril.

Contemporary efforts to put our great national purposes into words are disappointing. These purposes seem to find expression best in concrete realities rather than verbal abstractions. Some years ago the United States went through an extraordinary spasm of public soul-searching in an effort to reformulate the essential goals of the nation. The results were less than electrifying. Yet in the preceding decade our national goals were made brilliantly explicit in the concrete programs of action, the grand strategies, the solemn commitments to others that together made up the post-war American response to the most direct challenge in its history. These gave form and shape to the purposes of the nation, each representing a grand consensus growing out of all that had gone before.

Yet there are reasons why we should continue to try to formulate national purposes and goals in an orderly and systematic fashion. One in particular is that it helps us to develop a strategic doctrine embracing the many-sided scope of foreign policy. In contrast to military planning, civilian planning has always been weak in our country. We have tended all too frequently to fall into a trap of our own making in which so-called purely military objectives take precedence over political ones in strategic matters, forgetting the Clausewitz maxim that "the political design is the object, while war is the means, and the means can never be thought of apart from the object." The Communists have rarely committed this blunder.

National strategy needs to embrace the range of both civil and military purposes. The uses of military power have become complicated beyond recognition. Deterrence of general war is perhaps the highest order of use of military power today. So is arms control. Both depend on the establishment of what are usually called political objectives and on the purposeful design of military as well as nonmilitary instruments to achieve them. The accelerating rate of advances in science and technology poses a still newer danger to the unity of the national planning process.

Finally, in discussing national goals we must be clear about time spans. Since policy-makers and bureaucrats must face short-term deadlines, they are characteristically inhospitable to plans extending much beyond the next fiscal year or the next sessions of Congress, the United Nations, or the NATO Council. Scholars and seers like to breathe the more rarefied air of the long range. But perhaps the most imperative planning need is in the *middle* range – five to ten years off – where planning can be done with some sense of attachment to current realities but is somewhat free to escape from the dense gravitational field of present strategic concepts where the half-life of policies, as it were, is long and institutional inertia is monumental. Bismarck once said that political decisions should not be concerned with periods of more than three years. But the lead time of a new weapons system or space program is today in the neighborhood of eight years. The gestation period of a new industrial power is one generation. Everything argues for better planning, and for better planning we must have a clear picture of where we want to go in the foreseeable period ahead.

It is not impossible to derive a lucid and operationally meaningful interpretation of American external goals from our historical situation. The evidence suggests that the chief purpose for which our foreign policy operates is to develop an international environment in which we can enjoy our prosperity and cultivate our internal societal values without excessive disturbance or threat from the outside. To achieve this goal under present conditions, we are required to take measures to protect the physical base of American society. This is the essential rationale of defense policy. The international posture that results from this goal is one of discouraging rather than fomenting or encouraging violent changes by war, revolution, or other methods of dislocation or upheaval. As an entirely logical result, Western action policies are principally designed to stabilize, restore, and retain, as contrasted with the Communist purposes of unbalancing, revolutionizing, and seizing.

The logical consequences of such a policy preclude actions that would sharpen contemporary conflicts. They logically favor actions aimed at blunting and converting to acceptable and tolerable forms the thrusts of forces of revolution and change. In any overview of American policy today, all rhetoric aside, these are the basic contours. But because of the principles we feel to be at stake, and also because of emotional factors that reside in the process of domestic consensus and policy formulation, we have at times felt impelled to pursue at the same time unbalancing policies, at least on the verbal level, calculated to sharpen and intensify the conflict of forces. Because we *do* favor the restoration of self-determination to the East European satellites and of a friendly regime on the Chinese mainland, we have not formalized the present situation as Communist leaders would have us do. But the embarassing consequence is that we appear to be in favor of change in theory but in favor of the *status quo* in fact.

We are rescued from this uncomfortable dilemma by the changing nature of the situation. We do not need to remain trapped between acceptance of the *status quo* and the fomenting of revolution in Eastern Europe and China, the price of which we are unwilling to pay. The *status quo* is never permanent, and our long-term program must actively collaborate with that eternal historical verity. At the same time, the short-term objective of stability is also of great validity, and on the occasion of any major threat to this objective, we are sometimes forced to run risks of involvement that verge on the intolerable.

I would therefore formulate the grand strategy that follows logically from our fundamental national interests in the following way: For the Communist states we seek stability in the short run but change in the long run, exploiting the vulnerabilities and encouraging the trends which seem to favor our long-term objective. But our policy toward the forces of anticolonial, anti-Western nationalism logically is the other way around – in the short run to favor and to assist in the changes that are taking place anyway, with a view to long-term stability and the restoration of favorable relationships.

THE LARGER NATIONAL INTEREST

The nature of the world today is such that no great and powerful nation makes a decision that fails to take into account the interests of others. The revolution in technology and therefore in instruments of warfare may have already produced a situation in which the interests of a single nation are almost indistinguishable from the interests of the whole community – even if the community does not behave like one. At the same time, no nation, including our own, will act in serious matters in a way that runs contrary to whatever clear sense it has of its own national interests. Superficially, this produces a paradox and encourages the belief that the concept of the United Nations – the prime symbol of internationalism and common interests – by definition clashes with the notion of national interest with its traditional connotation of unilateralism and inevitably selfish and narrowly conceived national behavior.

But a nation's interest is not necessarily limited to the classic goals of seeking power and prestige. There is no automatic and self-regulating mechanism in history or politics that limits interests to a narrow spectrum. The broader concept of national interests represents the highest degree of self-interest for a nation in our circumstances in history, a nation that wishes to retain its power but sees that to do so it must seek common interests with other nations. The overriding American interest in a more satisfactory and durable world in which to enjoy what it has leaves this nation with little responsible choice between the political strategies that represent narrow and broad concepts of the national interest.

The significance of the United Nations to American foreign policy rests in great part on this insight. What cannot be done is to disconnect the notion of national interest from the notion of common interest and to regard the United Nations as the natural enemy of one and friend of the other.

Common action through the United Nations rather than unilateral action is politically feasible on major political matters when the common interest involved has been made clear not in terms of its virtue as an abstract good but as an explicit national interest. The connection between the common interest and the national interest is made when the national interest is defined in such a way that U.S. policies both inside and outside the United Nations will more effectively serve broad national concerns. This process can take place only when national goals and objectives are more clearly perceived, and when policies necessary to move toward attainment of the goals are better matched with the capabilities and limitations of the international institution. It cannot succeed unless the sought-after ends are distinguished from the diplomatic and institutional means; and it cannot acquire meaning in terms of specific policy problems facing the nation until these in turn are sorted out, the short-term from the middle- and long-range, the military security issues from the nonmilitary issues of evolution and welfare, and the ideal of law and order from the preliminaries of community building.

The task is at once made easier and harder by the fact that, both as an idea and as an institution, the United Nations has the peculiar and perhaps unique quality of itself serving as an embodiment of long-range objectives. So far, the long-range goals embodied in the Charter have at best served as occasional moral guides, at worst as an excuse for complacently viewing history as a story with an inevitably happy ending. In this sense the United Nations has served to deepen frustrations and feed the human sense of futility. But if the United Nations is viewed not as an end in itself but as a means to socially desirable and politically valid ends, it may have a more significant role in working toward goals of our own national interest than we have so far attributed to it.

AMERICAN GOALS

America's external purposes can be summed up as being aimed at *creating the sort of world environment in which the United States not only can survive with its own values intact but also can enjoy its survival both politically and spiritually.* The first charge on American leadership is thus *national survival in a form that reflects our cherished national values.* National security is the prime yardstick. And thus some policies pressed on the political center by the extremes simply cannot be contemplated by responsible leaders. It is, for example, not in the national interest to crush our enemies by launching a surprise nuclear attack likely to take hundreds of millions of human lives. Neither can a President indulge in acts of extreme renunciation such as unilateral disarmament. Neither complies with his basic charge of survival with our cherished values intact.

Looking ahead, a present or future President might legitimately perceive seven paramount middle-range objectives of the United States in the world arena, the quest for which represents the national interest of the United States.

Objective Number One is *the prevention of a general thermo-*

nuclear war. If this goal is not attained, clearly all other goals – including "winning over" communism – become relatively meaningless. This objective does not, as some assert, automatically imply that military power is itself irrelevant or obsolete or that the chances for world peace would necessarily improve by dismantling all military establishments. Besides being essential to the pursuit of such other national objectives as the maintenance of stability in various parts of the world, military power serves the national interest at the highest level as a deterrent of major aggression.

Given a conflict the intensity of which has not been matched since the religious wars of the sixteenth century, it is probably only the existence of nuclear weapons that has prevented World War III. The Cuban crisis of 1962 was a powerful convincer of the painful truth – missed by many dedicated to peace – that such peace as we have is presently saved by our occasional willingness to risk nuclear war.

The continued deterrence of major aggression depends on the maintenance of a strategic equilibrium which no one can benefit from challenging. In specific terms this means maintaining a well-protected, well-controlled nuclear second-strike capacity; and if there is ever a disarmament agreement, this capability will still be needed by any governing authority. So the first of two prime sub-goals in the category of security is *to maintain a military capability that deters major aggression and can deal effectively with lower-level conflict situations.*

But having accepted the vital necessity of military power even in a disarmed world and above all today, the United States is caught in the dilemma that actually to use our strategic nuclear weapons would be wholly irrational. Moreover, the population explosion in nuclear weapons is changing the meaning of security itself. As the President's Science Advisory Committee implied in its extraordinary statement in support of the limited test-ban treaty in 1963, the point has now been reached where each new weapon that enters our arsenal and each new idea in military research and development may serve ultimately to diminish rather than to enhance our security. Thus the twin sub-goal of American security policy in the middle range must be *to master the arms race: to moderate it, preferably to reverse it, and to create new arrangements for political and military security which conform to the new realities of our age.*

This cannot mean anything as nonsensical as general and complete disarmament. It means regulation, limitation, and balanced reduction of armaments. It means a wide variety of arms-control measures, some taken unilaterally to stimulate reciprocal action. It means trying to control the environment around us which, if uncontrolled, will allow an increasing number of countries to acquire the ability to provoke war or entangle the superpowers. The achievement of our strategic goal calls for the prevention of the spread of nuclear weapons at almost any cost, which in turn raises the bitterly hard problem of forcing others to comply with any agreements that may be painfully reached between the superpowers aimed at decreasing the dangers of nuclear war.

The second great middle-range objective of United States policy is *to find a more tolerable basis for relationships with the Soviet Union.* If the United States is unable or unwilling to crush the physical power of the Soviet Union, there appears to be no other rational alternative. U.S. objectives can be served only by a strategy that encourages the process of change in the Communist world but does not provide the opportunities for the renewed thrust. Clearly one of the paramount policy tasks is to find ways of exploiting the Sino-Soviet break, with its historic shattering of the Communist monolith. The encouragement of diversity in the Communist world can only serve our interests.

General de Gaulle, with his occasionally irritating proclivity for being right, sees the Russia of the future as an essentially European power, purged of her messianic drives. But this prophecy is not necessarily self-fulfilling. It is in the American interest to bring Russia into Europe and out of Asia, particularly as the Westward momentum is supplied by the Chinese. American planning for the 1970s ought not to exclude the contingency of U.S.-Soviet combined military or nonmilitary action against China if, as seems likely, American interests will have more in common with the Russians than the Chinese – particularly if this is the only mutual way to enforce a desired moderation of the arms race or a new joint commitment to peacekeeping.

But if it is possible that the Soviet leadership in the late 1960s and early 1970s may be less inclined to destroy the *status quo* because its own stake in the established order will have increased even to the point of some new relationships with the West, there is no evidence that the Chinese Communists are even beginning to follow this path. Two profoundly vital American interests are involved here, leading to the third and fourth objectives of U.S. policy, which must be stated together: *to contain Communist China* and *to avert a worldwide racial war.*

The military strategist may or may not be correct in continuing to rate mainland China as of only moderate concern for a decade or so in terms of efficient nuclear-weapon-delivery systems, sophisticated warheads with economic yield-to-weight ratios, invulnerable launching platforms, advanced early-warning systems, secure command and control, and all the other paraphernalia of superpower military capacity. But it is China in two other roles that must preoccupy both civil and military American planners in the meantime: first, China as an expansive and therefore unstabilizing force in Asia; and second, perhaps more crucially, China as a catalyst for that which mankind as a whole may need to fear more than nuclear weapons themselves – a fundamental conflict between the races. For there have been ominous hints that Peking is well aware that the preconditions for racial conflict can be felt in the awakening of nonwhite races around the world to all the implications of power, influence, and affluence that long were the monopoly of the white man, and may see this issue as the key to future political power.

The great strategic objective of the United States must be to see that this crystallization of latent racial antagonisms, this mobilization along blood lines, of continent against continent, never takes place. And to work toward this objective, the United States must face squarely an issue seemingly unrelated, but in reality intimately connected – the problem of South Africa.

South Africa has a dual meaning to American national strategy. It is a time bomb in the African subcontinent that could open the way to chaos and communism; and it could one day be the trigger for the larger racial tidal wave on which Communist Chinese leaders fancy themselves the riders of the crest.

Vital United States interests will be served here by detailed policy goals aimed at both of these problems. First, an expansionist Communist China must be checked. That same strategy recommended by George Kennan *vis-à-vis* the fluid stream of dynamic Soviet power should be aimed at by the West in this situation: Chinese pressure against non-communist nations on its periphery should be contained by "the adroit and vigilant application of counter-force at a series of constantly shifting geographical and political points. . . ." [5]

China's capacity to inflame already explosive racial passions into a holy war of the races must also be reduced. It is already late for this. The sleeping princess that was China has already been awakened, as someone put it, by the wrong kiss. The isolation of China from the West and in particular from the United States can only add fuel to the racial fires. The United States should make — and is beginning to make — deliberate moves aimed at demonstrating to Peking that normally acceptable behavior will be a passport to tolerable relations with us. Chinese behavior has implied unwillingness to accept the ground rules that undergird diplomatic relations, U.N. membership, and other multilateral relationships. On balance, a combined strategy of containment and efforts to bring China into the established order seem appropriate to the facts.

The related objective is to prevent the tragedy of South Africa from unfolding to its predictable climax by whatever diplomatic, propagandistic, economic, and military means can be devised. Given the obduracy of the Capetown regime and the growing impatience of black men in Africa in the face of that monument to their continued humiliation and servitude, this objective will not be met without a strategy designed to avoid the nightmare alternatives of a colored war against whites and the equally nauseous white efforts systematically to suppress nonwhites. As things get worse in southern Africa — starting with Rhodesia and leading like a powder train through South-West Africa, Angola, Mozambique, and finally South Africa itself — as communism seeks to capture the color revolution for its own purposes, as a do-or-die stand for the white man is posed as the only available policy, the United States will find itself increasingly asked to make nearly impossible choices.

The objective of American policy is to see that it never comes

[5] George F. Kennan, *American Diplomacy 1900–1950* (Chicago: University of Chicago Press, 1951), pp. 119, 120.

to that. Rather than being at the mercy of the extremes, the United States should work out its own preferred alternative for South Africa, one that will appeal to moderate whites and, indeed, to all reasonable men as a standard to which all can repair.

The next middle-range goal is *to win the battle of modernization in the developing societies.* Here is one place where "winning over communism" has clear and specific meaning. Our aim should be to lay the foundations now for good relations with those countries *after* they have passed through the first rude stages of transition from colony to nation. We seek, in the long run, the establishment of societies in the new countries that will be friendly to us and preferably democratic in their political complexion. Such a goal requires the investment of resources, a commitment to peoples, and a willingness to encourage peaceful revolution without any assurance as to the outcome.

The next basic U.S. vital interest, expressed as a middle-range objective of policy, is to make progress toward the longer-term goal of *transforming international society into true community.* In its broadest sense, this is what Dag Hammarskjöld called the overriding problem of "the relations of man to man, of man to his environment, and of groups to groups." [6]

The objective is not necessarily to form a larger polity, anticipating the end of smaller national units. This age of neonationalism does not yet look like fertile soil for drastic supranationalism. Nor is world government necessarily desirable. It is, for example, by no means clear that world-government enthusiasts have sufficiently examined the implications of tyranny on a global scale. Here, more than anywhere else, the perfect is the enemy of the good, and the good is desperately needed. Nationalism can be even a positive good. The vices of extreme nationalism are mirror images of its virtues, virtues that are creating the beginnings of a new and freer pattern for the Eastern European states.

In the middle run of time and planning, then, barring a great catastrophe, the goal should not be the utopia of world government. But having said that, one can establish reasonable and even exciting goals of community building that, in recognizing the growing web of interconnected purposes and activities in which

[6] *United Nations Review,* March 1959, p. 29.

all mankind is bound, offer creative political substitutes for historically destructive nationalism of the virulent and exclusive type.

A more reasonable picture of a middle-range political future would appear to be a society of independent states that would have agreed in advance to submit on some issues to the will of a highly qualified majority, but with some form of national veto retained *in extremis.* Universal collective security remains a rational ideal, but in this age it has to be — and has been — modified. In the realm of cooperation the American goal should be, first, to create the consensus without which there can be no community, and then to encourage the formation of the community institutions, regional and global, that give political life to the consensus. This is a broad-spectrum goal applicable to regional organizations for Western Europe, Central America, or Africa, or to those organizations embodying worldwide programs polarized not around abstractions, but around concrete international tasks based on shared interests, whether they be trade, science, space, or the control of armaments.

In this connection the role of Europe retains a special, crucial importance for the United States. But the Western Europe of the 1970s will only partly resemble that of 1945 on which American attitudes in many ways are still based. The U.S. sub-objective here must be *to develop a genuine partnership with Europe that conforms to the realities of the changed relationships.* A host of events in the 1960s demonstrated that a prosperous and proud Europe, freed of what has become the disabling onus of overseas colonies, cannot be an appendage of American power.

The unification of Western Europe continues to be a legitimate and desirable American goal, and we may properly regard the Gaullist version of a *Europe des Patries* as only a temporary obstacle to real unity. John Foster Dulles correctly described Europe as historically the world's greatest fire hazard. Though his policies and style may have been inadequate to his insight, it is still the U.S. aim to support arrangements in Europe aimed at ending that menace for all time. A stake in something larger than itself remains a prescription not only for Germany but for every country in Europe.

The final vital middle-range objective of U.S. policy is *to capture the technological revolution before it captures us.* The time has come to question the unbalanced worship of science for science's sake, a cult that could end in annihilating us. Just as military actions are meaningless without political purposes, so science may end up having no meaning apart from its values for the individual and the community. For we have not always been well served by the scientific mystique which insists on the right to make vital national choices for us but at the same time scorns politics as a dirty word, diplomacy as a pejorative, and military power as an evil.

Some areas where applied science needs to be better harnessed to national purposes are population control, food supply, power and water supply for the arid zones, and low-cost housing supply for a world that needs it desperately. To include in national strategic doctrine the setting of goals related to solving these problems will generate pressures on technology to adapt itself to socially valuable purposes. This is not to advocate Lysenkoism and related totalitarian diseases. Science must remain free. But government in the United States is virtually supporting science, and without a better-thought-out linkage between their respective values and purposes, statesmen and people the world over will continue to be confronted and increasingly threatened with the products of politically mindless choices made in the laboratory or on the drawing board ten years earlier.

With these major external policy goals in mind, we can become more specific in ordering concrete programs that represent in their totality a definition of the national interest. They fall into four operational categories: Military Security, Political Security, Stability and Welfare, and World Order. These categories are not mutually exclusive. All have obvious implications for United States security in the broad sense. All of them are relevant to the East-West conflict, and many exist as goals only because of the motivations supplied by that conflict. All of them are related to the kind of world we wish to see emerge from the present dangerous and unstable period.

Under these four headings, I have attempted to render a summary catalog of national foreign-policy goals against which one can test the present and future utility of the United Nations as an instrument of diplomacy and an agency of political action. In each category are sets of programs that together make a total agenda. For convenience, the scheme is listed in its entirety in the appendix to this Part.

APPENDIX TO PART I

United States Policy Goals

OVERALL OBJECTIVE: *To secure the kind of world environment in which our nation — and, by definition, other nations — can cultivate their societies without excessive insecurity and external threats of disruption.*

MILITARY SECURITY

BASIC OBJECTIVE: To preserve the zone of freedom and at the same time to minimize the chances of an all-out war.

Specific Objectives:

1. To discourage deliberate Communist military risk-taking by maintaining a consistently stable power relationship *vis-à-vis* the Soviet Union and Communist China to neutralize Communist military capabilities of launching a successful military attack, surprise or other, on the United States or other nations and in order to discourage Communist intentions to do so.
   a. To maintain an adequate deterrent in the form of military and technological strength.
   b. To back up the physical deterrent with maximum national will and determination.

c. To make military adventure prohibitively costly, politically and morally as well as militarily.

2. To bring the arms race under control by safeguarded international agreements, tacit understandings, or unilateral arms-control measures aimed at encouraging reciprocity.
   a. To work toward demilitarization of outer space.
   b. To discourage the spread of nuclear weapons to additional countries.
   c. To develop automated inspection devices that will minimize physical intrusion.
   d. To encourage regional agreements in the underdeveloped parts of the world to limit arms to those needed for internal security purposes.
   e. To aim at the ultimate withdrawal of all foreign military forces stationed on the territory of states.

3. To prevent accidental or inadvertent large-scale war from developing out of local hostilities either involving the Soviet Union and China or within the non-Communist states by improving military and diplomatic techniques of prevention and localization of dangerous situations.
   a. To prevent hostilities involving the great powers from leading automatically to all-out war — assuming a chance exists to localize them — by developing better military capabilities for limited warfare.
   b. To create the maximum political deterrence to expansion of hostilities by developing the widest possible international support in the event of such hostilities.
   c. To develop more effective means of dealing with smaller-scale breaches of peace involving non-Communist nations, including the exploration of regional pacific-settlement agencies.

4. To find more effective ways of preventing and repulsing externally directed insurgency, subversion, and other indirect aggression against political independence and territorial integrity.

5. To conduct hostilities, should they break out, in such a way as to attract maximum military and political support, limit the

scope and aims of the hostilities, and terminate them as quickly as possible under the most satisfactory political conditions.

a. To ensure maximum international military and political support in the event of general war.

b. To hold war aims that permit reduction and liquidation of a given conflict rather than demand its enlargement.

6. To maintain the maximum political and military support and unity in the face of a continuing Communist threat.

POLITICAL SECURITY

BASIC OBJECTIVE: To ensure the survival and prosperity of our political and social values in an era of protracted international disequilibrium.

Specific Objectives:

1. To moderate the hostile quality of both Soviet and Chinese communism toward non-Communist states.

   a. To seek and cultivate common interests with the Soviet Union with a view to a protracted *modus vivendi,* including above all the common interest in reducing the fear of military aggression by the other side.

2. To encourage the continued evolution of the Soviet system to internal liberalization and external détente.

   a. To expose Soviet personnel, particularly the emerging elites, to the advantages of personal freedom and an international philosophy of "live and let live."

   b. To offer alternatives to the Soviet government that involve collaborative relationships with other countries.

   c. To hold before the communized nations the alternatives of genuine coexistence rather than ultimate conflict.

3. To work toward the evolution of the Chinese Communist regime to a tolerable relationship with the United States.

   a. To discourage Peking's expectations of successful destruction of Western power and influence.

b. To encourage Peking, by rewarding acceptable behavior, to come to terms with the non-Communist world order.

4. To neutralize the ideological thrust of communism by improving the capacity of free societies to furnish human and social satisfactions, both material and nonmaterial.
   a. To demonstrate through political, economic, technological, social, cultural, and humanitarian policies that a free, open, and competitive society is capable of supplying acceptable leadership in these fields and can yield more ultimate satisfactions to the individual than a totalitarian system.
   b. To sustain the validity of our own form of society and government as a model by purposefully working to remove its blemishes.
   c. To give other peoples, particularly those in unaligned countries, a demonstrable stake in freedom and cooperative relations with the West, as well as confidence in voluntaristic rather than coercive methods in the creation of their own social orders.
   d. To defend ourselves successfully against hostile propaganda, systematically revealing the fundamental fallacies of Communist doctrine.

STABILITY AND WELFARE

BASIC OBJECTIVE: To develop greater stability and less friction in international relationships.

Specific Objectives:

1. To find ways of minimizing resort to violence as a technique for settling international disputes.
   a. To reduce the present and potential sources of tension and political instability in the non-Communist states.
   b. To remove from future conflict such potential sources of dispute as international waterways, outer space, and the seabed.
   c. To improve international capabilities, preventive and remedial, for resolving territorial and other disputes more effectively, predictably, and justly.

2. To achieve effective and dependable means of peaceful change with the aim of preventing dissatisfactions with the *status quo* from leading, as in the past, to war.

3. To create conditions of economic stability, with the particular goal of satisfactory and durable relationships with the underdeveloped countries, by fostering economic and social progress.
   a. To develop a more effective and predictable flow of capital to underdeveloped countries.
   b. To develop an international trading system in which all can survive and prosper, including arrangements in the fields of trade, currency, and the price structure of internationally marketed commodities.
   c. To maintain just international arrangements aimed at retaining free access to raw materials for the United States and other developed countries.
   d. To work urgently toward the solution of problems arising from conditions of excess population and from the decreasing ratios of population to available material resources and human opportunities.

4. To expedite liquidation of the remaining Western colonial-type holdings and the substitution of more durable and mutually satisfactory relationships.

5. To channel contemporary forces of nationalism toward constructive rather than destructive tasks and purposes.
   a. To design and help execute constructive tasks for underdeveloped countries.
   b. To foster the growth of loyalties to broader communities of common interest, both political and functional, through the processes of integration.
   c. To develop concepts of greater responsibility by states, particularly the newer ones, regardless of size or strength.

WORLD ORDER

BASIC OBJECTIVE: To build a more reliable, predictable, and tolerable world order based on values reflecting freedom and voluntarism rather than totalitarianism and coercion, and combining the values of unity with the values of individual dignity and social and political diversity and pluralism.

Specific Objectives:

1. To substitute processes of cooperation, order, and eventually world law for the anarchy and narrow nationalism that continue to endanger world peace and stability.
   a. To make existing international and political and legal institutions more effective by policy, by example, and by use, with the aim of worldwide participation and compliance but without waiting for all the conditions of universality and without endangering short-run security requirements.
   b. To foster the growth of international institutions that reflect common interests in solving scientific and technical problems that transcend national boundaries.
   c. To work steadily toward the concept of international participation as a universal obligation of all states rather than as a reward for good conduct.
   d. To encourage regional, functional, and other forms of freely entered-into political and economic integration, particularly in Europe.
e. To promote and encourage the expansion of human loy-
   e. To promote and encourage the expansion of human loyalties on a widening basis, preserving the values of diversity, but steadily broadening the area of common responsibility.
   f. To encourage the formation and realization of common interests among nations to form the bases for community that underlie law and order.

PART II The United Nations and National Security

CHAPTER FOUR

The Setting for Military Strategy

CHAPTER FIVE

General War and Limited War

CHAPTER SIX

Lesser Conflicts and U.N. Peacekeeping

CHAPTER SEVEN

The U.N. and the Problem of Counterinsurgency

CHAPTER EIGHT

Disarmament and Arms Control

CHAPTER FOUR

The Setting for Military Strategy

THE SECURITY "MIX"

National security conceived as a military problem is concerned with a variety of things. Overriding all else, in the absence of effective disarmament and arms-control measures, is the deterrence of armed attack on the United States. But we moved in the 1960s from a strategy based almost wholly on the likelihood of all-out military aggression by the Soviet Union to one based on the greater likelihood of limited Communist-supported indirect aggression and of outbreaks of violence of the brushfire variety, not necessarily Communist-inspired, elsewhere in the world. With the fundamental issues of national military strategy partially — but not entirely — resolved, efforts are still being made to determine the right "mix" of strategic and tactical forces and of the allocation of resources to create and support them.

Throughout the continuing debate the emphasis has been almost exclusively on the composition of American and Western strength. Even among those who have successfully advocated an improved capacity to deal with military situations of the less-than-total variety, little serious attention has been paid to the potentialities of the United Nations. Its limitations have generally excluded it from serious attention in the context of national military strategy. There are two fundamental reasons why such reasoning may be faulty.

First, experience in our era has demonstrated once again the historical significance of military forces as makeweights in the realm of political action – military forces that may never be used for actual fighting. The policy of deterrence is the outstanding example of this relationship in that nuclear weapons are commonly "used" to achieve maximum political fallout, so to speak, without ever exploding. The presence of nonfighting international contingents in the Sinai Peninsula, the Gaza Strip, Sharm-al-Sheik, Lebanon, Cyprus, and, for a while, the Congo has illustrated lesser – but no less valid – degrees of "deterrence." One of the crowning ironies of modern history is that whereas in 1945 it was assumed that the maintenance of peace would depend on decisively involving the great powers, events such as the Congo, Suez, and Cyprus have suggested that world peace may be dependent upon keeping the United States, the Soviet Union, and ultimately Communist China out of military situations that initially do not involve them. If this is so, a vital problem for national as well as international security is to supply the capability for non-great-power military intervention.

Second, one of the most significant consequences of the revolution in military technology is that the objectives of warfare must be regarded as having changed. Mankind can no longer accept the risks implied in a doctrine of victory at all costs – or of unconditional surrender. The pressing awareness that any purpose for which military action takes place will probably be furthered not by the extension but by the termination of hostilities suggests that war aims must be formulated on a more complex and sophisticated basis than the conviction that there is no substitute for victory. This was the lesson – imperfectly learned – of the Korean War and relearned in Vietnam.

Moreover, the revolution in military weaponry has changed not only the kind of war most likely to be fought but also the attitudes of the great powers toward war itself. The political *status quo* of the West is anathema to its enemies, and the territorial *status quo* of the great Communist powers is unacceptable to us. Yet as general war becomes increasingly irrational for both parties, the *de facto* truce line which exists between the divided spheres has hardened. When it is crossed overtly, as in Korea, most people seem to recognize such action as a manifest violation of the peace and counteraction becomes politically feasible. Even India and Egypt voted initially to oppose the Communist aggression in Korea. On the other hand, as we saw in Hungary, a general military counteraction across the line is quite impossible politically, even if we are willing to lead it. If the truce line is politically ambiguous (or difficult to patrol) or the external infiltration is confused with a civil struggle – all of which were true in Laos and Vietnam – world opinions are by no means unanimous as to what has happened or as to the rights and wrongs. When the truce line is unmistakable – as in Berlin – one of the more stable situations of confrontation exists, at least in the short run.

To sum up, then, it would appear that barring a drastic change in Soviet and Chinese estimates of Western power and the will to use it, the paraphernalia for all-out war has more political than military significance in the period immediately ahead.

But military actions arising out of outbursts of violence largely within the non-Communist states have proven to contain a significant potential for menacing world peace, and the more likely contingency has become not premeditated all-out war but the spread of what are initially small-scale hostilities. Thus lesser instruments for exerting power assume increasing importance, and among them is the military and quasi-military potential of the United Nations.

It is not easy or natural for Americans of the present era to consider in the same breath the problem of national security and the possible uses of the United Nations. In 1945, when the United Nations was founded, its *raison d'être* was to provide greater security for its member nations. As the basic conflict of interests between Soviet communism and the free nations unfolded, the cold war rapidly came to suffuse the entire organization like a sort of nerve gas, paralyzing but not killing. In a relatively short time the United Nations was seen to be incapable of resolving or even seriously affecting the dominant world conflict. The United States and its principal allies were forced to conclude that, except as it provided a forum for counterpropaganda, the United Nations was irrelevant to their overriding short-term military and security problems.

The Korean War threw a new light on the capabilities of the United Nations as a political mechanism for organizing and demonstrating worldwide resistance to limited Communist aggression. But the disproportionately large contribution that the United States had to make to the conflict strengthened doubts that the United Nations could play a central role in the short-run protection of American national security. It continued to exercise a powerful attraction for many Americans since it exemplified their great will for peace, but as the custodian of the peace it seemed to be in a fiduciary relationship not to us but to an unborn generation who might have a capacity for managing its affairs more harmoniously.

THE CONCEPT OF "COLLECTIVE SECURITY"

This general disposition to separate sharply U.S. security and U.N. potential is symbolized by the disrepute into which the concept of "collective security" has fallen. It is a concept whose past historical meanings have weakened its utility today as a tool of thought. For one thing, the notion of universal collective security evokes images of failure in the 1930s that becloud the issue of future prospects. More to the point, the notion of universal collective security based on an abstract commitment to fight anyone, anywhere, anytime on the call of a majority has not yet entered the realm of reality. In the absence of a true world community and given the wide variety of meanings ascribed to the concept of justice, it has never really been a legitimate expectation.

The basic foundation for a successful universal collective-security system was — and is — either a consensus on political values or the reliable availability of the power to coerce. President Franklin D. Roosevelt in the naïve spirit of the day liked to conceive of it in terms of "Four Policemen" — the United States, the Soviet Union, Britain, and China — who would, by cooperating to enforce the peace, somehow see to it that the rest of the world was peaceful. The responsibility would be entrusted to a council in which the great powers (to which the still enfeebled France should be added in due course) would make the decisions, furnish the chief resources and — assuming they were all in agreement — take action up to the waging of war on aggressors and violators of the Charter. (It will also be recalled that the veto on the use of force by the Security Council was the condition for United States as well as Russian membership. The congressional delegates at San Francisco made it clear that the Senate would not ratify a Charter unless it contained such a clause.)

As it turned out, the condition required to make the system work did not exist. So long as the Soviet Union considered itself to be virtually at war with the non-Communist world, it was quite impossible to conceive of common military action against some third party. At the same time the organization did not have (nor was it ever meant to have) the capacity to bring to book either of the two superpowers. Realizing that the main security arrangement as foreseen at San Francisco had lost its principal meaning, the United States sought ways of rebuilding security machinery through alliances in order to deal directly with Communist aggression, whether overt or by means of subversion, guerrilla warfare, and the other forms of limited war.

As the United Nations has evolved, however, its role in contributing to the maintenance of international peace and security has not been restricted to relying on the enforcement powers of the Charter. Most of the United Nations' business in the political field has in fact arisen from its efforts to deal with international differences before they irretrievably escalated into open warfare and to patch up conflicts among the smaller powers. The history of the organization to date constitutes a long and often impressive list of recommendations and actions with regard to international disputes "the continuance of which is likely to endanger the maintenance of international peace and security," as well as to situations "which might lead to international friction or give rise to a dispute," to quote the relevant Charter language. The parties to a dispute have often been encouraged to seek solutions first by all methods of their own choosing — a point frequently lost on those who believe that every dispute should immediately be handled by the United Nations. The Security Council has then been empowered to recommend appropriate procedures or methods of adjustment — a device used many times in dealing with the perennial disputes between Israel and its Arab neighbors.

In general, what has happened under the overall rubric of "collective security" has been, first, the deterrence through national and alliance strength of overt great-power aggression; second, some major efforts in the early U.N. years of peacemaking, as in Palestine, Indonesia, the Italian Colonies, Kashmir, and so on; and third, in what might be called the "Age of Peacekeeping" commencing in 1956, a new format for quasi-military operations in the name of international security.

SECURITY IN A DISARMED WORLD

The issue of security acquired a new dimension of complexity as plans were presented in the late 1950s by both the Soviet Union and the United States for "General and Complete Disarmament" (GCD). Soviet Premier Khrushchev's proposal to the 1959 General Assembly for "total" disarmament suggested to logical Western minds the obvious corollary of such a scheme: a world police force to fill the vacuum that would be left by the elimination of significant national forces. As the American Secretary of State put it in February 1960, the stage of actual disarmament would be approached after initial arms-control measures designed to avert the danger of surprise attack and the spread of nuclear weapons had paved the way for "progressive, gradual, and balanced reductions" in national military forces.

Our objective in this second stage should be twofold:

> First, to create certain universally accepted rules of law which, if followed, would prevent all nations from attacking other nations. Such rules of law should be backed by a world court and by effective means of enforcement — that is, by international armed force.
>
> Second, to reduce national armed forces, under safeguarded and verified arrangements, to the point where no single nation or group . . . could effectively oppose this enforcement of international law by international machinery.[1]

In the fall of 1961 the United States and the Soviet Union circulated a "Joint Statement of Agreed Principles for Disarmament Negotiations." [2] One section specified that under the program for GCD states would maintain only those nonnuclear weapons and facilities necessary to preserve internal order and the personal

[1] Secretary Herter before the National Press Club at Washington, D.C., on February 18, 1960. *Department of State Bulletin,* March 7, 1960. p. 357.

[2] U.N. Document A/4879, September 20, 1961.

security of citizens. It also said that states would supply agreed-upon manpower for a U.N. Peace Force to be equipped with agreed-upon types of armaments. Section 7 asserted:

> Arrangements for the use of this force should ensure that the United Nations can effectively deter or suppress any threat of use of arms in violation of the purposes and principles of the United Nations.

Subsequently at Geneva the United States presented a treaty outline embodying these themes and looking to a peace force which

> would be progressively strengthened until, in Stage III, it would be fully capable of insuring international security in a disarmed world.[3]

The draft treaty contains other references to such a force, which remains a presumably serious United States commitment, although there has been little discussion of it and even less negotiation.

Without repeating in detail here my conclusions published elsewhere about what such a force might look like if this policy should ever become operative,[4] analysis has suggested a number of far-reaching implications. To be able to fulfill its mission, there would need to be a relative monopoly of political power, accompanied by preponderant military force, at the center of the international system. Since the capacity would still exist for the clandestine production of nuclear weapons, the central authority would need nuclear weapons and delivery systems to deter clandestine violations and any subsequent attempts to disrupt the new system. Such an authority, with such a capacity, would by any definition be a world government, however limited. One can only predict that, short of some transforming catastrophe, in this age of rampant nationalism the chances of nations taking this major step from national sovereignty to supranational authority are slim indeed.

[3] "Blueprint for the Peace Race," USACDA Publication 4, General Series 3, May 1962.

[4] See Lincoln P. Bloomfield *et al., International Military Forces — The Question of Peacekeeping in an Armed and Disarming World* (Boston: Little, Brown, 1964).

Even assuming a willing acceptance of limited world government by the great powers and its acceptance by or imposition on all other states, there is no reason to assume the subsequent disappearance of the dynamic factors that create political instability. There would continue to be economic disparities and racial and ethnic tensions, not to mention irrational behavior, political ambition, and inequalities – any of which could lead to the use or threat of violence. There would therefore be continuing pressures on a world government, some of which could lead to civil war on a global scale.

Since it would be of the utmost importance to ensure that no large-scale civil war did occur, it seems that unless and until man finds a satisfactory substitute for war as a means of effecting changes in the *status quo,* world government offers the nightmare possibility of world tyranny no less than a rational solution to the problem of international governance. The problem of modern history continues then to be to devise ways of accommodating the dynamic forces making for change without allowing them to lead to war.[5] Until there is a breakthrough in this realm, nothing else about world order has meaning in terms of the efficacy of the system or the values by which we would continue to live.

Even in the theoretical event of such a breakthrough, there would remain the possibility of conflict over the single remaining legitimate stock of decisive weapons. To centralize such power contradicts everything we have learned about diffusion and balancing of power, pluralism, and diversity.

All of this illustrates the complexity of the security equation, in the future as in the present, as the variables of politics and power interact to produce new meanings for a relationship traditionally considered to be simple or, at the least, straightforward.

It would be tragic if we were to allow the still utopian prospects of total disarmament and international armies to divert our attention from the pressing need to integrate more rationally into current strategic thinking the possible uses of limited and admittedly imperfect international machinery for specific tasks which confront us today. Once limited steps are achieved, further

[5] See Lincoln P. Bloomfield, *Evolution or Revolution – The United Nations and the Problem of Peaceful Territorial Change* (Cambridge: Harvard University Press, 1957).

progress may be encouraged toward larger international responsibilities in the future, although it is by no means demonstrably a linear process. For the task at hand, U.N. machinery should be considered in terms not of what it might be under wholly different circumstances, but in terms of enhancing its usefulness under present and foreseeable conditions and of constructing better foundations for its future development.

In doing so, the touchstone for planners is to be found in the various relevant American policy objectives ranging from the prevention of thermonuclear war to the improvement of prospects for a more reliable and responsive international order.

CHAPTER FIVE

General War and Limited War

One implication of present world tensions is that general war can arise not only as a result of a deliberate all-out assault which could be met only by the application of total countermeasures but also as a climax to an unplanned and undesired chain of events growing out of one of the interminable crises of our age. A revolt in Hungary or East Germany, a Congo, a Chinese-supported aggression in Vietnam — all these automatically pose the issue of great-power engagement and could lead to incalculable consequences in view of the military capacities of the United States and the Soviet Union. At the extreme the consequences of either planned or accidental general war would be the same: a generalized military engagement between East and West.

The prime American objective since World War II has been to minimize the chances of the calculated all-out assault. The prime strategy for achieving this objective has been a policy of military deterrence in the hands of the United States. Has the United Nations any role in this area?

DETERRENCE

Deterrence involves both neutralizing Communist military capabilities to launch a successful military attack and influencing

Communist intentions to commit such an act. These are beyond present-day U.N. capabilities. In the short run and under foreseeable conditions both are tasks that can be performed only by the United States and its allies.

In order to play a significant role in this area of American and free-world security the United Nations would have to have an independent military capability of its own, something that only a drastic alteration of the present situation could achieve. Although it is conceivable that in time sufficient disarmament will have taken place to make the creation of such a force a serious possibility, we cannot count now on such a revolution in political arrangements as a foundation for serious planning in the short range or even in the middle range of policy planning, *i.e.,* the next three to ten years. This would seem to be true even of suggestions for limited world government, such as those advanced by Clark and Sohn.[1]

Thus, without any military force of its own, the United Nations would seem of little use in the objective of reducing Soviet or Chinese military capabilities. At the most it can affect those capabilities only indirectly by furnishing a forum for negotiation on the limitation and regulation of armaments and on the restriction of the use of outer space to nonwarlike purposes. Agreement on either of these, of course, affects national military capabilities. Despite the essentially bilateral nature of such agreements, the wide choice of means of negotiation offered by the United Nations should not be undervalued. The importance of these avenues was illustrated, for example, when the Soviet Union used U.N. facilities in early 1949 to put Ambassador Malik in private contact with Ambassador Jessup with a view to liquidating the Berlin blockade and when U Thant's office – and good offices – provided desired "outs" for both Washington and Moscow in defusing the Cuban missile crisis of 1962. However, the U.N. role in these superpower confrontations is necessarily marginal, and a United Nations without military force of its own will remain at a distance from this central struggle.

However, as I have said, the relationship between military capabilities and deterrence is a shifting one. When the chances

[1] *World Peace through World Law,* 3rd ed. (Cambridge: Harvard University Press, 1966).

are high for a deliberate military assault, the military component of deterrence is paramount and the significance of other instrumentalities such as the United Nations is low. This was the situation in the earliest postwar years when Western strategists rated as high the probability of Soviet attack, and it may again be the case if Peking combines growing nuclear power with a policy of external aggression.

But a successful deterrence policy by definition results in lowering the chances of such an attack. Military deterrence, when it works, is a shield behind which the battles are fought out by primarily nonmilitary means. Limited wars and insurgency situations become the central military issues, while nonmilitary strategies and nonmilitary "weapons" become the increasingly operative determinants of the success of foreign policy. Under the shield of deterrence to general war the political and economic offensive has replaced the Red Army as Moscow's primary agency for political and territorial change. And because of the great-power deterrence relatively weak states such as the United Arab Republic, Indonesia, Algeria, Cuba – and Communist China – have exercised disproportionate influence in the world and have been able to get away with behavior which great powers in another age would not have permitted. It is not the United Nations that gives the small states the means for independent national behavior today; it is their relative immunity under conditions of *mutual* great-power deterrence.

Under these conditions neither the United Nations nor any other nonmilitary institution of international action should be measured solely in terms of its contribution to military deterrence. There are other components of the general prevention of war apart from preponderant military strength and making credible the will and determination to use it if necessary. There is, for instance, the objective of making military adventures prohibitively costly politically and morally as well as militarily.

Such a deterrent is not comparable in power to the Strategic Air Command, but there have been too many examples of Soviet sensitivity to world public opinion to discard it as meaningless. The Afro-Asian States that were meeting at Belgrade when the Soviets unilaterally broke the nuclear-test moratorium in 1961 were shamefully silent in comparison with their chronic criticisms of the United States. But it is not always remembered that the U.N. resolution condemning Soviet intervention in Hungary was supported by fifteen Afro-Asian states, with none in opposition.

Primary responsibility for implementing the commitment in the U.N. Charter to oppose aggression has, as I have said, passed during the 1940s into the hands of the regional and collective self-defense arrangements that have constituted a strong element, both military and political, in the generalized deterrent. Such organizations might have developed without that governing principle; but there is no doubt that the negotiation and development of such a security system was made easier because of the already existing principles from which it could borrow and in whose name it could act.

To sum up, the principle of collective resistance to aggression embodied in the U.N. Charter has played an obvious role in postwar Western policies. The fact that the United Nations concept exists can be set down as a consideration affecting Soviet calculations about the profitability of military operations, even though it hardly figures as a prime factor.

GENERAL WAR

We can deal briefly with the role the United Nations could play if an all-out war took place either by calculation or by accident. We are prone to believe that general war would mean the end of the United Nations, and this may be so. Yet as Korea illustrated at a less than all-out level, the United Nations can serve as a symbol under which the United States and other free nations can legitimize their military response to Communist aggression at whatever level. It can arm our side with the banner of moral right — a force still very much alive beneath the surface of contemporary world politics. It can make neutral nations available for the imperative tasks of disentangling the combatants. It might have great political significance in providing a legal and acceptable way of replacing Communist U.N. representatives with spokesmen for free and democratic regimes. Indeed this seems far more sensible than trying to expel the offending power, under Article 5 or 6 of the Charter, in a war situation, since such a step — while perhaps being more emotionally satisfying — would deprive our side of one of the organization's most valuable symbolic uses.

I have tried to make the point that under present and foreseeable conditions no national objectives would be served in any major conflict by the traditional aim of destroying the enemy regardless of political consequences. If political war aims were defined by a U.N. majority rather than by any single nation, including our own, hostilities might be brought to an end more promptly than otherwise and a chance bought to try again with the weapons of diplomacy.

The continued failure of Americans to absorb the Clausewitz dictum of the interrelation of war and peace, long a centerpiece of Communist doctrine, has in the past made it almost impossible to plan rationally for a fully orchestrated political and military strategy in the event of war. It explains American resentment at the restraining influence of both our own policy-makers and the U.N. majority in the Korean War. It also explains the decade-long failure of the United States, prior to 1965, to put the Vietnam situation formally before the United Nations. But it is conceivable that U.S. interests would be best served in some future conflict by having restraints placed on any claims one or another party to a conflict might make for the right of hot pursuit, for invading a privileged sanctuary — or for total victory. The United Nations, inconsistent as conflicting policies might make it, and not itself carrying the prime burden, might in fact make a greater contribution to our broad objectives than those who define our war aims by claiming primacy for military over political objectives. We should not be ashamed of planning against the possibility that unreason could again whisper to us that there is no substitute for total victory and unconditional surrender. The United Nations' very existence can protect us from taking an untenable position.

Above all, the continued existence of the United Nations even in an all-out war could give the world a framework to which to return for the task of patching up the shattered peace and carrying on. Our planning must not ignore this possibility, and we must assume there would be a postwar world to organize.

LIMITED EAST-WEST HOSTILITIES

Some of the same considerations apply to direct military confrontations on a limited scale with the Soviet Union or Communist China. There are two possible avenues to limited war of this dangerous sort. The first is a calculated military move by the Soviet Union, Communist China, or one of their allies that is clearly intended to achieve only a limited objective. Several means exist for them to convey such an intention: proxy aggression, such as that by North Korea in 1950; guerrilla warfare, as in Greece in 1947, Malaya in the 1950s, and Vietnam; or militarily ambiguous testing action such as the 1948 Berlin blockade, the Laos probe of 1960–1961, the Cuban missile emplacement in 1962, and the Chinese stabs into India in 1959 and 1962.

The second avenue is unplanned involvement resulting from the highly dangerous brand of crisis diplomacy periodically practiced by Communist leadership. The possibility of the continuation of this hazardous policy should not be discounted so long as the several brands of Communist leadership remain confident of their capacity to draw back before making a fatal commitment.

Whatever the event – the deliberate limited probe or the unplanned military encounter arising out of diplomacy at the brink – an objective of U.S. policy must be to keep such limited hostilities from spreading. The question that arises embraces both the possibility and the means of achieving that end.

One school of thought discounts the possibility. Another view holds that an open conflict need not become general since there would still exist a common interest between the combatants not to go all the way. A third view is that limited war is even desirable as an alternative to all-out war.

Khrushchev's famous speech of January 6, 1961, rejected all-out war as intolerably dangerous and limited war as leading to the former. But the leaders of Communist China have not followed suit. While Moscow behaves with increasing circumspection, Peking reiterates that "political power grows out of the barrel of a gun." [2]

[2] "Problems of War and Strategy," *Selected Military Writings of Mao Tse-tung* (Peking: Foreign Language Press, 1963), p. 272.

To an even greater extent than in a general-war situation, the key to the matter of Western response in a limited war is in our war aims. Shall the purpose for which we fight be the repulsion of aggression or the accomplishment of an otherwise unattainable political objective, such as our intent to unify Korea in the early fall of 1950? Can we be satisfied with aims that go no further than the restoration of the *status quo ante?* We eventually were in Korea; and by and large we have accepted such an aim as the only realistic basis for American policy in Vietnam.

A strategy of restraint is far from easy for a nation's leaders, as American Presidents learned in both the Korean and Vietnamese wars. A strategy of restraint involves keeping alive opportunities for settlement during hostilities. Diplomatic contacts must be maintained, as the 1964 "Hot-Line" Agreement explicitly recognized. The enemy's retaliatory forces remain immune. Sanctuary areas must be preserved. These are of course the conditions that many Americans found supremely difficult to accept during the Korean and Vietnamese Wars.

This dilemma cannot be evaded, nor can it be resolved, for it sums up the grand conundrum of the age: the prospect of choices – none satisfying, all implying undesirable alternatives. But we can be sure that the classical notion of military victory can only reproduce Pyrrhus's lament: "Another such victory and we are undone." Military victory in any major war between the United States and the Soviet Union is, as all recent U.S. presidents and Soviet political leaders have conceded, no longer really possible, and as a goal it does not serve national or international ends.

We come, then, to a threefold proposition: preventing the spread of limited East-West hostilities is not a hopeless objective; a decisive factor in achieving that objective will be our own doctrine of response to enemy action; and the key to our response is war aims short of military victory, aims which are summed up in bringing hostilities to an end as quickly as possible so that political processes can be substituted for military action.

It is in the light of this proposition that we consider the possible role of the United Nations in achieving the U.S. objective of limiting East-West hostilities if they should break out.

The first and major value of the United Nations in such a

situation is, as in general war, chiefly psychological and symbolic. By turning to the United Nations, a nation can communicate to its opponent that it does not wish the conflict to spread into a general war. The scope of hostilities would still be largely determined by the estimates each side makes of the intentions and the capabilities of the other. But given the will of each to keep them limited, the United Nations can then offer the advantages it did when the United States made its decision to resist in Korea.

First, the United Nations furnishes one means to secure maximum political support. This support is indispensable if we are not to lose the sense of legitimacy and moral right that we as a people particularly need in order to sustain a military effort. The ambiguities concerning Vietnam in the minds of most other countries were reinforced by the fact that the fundamental U.S. commitment in South Vietnam was made without any reference to the United Nations. The second advantage is the opportunity afforded by the commitment made by all U.N. members to assist the organization in any action it takes in accordance with the Charter. This does not have to mean "action" in the legal sense of Security Council enforcement. Marginal offers of bases, transit rights — even "a sharpshooter on a camel" — can not only demonstrate the breadth of international disapproval of an act of aggression but can also pay important strategic dividends. Economic sanctions could have a worldwide impact on the aggressive party. Thirdly, the mere fact that the conflict is before the United Nations might discourage participants from expanding the scope of the war recklessly or setting extravagant war aims.

The U.N. involvement in Korea served the American national interest by legitimizing and broadening the political and moral base of a military action the United States felt was imperative. The price of such broadening was the imposition of constraints on American policy-making, some of which seemed irksome at the time. The General Assembly's will was quite broadly interpreted in the early fall of 1950 when MacArthur drove his seemingly victorious forces toward the Yalu. One suspects that there were many in that U.N. majority who were as glad as we to use the occasion of a military victory over the North Korean forces to implement the previous U.N. resolutions calling for extension of U.N.-supervised elections and, ultimately, democracy to North

Korea. But this failing, if you will, of human nature only points up the difficulty of prescribing in advance rigid rules for transmitting political guidance to military commanders. When the Chinese Communists entered the conflict and drove the U.N. forces back to the South, the political guidance, particularly from those not involved, became far more pointed. It was then that the influence of the Assembly majority bore down hard on negotiation and limitation of the objective to restoration of the *status quo ante.* This was action which, in any realistic appraisal of the war in Korea as a reflection of the larger stalemate, was of great value to the United States and had its payoff when both sides came to share an interest in seeking a way out.

Conversely, it may not be an exaggeration to say that the United States earned unnecessary opprobrium and internal dissension by going it alone — or virtually so — in Vietnam. The distinctions among several types of conflict situations is all important, and there seems no realistic way in which the 1961 Berlin confrontation or the 1962 Cuban crisis could have been resolved without war had not the United States acted quickly, resolutely, and practically alone. But for the less direct clash, the pre-escalation situation, and, perhaps increasingly, the Chinese threat, it would be shortsighted to exclude from U.S. planning the possible values of active U.N. involvement.

This discussion has emphasized the political role of the United Nations, with the understanding that meaningful collective security in terms of military capabilities is not now or foreseeably a prime function of a global U.N. organization. The military capacity to resist military or parliamentary aggression comes chiefly from the national forces of the United States and its allies, for which the United Nations offers no substitute. But neither do national military forces substitute for the political role of an essentially peace-favoring organization, with its peace-favoring majorities, in the paramount task of staying the hands of the antagonists in any fight that threatens the whole fabric of world peace, a task that conforms to the vital political objectives of the United States. The political role of the United Nations can thus be a major consideration in policy-making within the larger framework of limiting East-West conflicts.

CHAPTER SIX

Lesser Conflicts and U.N. Peacekeeping

A vital lesson being taught by contemporary history is the possibility of involvement of the superpowers in a military outbreak that does not originate as an East-West conflict. What is the potential role of the United Nations in this context?

In significant ways the political history of the United Nations is the history of conflicts in the non-Communist world that were aborted, stopped, suppressed, or in a few happy instances resolved. The U.N. machinery of investigation and conciliation, the calls for cease-fires, the use of uniformed personnel to observe and report – all of these techniques have with a few exceptions (such as Greece and Laos) been applied chiefly to intra–free-world disputes. Indonesia, Palestine, Kashmir, Suez, Lebanon, Yemen, and Cyprus all involved U.N. machinery designed to moderate conflict and separate the parties long enough for them to cool off and resume a less violent dialogue. Each represented innovations in the techniques used, and each in its own way was a success in terms of suppressing overt violence.

THE AGE OF PEACEKEEPING

The beginning of the peacekeeping era coincided with a new, rising confidence on the part of the Soviets. As former Premier

Khrushchev put it, "The correlation of forces has changed rapidly in favor of socialism." With the death of Stalin and the initiation of policies of relative internal relaxation and external détente, the Soviet Union began to develop some variations in its previously monochromatic U.N. performance. The more flexible approach coincided with the beginning of the missile age and its implications of mutual deterrence. This led Soviet (and to some extent Chinese) policy-makers to become more cautious, although both continued to pursue some destabilizing policies and to exploit short-of-war situations to the hilt.

After the initial period of Trygve Lie's energetic – though often frustrated – leadership, the United Nations from 1953 on was under the guiding hand of Secretary General Dag Hammarskjöld, whose dynamic and inventive views of the role of the organization had great influence in shaping the peacekeeping age. Hammarskjöld laid down as his basic injunction "that the United Nations simply must respond to those demands which must be made of it . . . . and should have confidence in its strength and capacity to respond." [1] He took initiatives in quiet "preventative" diplomacy, mostly at the request of organs of the United Nations but sometimes on his own, and he himself became a central part of the "U.N. presence" of which he often spoke. (Sometimes, as in Jordan in 1958 and Laos the following year, the presence was a single individual representing him.) A genius in formulating his own mission in politically acceptable ways, Hammarskjöld for the first time articulated the Secretary General's right "to express what may be called the independent judgment of the organization." [2]

The event that opened the Age of Peacekeeping in its contemporary sense was the invasion of Egypt in the fall of 1956, first by Israel and then by Britain and France. The U.N. Emergency Force (UNEF), created at the United Nations in the midnight hours of the crisis by Lester Pearson of Canada and the Hammarskjöld "team," created a far-reaching precedent in sending a U.N. force into a member country, with its consent of course. The full complement of the Emergency Force consisted of 6,000 soldiers from ten small and medium-sized countries. It was sent to moni-

[1] Press Conference April 2, 1959.
[2] May 2, 1959, U.N. Press Release SG/812, May 1, 1959.

tor a cease-fire between the parties by getting between them and staying there. A decade later, UNEF was still stationed in the Gaza Strip and on the international frontier in the peninsula, continuing to fill a vacuum that if left unfilled would create new dangers. There was no sign that either party wished it to leave.

In 1958 other units, again drawn from the smaller countries and again wearing blue U.N. armbands and white helmets, were dispatched to Lebanon with a mission not of war but of observation, patrol, and reporting. The U.N. force in the Congo, known as ONUC from its French initials, was the largest and most controversial of all the peacekeeping enterprises. For four years beginning in 1960 a uniformed force of up to 20,000 men sought to execute the mandate laid down by the Security Council in July 1960 and in subsequent resolutions to assist the Congolese Government to keep order.

In addition, two other missions using military personnel "borrowed" from member countries were fielded for special administrative and observation roles. In 1962 the U.N. Security Force (UNSF) in West New Guinea, chiefly made up of Pakistani troops and a small naval detachment, oversaw the transfer of that territory from the Netherlands to Indonesian administration. And in 1963 perhaps the least successful U.N. field operation took place in Yemen, with an observation mission consisting initially of 200 Yugoslav and Canadian soldiers and airmen, subsequently reduced to 25, then withdrawn.

In 1964 a more than 6,000-man U.N. force (UNFICYP) – comprising Austrian, Canadian, Finnish, Irish, Swedish, and principally British troops – was organized on the island of Cyprus and remained to keep order as efforts at mediation and conciliation were tried, failed, and were tried again. In all, there have been five major operations involving some form of U.N. peacekeeping, and the troops employed in all U.N. field operations and peace observation missions have been drawn from fifty-four countries.

But ten years after the Age of Peacekeeping began, its future was in real doubt. In 1956 Moscow for the first time had seemed to share Washington's alarm at the dangers inherent in local explosions. UNEF was not an enforcement action, nor was it collective action against aggression. But it did provide a precedent for effective responses by the United Nations to conflict situations on the peripheries of the Cold War. It was generally agreed that the United Nation's newfound capability could contribute directly to the high purpose of avoiding head-on collisions between nations possessing the power to incinerate much of the planet.

Unfortunately, however, by carrying this logic of international intervention one step further, applying it this time to a situation of internal conflict in the Congo, the whole enterprise was brought close to disaster. The development of an effective "executive capacity" for the U.N. Secretary General – perhaps the single most hopeful aspect of the Age of Peacekeeping – was in jeopardy. It was not, after all, possible to divorce the "neutral third party" from the Cold War. Instead peacekeeping became one more topic of ideological dissension and the focus of fundamentally conflicting views about the proper role of international organization. The crisis thus precipitated threatened to bring down in ruins the device that had seemed for a moment in history to promise so much. All that followed – financial crisis, constitutional crisis, the Assembly's paralysis in 1964–1965, the denouement in August 1965 when the United States backed down, and the ominous doubts about the future – resulted from the effort to adapt the United Nations to the very sort of situation most likely to require the peacekeeping remedy in the years that lie ahead.

FUTURE PROSPECTS

Despite the grave difficulties of U.N. peacekeeping implied by the Congo operation and its aftereffects, there are no convincingly better alternatives in sight to help contain the endless agenda of lower-level conflict that our age has spawned. We can therefore predict that from time to time a majority of nations will still prefer it, warts and all, to other less palatable alternatives for two tasks in particular: pacifying violent quarrels between states other than the great powers; and stabilizing situations such as the Congo and Cyprus where internal disorder threatens to draw in powerful outsiders.

In both these kinds of situations unilateral intervention by any of the great powers seems fated to provoke an equal and opposite reaction, resulting not in a Newtonian equilibrium but in potentially uncontrollable violence. Regional organizations perhaps offer an alternative for the more distant future, but today they appear to be either impotent or inappropriate for peacekeeping missions. Planners, then, need to continue to include in their calculations the necessity of U.N. peacekeeping for a range of potential crisis situations to which there is no foreseeable end. Some obvious candidates are Kashmir, if a third round ensues; Rhodesia, Angola, and/or Mozambique; South-West Africa; Palestine; Aden and South Arabia; any one of a dozen African states that, like the Congo in 1960, are far from being nations; and South Africa, where the dreadful alternatives may someday be the arming of the blacks by Communist states or Western intervention to protect the white race.

We can expect the continuation of border disputes in new states with artificial and unnatural boundaries. There is a growing prospect of new-style imperialism at the hands of black, yellow, or brown peoples where ambition coincides with power. And there are the chronic vacuums which develop when colonial power departs and nothing exists that can truly replace the old order, thus offering irresistible temptation to external troublemakers. And in the world as a whole there is a discernible trend toward unilateral acts of force, whether under the banner of revolution, reprisal, or a policing function.

Even in areas of great-power confrontation a U.N. role should not be automatically ruled out. In Vietnam such a role could not substitute for American power; without the latter the United Nations was incapable of persuading Asian communism that it cannot take over South Vietnam by terror and force. But there can be an important peacekeeping role for the United Nations wherever fighting can be stopped.[3] One can even imagine a comparable role in that very heart of the Cold War — Berlin — if ever things should get out of hand and both sides suddenly discover that military disengagement under the cover of a neutral presence is preferable to nuclear war.

All in all, then, eyes may well turn toward the East River for action in at least some future crises. There the United Nations, without any fundamental consensus on political values and lack-

[3] A Gallup poll released in January 1966 reports that 49 percent of those Americans questioned thought it would be a good idea for the United States to accept any U.N. decision about Vietnam, with 37 percent disagreeing.

ing the basic foundations of community agreement about law and order, may once more be expected to act as if it were a form of government. Statesmen and diplomats, gathered some midnight and reading with mounting alarm the tickers and cables, may once again ask, as Adlai Stevenson reported that Adam asked when Eve hesitated for a moment after his proposal of marriage, "Is there someone else?"

If, despite its drawbacks, U.N. peacekeeping will nevertheless be turned to again in our time, we need to take a sharp look at what it can and what it cannot do.

The most important ingredients of effective peacekeeping – firm political support, a workable directive, and consistent revenues – are likely to be missing. Their absence reflects accurately the divided world and its insufficient sense of community. They also explain why the realistically cautious ground rules constructed by Dag Hammarskjöld for UNEF remain generally valid for U.N. intervention today and probably tomorrow as well. In essence these called for at least a tacit agreement among the great powers; for the consent of the "host" government, however prostrate the host might be; for the force to be *ad hoc* in nature; and, in general, for the prime function of U.N. peacekeeping forces to be better comprehended by the word "police" than by the word "military."

Some elements of the ground rules have had to change. In the Congo, unlike Suez, the United Nations eventually reserved the right to decide the force composition without the detailed concurrence of a kaleidoscopically shifting government. Because British forces were already in position in Cyprus, they were absorbed into UNFICYP (without necessarily setting a precedent for great-power participation). The Congo operation developed a "sliding mandate" for ONUC that in the end authorized the use of limited force.

It remains theoretically possible for a U.N. peacekeeping operation to be launched without the host's consent. The restraining power of the domestic-jurisdiction barrier as defined by the Charter has been crumbling since racial discrimination in the southern half of Africa began to be accepted by large U.N. majorities as constituting a threat to international peace and security. But without United States financial and logistical support, operations that disregard the Charter seem remote for the present. It also seems unlikely that any new U.N. mandate would authorize the use of force, at least initially.

But the chief difficulties today relate to decision-making and financing. Both problems were profoundly affected by the recent constitutional crisis over financing peacekeeping.

We do not know the thought processes that led Khrushchev to go along with U.N. peacekeeping efforts in Suez, Lebanon, the Congo, and Cyprus. One factor was undoubtedly the generally favorable attitude of the Arab and African states. What we *can* reconstruct is the sense of outrage the Soviet leaders felt when in the late summer of 1960 they came to appreciate how damaging to their national purposes in central Africa a determinedly non-partisan U.N. operation could be. Above all, Moscow had not calculated that the U.N. Secretary General could act as a genuine power factor in world politics, moving events in ways they could not control. Dag Hammarskjöld was henceforth the target of savage Soviet attack and unrelenting opposition, with Moscow urging for the Secretariat the rules of control that applied to all other international power structures into which the Soviet Union had entered. Soviet policy came to a head in adamant refusal to pay assessed shares of the cost of mounting the UNEF and Congo enterprises, both retrospectively branded as "illegal."

It may be that if Moscow had acted alone and without support, its assault on the new peacekeeping would not have made significant political headway. Coinciding as it did with General de Gaulle's sweeping *recul* of the French position in all international organizations smacking of supranationalism, the Soviet drive was potently reinforced by France's refusal to pay its share of the Congo operations. The Soviet position, which in its doctrinaire rigidity should have been isolated, thus acquired the force of a movement.

It was more than coincidence that during the same period the United States itself was having second thoughts about the decision-making process in the United Nations. Washington has increasingly seen renewed potential in the Security Council, where it retains the veto, away from the "swirling majorities" of the Assembly. There have even been unofficial suggestions that the Military Staff Committee be revived for peacekeeping direction.

Yet with the memory of Korea still vivid and the cold war far from over, the right to mobilize the Assembly must be reserved. With Peking in the United Nations, the Uniting for Peace procedures of 1950 would probably prove indispensable. Thus the United States has reaffirmed the primary responsibility of the Council, but it has also upheld the Assembly's authority to act when the Council is paralyzed.[4]

In many ways the American stand on collective financial responsibility for peacekeeping reflects a steadfast posture of support despite the sobering implications of U.N. troops engaged in actual combat operations and the unpleasant possibility of a U.N. operation running contrary to American wishes. Today Washington can be virtually sure of a "blocking third" vote in the General Assembly, but this cannot be guaranteed for the future. Still the United States was prepared to run that risk in support of Article 19 and the principle of collective responsibility.

The disappointing fact was that with a few notable exceptions there was little support for either a showdown on this issue or on the United Nations' financial needs in general. As the crisis wore on, it became evident that Washington's options were in fact between a badly fractured world organization and the humiliation of backing down. Washington chose to accept the short-run defeat.

But a price was charged in terms of American support. Others had insisted on making exceptions to the principle of collective financial responsibility for activities repugnant to them. Henceforth, the United States reserved for itself the same option "if, in our view, strong and compelling reasons exist for doing so." [5] The sobering reality was that in one vital sense the United States had accepted the Soviet-French conception of a United Nations in which any member could "opt out" when a majority, however constitutional, set it on a course the member believed ran counter to its fundamental interests.

Mandatory assessments are not the only way to pay for peace-

[4] Statement of Ambassador Arthur J. Goldberg to U.N. General Assembly, November 24, 1965.

[5] Statement by Ambassador Arthur J. Goldberg to Special Committee on Peacekeeping Operations, August 16, 1965, U.S. Mission to the U.N. Press Release No. 4615, August 16, 1965.

keeping operations. The Yemen force was paid for by the two parties involved, the Cyprus force by voluntary contributions. Some proposals have called for centering the financial responsibility in the Council, as the Soviets and French prefer, or for a mixed Council-Assembly decision. Canada has suggested fund-raising conferences such as are used for technical assistance. Other suggestions propose special peacekeeping funds, an endowment fund, payment only by those who take part, and – the position favored all along by the Soviets – payments by the "aggressors" in each case.

Intensive deliberations since the crisis point to the evolution of new and rather different procedures for peacekeeping operations. It can be predicted that the role of the Security Council will continue to be central – and also that the Assembly will still occasionally be turned to, particularly if Peking takes China's Security Council seat. But whatever the arrangements, it will be the rare peacekeeping operation that can be launched without at least the passive acquiescence of all the great powers. Financing may be arranged in several different ways depending on circumstances. These include voluntary contribution, payment by the parties directly affected, perhaps eventually new sources of international revenues derived from "farming" the sea and "mining" the seabed under international waters.

When the way chosen involves assessing the member states, we can assume a special scale that requires only the most token contributions from the 90-odd under-developed countries; they may pay no more than 5% of the total. And it would be wise to exempt other members – the United States no less than other great powers – from any payment at all if they do not support the operation in question.

INITIATIVES TOWARD A U.N. FORCE

The worsened climate has thrown into doubt even modest proposals for nonstanding U.N. forces.[6] There is still no reliable supply of units skilled in the arts and techniques of peacekeeping

[6] See for instance the author's detailed proposal contained in Chapter 7 of *International Military Forces – The Question of Peacekeeping in An Armed and Disarming World,* by the author with others (Boston: Little, Brown, 1964).

(crowd control, civic action, intelligence) and drawn from politically appropriate parts of the world. The U.N. Secretariat does not include an adequate staff to preplan the logistics, deployment, and support of possible future operations. For the frustrated commanders who have to make U.N. peacekeeping operations work, life would be easier if contingency planning focused on ways of providing a diversified and skilled command, arriving on schedule, wearing the right weight uniforms (and perhaps born with the politically right color skins), and equipped with uniform caliber rifles and uniform size wheels on their vehicles.

Over the years several efforts have been undertaken by the U.N. Secretary General to encourage member states to earmark units within their national forces for ready availability. The list of countries responding to the most recent appeal contain no surprises. Canada, which has supplied virtually all the signals units for U.N. field operations to date, has reported that it has formed a 29,000–man mobile command specially trained for peacekeeping duties. The Netherlands earlier designated a unit of 600 marines and subsequently a supply ship with four helicopters, patrol and scout ships, a light armored carrier, an armored infantry battalion, a medical company, a transport plane, and three jet helicopters. Iran, Italy, and New Zealand have earmarked units. London has taken some steps under the Labor Government that perhaps mark the end of Britain's case of post-Suez sulks toward the United Nations. Substantial British military units have been pledged, though on a highly contingent basis. The British have also signified a willingness to provide significant logistical support. Perhaps most usefully, they have led the way in contributing to a rescue fund to wipe out the existing deficit.

It is the Scandinavians, consistent with their splendid record of enlightened international behavior, who have gone the furthest to build a more reliable international peacekeeping capacity. The parliaments of Denmark, Norway, and Sweden, and Finland as well, have all passed bills that set in motion a training program involving approximately 1,000 men each that can operate either jointly or separately. All four states now have officers working full time on technical planning, with Defense Ministers' meetings twice a year. The training proceeds along the commonly accepted lines of communications, riot controls, and related skills. (Although it developed that Denmark does not normally train its soldiers in riot control, the regiment that put down Copenhagen's last riot – in 1895 – remaining highly unpopular at home!)

Earmarking, training, and even organizing for prospective peacekeeping have thus increasingly acquired a do-it-yourself flavor, in part because their value has become more rather than less controversial. Initiatives that under different circumstances would normally be taken at U.N. headquarters have been taken outside the deadlocked U.N. setting. Several private conferences have been held among government and nongovernment specialists to help thinking and planning to develop on an informal basis. The World Veterans Federation, a worldwide nongovernmental organization accredited to the United Nations but privately supported, has undertaken to establish a clearinghouse in Paris of the various efforts in international peacekeeping research and development.

The United States itself does not have earmarked forces. A group of Republican Congressmen has proposed the creation of a small volunteer unit of 1,000 American servicemen to render on a standby basis "emergency technical support" for U.N. peacekeeping operations, styled the FIRST brigade (an acronym for "Forces for International Relief on Standby").[7] This notion of course runs the hazard of inviting an equivalent contribution of manpower by the Red Army (or perhaps eventually the Chinese People's Army) – a contingency that could spell the end of such neutral peacekeeping capacity as the United Nations has been able to muster. Yet it symbolizes a desire to move ahead beyond the logistical support the U.S. freely furnishes.

In general it probably continues to be true, as the innovators of 1956 sensed, that the cause of peace will best be served when the maximum number of smaller nonwhite countries have put themselves in the position of supplying disciplined, technically trained personnel backed by governments that genuinely support the principle of responsible neutral behavior.

REGIONAL PEACEKEEPING

The role of the Organization of American States in politically broadening the unilateral American intervention in the Domini-

[7] Statement dated June 16, 1965.

can Republic in 1965 raises a point that belongs on the agenda of middle- and long-term planning. As of today, regional organizations are an inadequate substitute for the United Nations in terms of capacity to mount and execute effective peacekeeping operations. One reason is that such organizations are characteristically incomplete, excluding Israel in the Middle East, the southern part of Africa in the case of the Organization of African Unity, and even, one might say, Eastern Europe on the part of NATO. The OAS operates in the shadow of one dominant country. The majority of Latin American states appear to have resisted recent American efforts to make an institution out of the figleaf the OAS spread over American troops in the Dominican Republic. Even without this recent history, collective operations of the sort the United States envisages run against the traditions and beliefs of most Latin American states, evoke fears of American intervention, and smack, whether justly or not, of counterrevolutionary purposes.

In Africa the OAU has yet to show itself capable of replacing the United Nations, however much some of its members would wish it to. At the same time, however, in its brief history several interesting things have been done: in Tanganyika, Nigerian and Ethiopian troops replaced those Britain had earlier sent on request; three disputes have already been settled under OAU auspices; the OAU has voted resolutions for enforcement action against Portugal and South Africa, which in time may become meaningful with the development of some genuine capacity for implementation. In the Middle East the Arab League actually did provide a mixed force of 3,000 that replaced British units in Kuwait in 1961 (although it did not work any better than most other Arab League collective efforts). Even in Europe a new note is being heard. Harlan Cleveland, the U.S. Ambassador to NATO only recently departed from his U.N. duties in Washington, called in the fall of 1965 for finding "new ways of relating the peacekeeping forces on duty within NATO to the flexible callup system which the United Nations has been developing for peacekeeping duties elsewhere." [8]

All things considered — including the likelihood that most re-

[8] Address in Paris, October 21, 1965. *Department of State Bulletin,* November 15, 1965.

gional organizations would employ such power as they developed against their own particular enemy in their region – the wisest policy would seem to be to begin now to work out formulas by which regional organizations would be encouraged to act in close coordination with the United Nations in performing tasks of pacific settlement of disputes, including negotiation, mediation, arbitration, observation, and even small-scale policing. The connection with the United Nations is extremely important both in terms of establishing the legitimacy of regional operations and of vesting ultimate responsibility in the larger body of states neutral to the particular conflict. Yet there are valid reasons for strengthening the regional means, not only because this may be an inevitable development, but also because of the positive desirability of giving more effect to the still sensible provisions of the U.N. Charter according to which regional agencies are expected to aid in trying to work out disputes before they become formalized as U.N. "cases" (Article 33). Such a division of labor might well contribute to making disputes more manageable.

Peace and security, we were told in 1945, were indivisible. As of the late 1960s, however, our best bet may be to divide security up into smaller pieces in order to keep the larger structure from being overloaded. The 1970s may see a resurgence of regional arrangements whether we favor them or not. The task for the foresighted is to design the crisis-tight compartments that, by making the peace divisible, may ultimately help to make peacekeeping synonymous with peacemaking.

All in all, a number of sobering conclusions emerge concerning the peacekeeping capabilities of the United Nations. First, on the assumption that U.N. peacekeeping will be invoked in the future yet will continue to rest on a fragmented political foundation, common sense favors arrangements that do not put the existence of the organization at stake each time such a task must be undertaken. One means of achieving this decoupling, so to speak, lies in procedures enabling the great powers to stand aside from a given operation – and from paying for it. Their political resistance may still be formidable, and if one of the superpowers is adamantly opposed to a particular goal, the United Nations probably should not be made the instrument for achieving that goal. But there may be other cases in which they only object mildly, and there the United Nations can possibly be used – as it has been in the past – with one great power's objections limited to rhetoric.

In this connection the American reservation of the right not to pay for U.N. activities for which it disapproves was distressing to friends of the United Nations. In fact, however, such explicit decoupling of decision-making and paying of costs may contribute to the salvation of the organization. It could preserve the principle of apportioning expenses while avoiding the adoption of taxing policies that would be enforceable only under a world government. At the same time, the possibility of independent revenue sources for the United Nations, through imposts on international mail or trade or royalties on exploitation of sub-sea or outer-space resources, should continue to be studied for the future.

The second conclusion is that the price of achieving genuine reforms in procedures for U.N. peacekeeping would be to restrict to the Security Council's authority the launching of such operations. This trade-off is unacceptable to the United States, which, while shedding some unrealistic earlier expectations about majority rule in the Assembly, wants an escape hatch available in extreme situations (with the bonus value of deterring the uninhibited use of the veto in the Security Council). So long as this is true, the Soviets and some others will also continue to be hostile to any significant strengthening of the U.N. Secretariat for contingency planning, stockpiling, training, or any other of the desirable preparations for operations in any part of the world.

Peacekeeping efforts outside the organization, limited as they are, should be encouraged. Work done now to assemble data, to encourage countries to earmark and specially train units, to plan the necessary logistics, and even to blueprint force structures and training programs could one day prove vital for the success of one or another peacekeeping operation. And it cannot be repeated too often that American military assistance to underdeveloped countries might be far better invested if it emphasized the aim, already to be found in the legislation, of improving the capacity of international organizations to carry out peacekeeping functions. By its nature such a shift in emphasis would strengthen the very internal-security and civic-action functions that appear far more functional than the status-symbol types of weapons that wind up with depressing frequency being used against internal rivals or close neighbors.[9]

The third conclusion is that the clear interest of the United States in supporting a U.N. capability for peacekeeping is tempered by the candid expectation that under some foreseeable circumstances this country may interpret the action as running contrary to its interests. In the Dominican Republic in the spring of 1965 the United States resisted the United Nations Security Council's attempts to assert its competence (while France, with perhaps the merest *arrière pensée,* assumed the pose of champion of U.N. peacekeeping). Looking ahead, a punitive U.N. expedition aimed at stripping political power from the whites of Rhodesia (or, perhaps later, South Africa) could create a grave crisis of confidence for American participation. A theoretical capacity exists now for mobilizing U.N. peacekeeping machinery at the service of a passionate Afro-Asian majority, perhaps in the process overcoming Soviet (or later Chinese) aversion to General Assembly enforcement actions.[10]

In the end the reasons why the world needs international peacekeeping, global or regional, for secondary and internal explosions are akin to the reasons why American power polices the peripheries of the Communist heartlands. It is not because the United Nations is ideally equipped to do its job – clearly it is not – any more than the United States has a natural right to act as a substitute for real collective security – which it does not. Both, however badly done and justly criticized in detail, fill the void in the absence of an effective world political authority. The price for both – and it can be heavy in political, moral, and human terms – is perhaps less than the price of uncontrolled violence, unpoliced disorder, and unlimited war. On balance, it seems not too great a price to pay.

[9] See Lincoln P. Bloomfield and Amelia C. Leiss, "Arms Control and the Developing Countries," *World Politics,* October 1965.

[10] And if the ominous General Assembly vote of December 22, 1965, on bases is prophetic, it may be on the basis of a simple rather than two-thirds majority.

CHAPTER SEVEN

The United Nations and the Problem of Counterinsurgency

In a world where ideologies are in conflict, yet resolution by force is increasingly debarred because of its disproportionate risks, the application of techniques of indirect rather than direct action toward attainment of strategic goals is increasing.

The Communist movement has long utilized techniques of indirection that both serve the need for concealment and favor the position of one who must operate from an initially inferior power position. Communist power has multiplied, but so have the risks of overt adventurism; and so long as an effective deterrent to such adventurism is maintained by the West, the process of change in the Communist states may do its work of draining away the movement's messianic spirit and revolutionary *élan*. In the meantime, Communist penetration into new areas of political conquest employs the techniques of indirect aggression – clandestine penetration, subversion, and takeover of indigenous insurgent and revolutionary movements and turning them into what the Communists call "wars of national liberation." The development of these subtle Communist takeover tactics coincided historically with the emergence of a host of new, weak, poor, and politically unsophisticated nations in which revolutionary movements have become widespread as protests against colonial rule, poverty, dictatorial rule, and general hopelessness.

The acuteness and complexity of the world-wide problem of stability with which U.S. foreign policy seeks to deal grows precisely out of this lethal combination: revolution or insurgency that may be non-Communist and reflect genuine popular grievances with which Americans are traditionally sympathetic, and efforts by skillful, well-organized and well-trained Communist minorities, local or Moscow- or Peking-oriented, to capture such movements and the societies in which they occur.

There must therefore be included in the catalog of paramount American security objectives the need to find more effective ways of preventing and repulsing subversion externally directed against the political independence and territorial integrity of other nations.

It might be reasonable to conclude that if it is to have genuine relevance and value for what is perhaps the most baffling and yet exigent contemporary political issue, the United Nations ought to focus on the area of insurgency — and counterinsurgency. But on close inspection it is not at all certain that the United Nations either could or should be used indiscriminately in the type of situation that, in its very ambiguity and its combination of internal and external elements, is the most likely to evade the classic description of the act of aggression. Efforts continue, inevitably without success, to define acts of aggression. A U.N. committee meets periodically to grapple with a semantic problem that by its very nature cannot be resolved without solving the underlying conflict. For in Western eyes "aggression" today must include acts of indirect penetration from the outside — the very category of acts that both brands of communism seek to legitimize as acts of "liberation."

One set of difficulties inherent in trying to draw up universally applicable rules in this area was well illustrated at the height of the 1958 Middle Eastern crisis. During the early part of the summer, according to reports in the American press, discussions were taking place within the U.S. Government as to whether the U.N. General Assembly, then about to meet in emergency session on the crisis, should be asked to do something tangible and dramatic about the general problem of indirect aggression. The specific issue from which general principles were to be inferred was the alleged infiltration of hostile personnel and arms into Lebanon from Syria under the political direction of the United Arab Republic authorities and to the accompaniment of hostile propaganda designed to undermine the stability of the Lebanese regime and encourage the rebellion then in progress.

In his speech to the emergency Assembly session, President Eisenhower called for an "end to the fomenting from without of civil strife." [1] His texts were two resolutions passed by the General Assembly in 1949 and 1950. The Essentials of Peace Resolution in 1949 called upon every nation

> to refrain from any threats or acts, direct or indirect, aimed at impairing the freedom, independence or integrity of any State, or at fomenting civil strife and subverting the will of the people in any State.[2]

The Peace through Deeds Resolution, passed on November 17, 1950, in the midst of the Korean action, reaffirmed that

> . . . whatever the weapons used, any aggression, whether committed openly, or by fomenting civil strife in the interest of a foreign Power, or otherwise, is the gravest of all crimes against peace and security throughout the world.[3]

But by the time the President actually appeared before the Assembly the decision had apparently gone against the notion of making indirect aggression the central theme of the American presentation. The press attributed this change of heart to the realization that the United States might itself be vulnerable, at least in a legalistic way, to the charge of "indirect aggression" in, for example, Eastern Europe. Clandestine activities sponsored by the United States, however idealistically directed toward the end of national freedom and justice, might be subject to precisely the same strictures the United States had contemplated applying to Nasser's political and paramilitary activity, as well as to the larger problem of traditional Communist subversive tactics.

The distinction that emerged was a useful and instructive one.

[1] *New York Times,* August 14, 1958.
[2] General Assembly Resolution 209 (IV), December 1, 1949.
[3] General Assembly Resolution 380 (V), November 17, 1950.

It was one thing to oppose external support for the Czechoslovak coup in 1948, for example, which by all evidence was a plot against an unwilling and free people to install an authoritarian regime stage-managed by a foreign power. But the lessons of the Czechoslovak coup could not be applied unqualifiedly to the Lebanese civil war of 1958, or to the subversive aspects of the pan-Arab movement as a whole, or to some of the movements in Black Africa that opposed oppressive white rule — or oppressive black rule, as in Ghana in 1965. Even the Cuban revolution of 1959–1960 could not have been opposed at the time as "Communist." The same dilemma brought contumely on the American head when U.S. troops took over in Santo Domingo in 1965 because Communists might be involved. Any government attempting to apply formulas developed to cope exclusively with traditional Communist methods of infiltration, subversion, and ultimate take-over would find itself facing a complex dilemma growing out of the generally "popular" nature of revolutionary movements that marched under the nationalist banner, however subversive their techniques.

The ambiguous and complex nature of "insurgency" plagues American foreign policy virtually across the board, from the Caribbean to Vietnam. The fundamental dilemma is a large one: how to ensure stability in the world without bottling up popular forces whose political expression might in fact represent more genuine democracy than the autocratic or feudal or totalitarian regimes now in power. The United States is torn in several directions when it comes to formulating in concrete terms workable ground rules about subversion and indirect aggression.

Ideally speaking, we would presumably wish to see *all* feudal or imperial or internally undemocratic regimes discouraged and popular and democratic rule enhanced. Thus we profoundly oppose aggression against friendly democratic regimes that is aimed at imposing undemocratic or tyrannical rule. We shall in such cases doubtless help to support the existing government in every way, as we are now doing around the world, and we shall oppose the forces of infiltration or subversion. On the other hand, we would certainly not agree in advance to support international sanctions against forces acting to support pro-freedom or pro-Western revolutionary movements, which some day may rise again in Cuba, in East Germany, and perhaps in the centers of Communism itself. There have been instances where the United States has itself sponsored the internal subversion of a foreign government, notably in Arbentz's Guatemala in 1954. And finally, given the variety of circumstances that conceivably might prevail, we are not ourselves always prepared to intervene in any way at all or even to express an official view.

Indeed – and this is the hardest of all to acknowledge – it could be that we would, for overriding security reasons, discourage external assistance from any source to genuine and even pro-Western forces of revolution: witness American self-restraint in East Germany in 1953, Poland and Hungary in 1956, and Tibet in 1959. In point of fact, for reasons of military strategy or political stability we have occasionally given aid and comfort to regimes repugnant to our democratic principles: for example, Tito's Yugoslavia, Franco's Spain, Gomulka's Poland, and before them to Trujillo's Dominican Republic and Batista's Cuba. It is easy to condemn such inconsistency as immoral. It is less easy to weigh the values in a complex situation involving at best a choice of varying evils. There are obvious and excruciating difficulties in attempting to generalize a policy on this score on the basis of either simple minded maxims or abstract rules of morality. The very ambiguity of the characteristic subversive situation has made the defining of indirect aggression no easier than the effort to define aggression, itself beset by semantic and political pitfalls.

If the United States cannot afford the luxury of a simple copybook morality on this subject, what alternative courses are open to it? Can it be selective in its approach to subversion and indirect aggression? This would mean closing an eye to externally caused disruption in the Communist world and in non-Communist regimes we do not favor while insisting on the principle of nonintervention in areas chosen as targets by Communist and other forces as well as in countries with undemocratic regimes with which we find it convenient to deal. This position, which roughly approximates the present reality, is not particularly attractive either politically or morally.

Another alternative would be to act consistently on our announced principles. But to oppose all forms of outside assistance to revolutionary movements would carry us back to the worst excesses of the Holy Alliance and breed the same reaction. It would retroactively put into moral question the substantial assistance given to the embryonic United States by France, for example, or the powerful indirect support afforded by England to revolutionary democracy in Greece in the 1820s or by the West to Hungary in the mid-nineteenth century.

The final alternative in generalizing a consistent rule is unthinkable in view of our profound interest in world stability. Complete *laissez faire* with respect to subversive movements would encourage perpetual turmoil and takeover by the best-disciplined and most determined minority – often the Communists. The removal of an important obstacle to those who oppose freedom of choice would frustrate our objective of preserving and, if possible, enlarging the present area in which noncoercive societies are at least permitted to develop.

What conclusions can be drawn from this analysis? The first is that we cannot live by a hard-and-fast rule with respect to insurgency and indirect aggression – a rule bearing equally on the just and unjust and administered with blind impartiality, like the law of the Medes and the Persians, regardless of whose ox is gored or which side wins out in the struggle. Our approach can only be a pragmatic one. We must be selective rather than general in our application of principles precisely because there is neither any overall political rule nor any unambiguous moral position which can be applied satisfactorily for all cases.

A second major conclusion is that, whatever action might be taken by multilateral agencies, the key to the problem of subversion lies within rather than outside of a nation's borders. The primary elements necessary to sustain the internal health of externally harassed regimes are widespread popular support, a stable yet adequately dynamic social and economic order, capable leadership, and, finally, military and police facilities to maintain internal order and guard the borders. After decades of unremitting propaganda, enmity, subversion, infiltration, espionage, and possibly sabotage, the Soviet Union, through the American Communist party and networks of Soviet agents, has made virtually no impression on the political, economic, or social fabric of the United States. The same has been true of every other Western democracy whose internal strength rests on solid foundations. But the non-Western societies that are the new targets of indirect aggression lack in varying degrees the conditions that make indirect aggression relatively profitless; and the development of their internal strength, in the final analysis their only sure protection against subversion, must be a self-generated process in which external assistance can be only marginal.

In the late 1960s one of the most promising developments is the awakening on the part of an increasing number of Asian and African states to the perils of Communist penetration. In one state after another — the Congo, Algeria, Uganda, Burundi, India, Indonesia, Ghana, even Guinea and the United Arab Republic — subversion efforts by Moscow or Peking have been identified as such and checked with varying degrees of severity and success. In Latin America and important parts of the other developing regions the process of recognizing and dealing with Communist subversion has only just begun; societies there are still weak, insecure, and vulnerable and will remain so for a long time to come.

What is the implication of these conclusions for the role of the United Nations?

We should not look to the United Nations for *general* rules regarding externally generated pressures in situations primarily characterized by civil strife. As suggested, our interests would not necessarily be well served by such rules in the present political state of the world. There is also doubt whether others would find such strictures desirable either. The political atlas includes countries governed by regimes ranging from democratic to totalitarian; it includes stable governments and weak governments; it contains countries sympathetic to neighboring regimes and countries implacably hostile. We could hardly expect widespread support of rules that would be examined by each country, not in the abstract, but invariably in terms of its own concrete policy problems.

But there is a role for the United Nations without imposing any such rules. The United Nations, along with other instruments of diplomacy and propaganda, can and should be used *ad hoc* where it would support our interests so to use it. There will continue to be many situations of blatant but non-overt interference from without by means of infiltration, subversion, and propaganda of a tendentious and revolutionary nature. If our object is to curtail and discourage such activity, U.N. debate may be the most effective agency of bringing these clandestine pressures to the widest possible public attention. This might have happened, for example, in Vietnam if the United States had not permitted itself to be persuaded over the years, first by France and later by its own unilateral involvement, to avoid until 1965 any formal reference of the issue to the United Nations.

We should keep alive the awareness that multilateral action thus has its uses in the complex circumstances and subtleties of indirect aggression even though the United Nations is only the stage on which the act, in preparation elsewhere, comes to light and presents other governments with choices and decisions. To regard such cases individually and in the light of national interest may appear unpalatably Machiavellian. It is, nevertheless, the only course that reflects present and prospective political realities.

CHAPTER EIGHT

Disarmament and Arms Control

DISARMAMENT

In a drastically changed world where all-out nuclear war and its devastating results are wholly disproportionate to the aims of any conceivable political objective, disarmament accompanied by a world police authority sounds like a good solution to the problem of national security. But how realistic is such a goal?

The Soviet Union and the United States have adopted verbal policies favoring General and Complete Disarmament (GCD) and have agreed on a joint statement of principles for GCD. In addition, the Soviets have realistically conceded the need for a nuclear "umbrella" throughout the disarming process. But GCD is confronted by powerful roadblocks – the force of inertia, the unresolved issue of Germany and Berlin, and the deep commitments to defense programs. Most of all, GCD runs afoul on the basic ideological cleavage between the Communists and the West, which leaves unresolved how to fill the power vacuum left by national disarmament. These formidable barriers to disarmament can be deplored – perhaps to a limited extent they can even be "designed around"; but they cannot be ignored.

One must therefore consider as utopian the possibility of a drastically revised international system in which nations will junk military power and subordinate national sovereignty and ambition to an international organization possessing a relative monopoly over the means of coercion. It may take a century or more – or even a trip over the brink of nuclear war – for man to evolve to a stage of higher development that will support such profound changes in his political ways. The towering problem for political creativity in the remainder of the twentieth century is to find realistic ways of bypassing this evolutionary period so that our world may gradually be made more tolerable. It is futile to pretend that there are already in existence the building blocks of fundamental consensus about the political, economic, and social arrangements that must underlie government, law, and its enforcement.

It will be recalled that the discussions on disarmament in the League of Nations, covering almost its entire lifespan, had no effect whatever on the realities of the armaments problem. Indeed, the only tangible effect was to soften the will and the capacity of the democracies to survive as they came to view weapons as villains rather than as only sometimes the tools of villains. The League debates never had any real-life effect because France never received the guarantees she sought from the United States and England against the possibility of standing alone in the presence of a rearmed and hostile Germany. No amount of words in Geneva in the 1920s could overcome this obstacle.

By the same logic, under conditions that can be foreseen for the years immediately ahead, the prospects of significant reductions and controls in armaments remain first and foremost a function of the relationship between the major powers, and thus at any given time are subject primarily to the special influences of Communist doctrine and tactics.[1] The problem is acutely complicated in the period ahead by the probability that Communist China will undergo an extended period of fanatical nationalism, expansion, and hostility to the Western world – possibly including the Soviet Union – to the point that even limited disarmament will long remain an impossibility. This prospect haunts

[1] See Lincoln P. Bloomfield, Walter Clemens, Jr., Franklyn Griffiths, *Khrushchev and the Arms Race – Soviet Interests in Arms Control and Disarmament: 1954–1964* (Cambridge: M.I.T. Press, 1966).

our planning, for despite efforts to include China in such enterprises as the World Disarmament Conference planned for 1967, there seems little hope for a durable agreement. No predictable end is in view to the mutual suspicions that would have to be significantly alleviated before even limited disarmament could become possible.

In the face of these prospects one may wonder why present efforts to reverse the security-disarmament equation should have any brighter prospects than in the past. If there is an answer, it lies in the awareness, hopefully general, of the irrationality of an open-ended nuclear arms race.

Some have deduced from this logic that a real possibility exists for complete universal disarmament. I would suggest that the conditions for such disarmament are equivalent to those for world government: (1) a climate of significantly greater world confidence; (2) the presence of international institutions of a police nature which would furnish adequate physical protection to all nations; and (3) a global political regime which, as in any community whose members have laid down their arms, would supply continuous and reliable justice to its members, including provisions for peaceful change through the process of legislation. Obviously, these are not priority topics of serious planning in terms of action in any reasonably near future.

As a practical matter, the short-run problem of disarmament in the second half of the twentieth century is to reduce the possibility of widespread destruction or contamination by nuclear and other mass-destruction weapons. Even more specifically, the problem is to minimize the power of any given nation to mount a surprise attack sufficient to effectively eliminate the capacity to retaliate, a capacity that has so far deterred such risk-taking. A crucial part of this problem is to limit the number of states possessing nuclear weapons. Thus another set of answers comes under the catchall label of "arms control" – measures aimed at lessening the chances of war by miscalculation of accident.

ARMS CONTROL

Arms-control measures aim at improving the capacity to delay military retaliation that could result from ambiguous signals which may or may not indicate an attack. They seek to enable measured reactions to provocation rather than apocalyptic spasms. Thus they foster tacit bargaining, better command and control, and the doctrine of "flexible response." They focus on the need to reassure both sides about intentions; and they see communication as the heart of bargaining (hence the "hot line," and unilateral actions to inspire a reply, such as the mutual cutback of fissionable materials in early 1964).

But in political terms two events must precede genuine agreements among the great powers, whether tacit or negotiated. Both the Soviet Union and China must come to the conclusion that success in their alleged historical missions will be possible without the military capacity to crush the capitalist world. They must abandon Lenin's dictum that "only after the proletariat has disarmed the bourgeoisie will it . . . throw all armaments on the scrapheap." [2] Furthermore, the United States must come to the conclusion that the dynamic nature of both Soviet and Chinese doctrine no longer carries an important threat to the West of overt military aggression to achieve political ends. In sum, both sides will have to agree to forego insistence on the kind of strategic advantage that has thus far aborted disarmament negotiations.

Let us first consider the prospects of Soviet willingness to forego the advantages it seeks. One assumption popularized by Bertrand Russell has been that the new weaponry, like George III's generals, tends to menace its owners as much as it menaces others. If this assumption were genuinely accepted on all sides, the prospects of agreement might be great. For a time it appeared that only the U.S. made such an assumption, a view that perhaps more than anything else tended to unbalance the negotiating equation. Some Communists apparently still deceive themselves on their ability to survive a global holocaust. Chinese Communist leadership has been quoted as anticipating with satisfaction that the 300 million Chinese surviving a thermonuclear war would inherit the earth, and as expressing confidence that a superior civilization could be created "in the debris of a dead imperial-

[2] V. I. Lenin, "Military Program of the Proletarian Revolution," *Collected Works* (New York: International Publishers, 1942), p. 366.

ism." [3] Soviet doctrine has wavered uncertainly between confidence that communism will emerge triumphant from a war and acknowledgement that no one would win.

For even limited arms controls, the greatest difficulty in acknowldeging a real mutuality of interests stems from the role of arms not in the field of battle, but of diplomacy. Until the Cuban missile crisis of 1962, Soviet leadership seemed confident that its will and nerve were sufficiently superior that it could threaten nuclear warfare without much real risk in a variety of tactical situations. If others overreacted, the threat could be readily withdrawn, a sequence that had recurred in Berlin several times. One of the most sobering facts in the political scene was the seeming confidence of Soviet leadership in its ability to handle its own weapons rationally and self-consciously and not be controlled or panicked by them or by fear of them. Chinese doctrine, perhaps to keep up morale while living under the threat of American nuclear power, has emphasized this same quality of self-assurance. Agreement on arms controls has also been inhibited by apparent Soviet and Chinese confidence that the United States could be kept from launching a preventive or preemptive attack.

Thus an indispensable condition for even limited arms control has been a weakening of Soviet confidence in their continued ability to manipulate American hostility. A genuine American willingness to put everything at stake, as indeed it did during the Cuban missile crisis of 1962, apparently convinced the Soviets that the situation was not so manageable as they had thought and that they would do well to reach an agreement before the Americans "lost their heads." For in the following year, there was for the first time some real progress: a limited test-ban treaty was signed, direct communication was established between Moscow and Washington, and both parties announced their intention not to place in orbit or station in outer space any objects carrying nuclear weapons or weapons of mass destruction. Later negotiations on treaties to demilitarize space and to block the spread of nuclear weapons were conducted in the same tone.

The acceptance by both schools of Communist leadership of arms control as an interest-based policy must consequently de-

[3] See articles in *Hung Chi* and *Jenmin Jihpao,* both quoted in *New York Times,* April 23, 1960.

pend on their willingness to forego the propaganda and diplomatic advantages conferred by military power, as well as on their willingness to forego the capacity to repel capitalists who suddenly turn out as Lenin predicted they would.

But it is not only the Communists who approach disarmament negotiations with an *arrière-pensée*. The attitude of the American military community toward disarmament has been largely that of any other nation, and equally inhibiting to the prospects of agreement. Americans who are responsible for the nation's security tend to ensure that any agreement will leave this country in a relatively favorable strategic position. Sometimes the quest for residual strategic advantage has been explicit, and sometimes so tacit as to be unrecognizable.

The changing technology of warfare may force an alteration in these traditional attitudes, particularly when, as Secretary of Defense McNamara has explicitly admitted,[4] a military establishment can no longer give assurances of its ability either to defend the nation successfully against attack or to attack the enemy in a way that will not invite crippling damage in return. The central problem of either arms control or disarmament, then, is how to devise a scheme under which neither side would receive or even retain a net strategic advantage, a scheme which could convince military planners on both sides that their mission was no longer to secure that net advantage.

This problem is intensely complicated by the spread of nuclear-weapon capabilities. The detonation of Peking's first atomic devices in the fall of 1964 provoked renewed widespread discussion of the dangers of the further spread of nuclear weaponry. Speculation flourished about who would be next — Sweden? Japan? Israel? Or perhaps India, which had become the first nonnuclear country to build a chemical separation plant? Cost estimates have put nuclear weapons within reach of even the poorest nations within a few years.[5] Governments have issued solemn pronouncements about the need to design further international agreements to prevent nuclear proliferation, and at sessions of the Eighteen-

[4] In a variety of statements including his notable speech at Ann Arbor, Michigan, June 16, 1962, and his annual defense reviews since.

[5] See Secretary of Defense McNamara's news conference of October 22, 1964.

Nation Disarmament Committee in Geneva in 1965, both the Soviet Union and the United States introduced draft treaties to prohibit nuclear spread.

There is good reason to become nervous about the prospect of a five-, six-, seven-, ten-, or twenty-nation nuclear world. Notwithstanding minority arguments that such a situation might increase stability, there seems to be a consensus that this environment would furnish individual political and military leaders of varying degrees of personal stability, integrity, or responsibility with new and potentially disastrous opportunities for mischief on a grand scale. The present proclivity of some small states to invoke the possibility of thermonuclear war if they do not have their way could turn from rhetoric to reality.

To have a threatening disease under control in one location, as we now temporarily have, by no means guarantees preventing its outbreak at a variety of other places. In short, the further spread of nuclear weapons must be regarded by responsible nations as a profound complication at best, as a lethal menace at worst.

In this situation what are the possible uses of the United Nations in achieving basic policy objectives in the field of arms control in the foreseeable future?

THE USES OF THE UNITED NATIONS

When the United States and the Soviet Union were the only major nuclear powers, the United Nations had only marginal uses in dealing with the arms question. The French have since acquired a modest nuclear capacity that they have adamantly refused to discuss in any international forum. After the Chinese success in mastering nuclear technology the United Nations sponsored a proposed World Disarmament Conference to include China. But the problem of bringing France and China into negotiations has not been solved in or out of the United Nations. Nevertheless the United Nations has become steadily more useful as a forum for negotiation and as a source of international pressure.

At first even the Russians boycotted the U.N. Disarmament Commission, until their demand for parity in representation with the Western alliance was met in late 1958 by the device of making the Commission representative of the total U.N. membership.

The parity theme posed difficult problems for the West, chiefly because of the derangement it implied across the board in multilateral diplomatic activity; but parity was soon granted in the form of a ten-nation group on disarmament established outside the United Nations by the Big Four Foreign Ministers in August of 1959. This in turn gave way again to U.N. debate after the Russian walkout from the 1960 Geneva meeting of the ten-nation group. And with their espousal of a three-sided world in the troika proposals of 1960 on, the Soviets influenced a new principle of representation in disarmament talks.

In 1961 agreement was reached between the two superpowers on guideposts for future negotiations. The agreement called for balanced disarmament by stages together with the establishment of procedures for the peaceful settlement of disputes, maintenance of international peace through a U.N. force, and control by an international disarmament organization.[6] The General Assembly endorsed these principles and approved an expanded Disarmament Committee of Eighteen (ENDC) to continue negotiations in Geneva starting in 1962. When a World Disarmament Conference was decided on in 1965 Secretary General U Thant pointed out that like the Geneva committee, it would meet independently of the United Nations; [7] in the latter case the reason was the invitation to nonmembers such as Communist China.

But where and how agreement is reached is of no particular consequence. More to the point is that bilateral or even eighteen-nation agreement (seventeen without France, whose chair has remained vacant) will still leave the Nth country problem – the problem of other countries that have already developed or are on the verge of developing nuclear capabilities. By definition the problem here becomes multilateral (evidenced by the adherence of virtually all states except China, France, and Cuba to the limited test-ban treaty of 1963), and a wide multilateral forum would be the only appropriate basis for extending the agreement to all countries and binding them by it.

The proposed World Disarmament Conference was designed to meet this need. In general the United Nations as a negotiating

[6] "Joint Statement of Agreed Principles for Disarmament Negotiations," U.N. Document A/4879, September 20, 1961.

[7] *New York Times,* November 30, 1965.

forum can be useful only to the extent that the great powers are in advance agreement, as they were in the test ban. It can of course keep pressure on the great powers, but more than two decades of such pressure has not seemed to have had a determinative effect. Perhaps the most promising use of the United Nations would be in negotiating suitable political and security guarantees to accompany a treaty restricting nuclear proliferation – guarantees that would be in the U.S. interest to have made, but not unilaterally.

When it comes to the implementation of arrangements already agreed to, some special problems arise. As pointed out earlier, Western disarmament policy has been guided by the fundamental assumption that significant disarmament, or other agreed regulation and limitation of armaments, cannot be safely undertaken without supranational machinery to oversee, monitor, supervise, and otherwise manage the program. This assumption has two roots. First, it grows out of the view, particularly characteristic of American thinking, that international relations and arms control are essentially organizational problems, matters to be regulated and, ideally, controlled by appropriate organizational structures. Second, pervasive historical suspicion of Soviet motives has focused Western arms-control proposals on organizational frameworks that would minimize the possibility that Communist countries could cheat. The Western powers have consequently emphasized the need for both structured international controls over disarmament and the corollaries to comprehensive disarmament in terms of international forces and international peacekeeping institutions – in a word, world government, but without calling it that.[8]

The Soviet and, we can surmise, Chinese views of international institutions differ from the American in significant ways. By any authentic interpretation of Communist doctrine, a powerful non-Communist supranational organization at this stage of history can only mean a plot by the capitalist powers to check communism's forward momentum and destroy its hard-won gains. By this interpretation, existing international organizations such as the United Nations must be checked when they go beyond a

[8] See the author's "Arms Control and World Government," *World Politics*, July 1962.

purely servicing function. If they cannot be checked, the Communists generally prefer that they be eliminated. Moreover, unlike the West, the Soviets have been explicit in refusing to see any necessary relationship between disarmament and world government.

Thus, whether or not the Soviets really want some significant disarmament, they tend to view with profound suspicion any attempt to impose a new and, by definition, anti-Communist international order which under the guise of disarmament controls would frustrate their movement. It is not even a question of degree. At the level of minimum arms control, the issue is still that of penetration into Soviet society by a necessarily hostile power. And when one goes up the scale toward truly comprehensive disarmament programs, the conflict sharpens acutely between the Western assertion that supranational institutions are required, and the Soviet determination to oppose them as well as the equally conventional Western thesis that the amount of inspection needed increases with the degree of disarmament.

Clearly, then, whatever the disagreements on anything else — and they are formidable — there is no real common meeting ground either on the issue of international political institutions or on the related issue of intensive inspection under an arms-control agreement. As long as this is so, it is difficult to test whether a consensus exists in regulating the arms race. The West has set as a precondition for reciprocal arms reductions the radical rearrangement of power and authority in the political world, but in fact it may not really want this, once conditions actually favor arms reductions. We can attack the problem through three avenues, all intimately related: inspection, enforcement, and administration. Are there other ways of thinking about each that might be in the common interest?

THE INSPECTION DILEMMA

The key to the control issue is inspection — that is, a means of verifying to one side's satisfaction that agreed measures have in fact been carried out by the other side. All else flows from this need.

Inspection is now generally recognized to serve two principal purposes, and its dual nature has complicated our thinking about control institutions. The most commonly cited purpose of inspection is to discover and warn against violations. In this sense the system is a "deterrent to crime." It is this aspect of inspection that has dominated Western thinking thus far.

The second purpose of inspection, particularly important where there is a high degree of suspicion, is to reassure both sides that a potential or actual violation will surely be detected. When suspicion exists, the *belief* that crimes will be detected is the important factor. A degree of penetration of the Soviet Union significantly greater than would be needed to detect a major preparation for war would not necessarily deter the Soviet Union from trying to violate any more than would a lesser but adequate penetration, but it would have the political virtue of substantially greater reassurance for the West.

The high degree of mutual mistrust makes it uncommonly difficult to estimate the objective requirements for adequate detection. But until and unless that objective need can be separated from the psychological need for reassurance, we cannot be certain of having developed a disarmament position that does justice to our own priority interest in reducing the level of armaments, the danger of accidental war, and the proliferation of nuclear weapons. Mistrust, the need for reassurance, penetration of national societies, and the question of sovereignty are all links in the chain of political logic.

The Western position correctly asserts that if we cannot discover whether the other side is complying or not, it would be foolhardy and even dangerous to gamble on their word. By this reasoning someone other than a Soviet national – whether a U.N. inspector or a Western observer – must be permitted to verify Communist compliance, and vice versa. But because of the great suspicion between the two sides we have gone considerably beyond the essential minimum in our approach to inspection. Some Westerners believe that only through uninhibited access – that is, only by transforming the Soviet Union into an open society – can we have confidence sufficient to substantially reverse the arms race. This was the real meaning of the American position, taken after the Soviet resumption of testing in the fall of 1961, that any agreement on testing must contain inspection provisions insuring that no nation could ever again secretly even prepare to test. This was an obviously unmanageable position and was subsequently dropped.

The central logic of the matter is essentially uncomplicated. The Soviet system will, we fervently hope, be altered by time and such influences as we can bring to bear, but it is unlikely to be altered as part of the arms control *agreement* unless we are able to impose such an agreement by force – which is doubtful. At the same time, there is general agreement that Western – and Soviet – security would in fact be improved by reasonably safeguarded controls on the arms race. We must conclude, however reluctantly, that such an improvement in our security cannot be achieved if our price is ideological and political surrender on the part of the Soviets.

If we are to find a sound position for achieving our objectives regarding arms control, we need to understand better the Soviet view of inspection. Doubtless military secrecy is a prime component. But Soviet and, *a fortiori,* Chinese resistance to intrusion by "foreigners" goes deeper. The very matrix of control by totalitarian regimes depends above all on the monopoly of authority. The greatest danger to that monopoly could well lie in the sudden presence, under a politically transcendent authority, of foreign inspectors with search and interrogation powers like those which had hitherto belonged only to the regime. This prospect, as well as pure considerations of military secrecy, may explain Communist aversion to inspection to the extent that it penetrates and intrudes into the interior fabric of Communist societies.

It follows that so long as Western demands for inspection appear to require maximum intrusion, or so long as disarmament is seen by either side as a device for politically defeating the other side, negotiations will be sterile. Western proposals should, then, consciously aim as low as possible consonant with safety, rather than as high as possible out of idealistic, utopian, espionage, or excessively suspicious motivations. This is, of course, not a new insight. But it seems to require new understanding.

To break this discussion down into manageable parts, one must make a clear distinction between inspection that is essential to verify compliance, and inspection that is proposed for other reasons. It is becoming possible to accomplish this on a technically sound basis.[9] One can then systematically reexamine disarmament and arms-control measures to discern those that can be verified with minimum penetration of Soviet — and American — society, and those that require a manifestly unacceptable degree of penetration.

One highly promising key to this minimum-intrusion approach lies in the unfolding technology of detection. The American observation satellite known as Samos could become the agent of a first-stage disarmament agreement under which inspection could be made from orbiting satellites and supplemented by existing national intelligence capabilities. This revolution in information gathering has limitations: present mechanisms are crude, objects can be hidden, and at best the ground resolution of prospective systems will not tell people everything they would wish in order to be wholly reassured.

But within a relatively short time, a significant degree of inspection by an observation satellite system may be technically possible with respect to such important objects as deployed ICBMs, anti-missile systems, the deployment of surface naval vessels and major military aircraft, and significant new construction on the ground. It is thus possible that such military activities can be verified with a reasonably high level of confidence by an agency *external to the sovereign territory, waters, and airspace of a country* — even over the objection of the country being inspected.

There are other means of inspection that are equally nonintrusive compared with the injection of alien inspectors into the interior fabric of a society — for example, attachés, tourists, other travelers. Soviet disarmament proposals have invariably included inspection of "declared facilities," and this poses no real control problem, nor does the invitation to witness destruction of agreed

[9] See Lincoln P. Bloomfield and Louis Henkin, "Inspection and the Problem of Access," in *Security and Disarmament,* Richard A. Falk and Richard T. Barnet (eds.) (Princeton: Princeton University Press, 1965). The book was based on several authors' work at the Woods Hole Summer Study of 1962, fully reported in *Verification and Response in Disarmament Agreements,* Institute for Defense Analyses, Washington, D.C., November 1962.

amounts of military equipment. Obviously none of these is reliable or effective taken singly. But in combination with the fruits of the new technology and unilateral national intelligence, they might add up to an integrated set of inspection devices.

The Western response to such proposals is usually: "We may see them destroy stocks, and we may be posted at declared plants, but how do we know how much is left, and about unreported activities? How can we find out without having complete access?" The answer, of course, is that it is impossible to have complete assurance. The only valid question is whether, risk for risk, contingency for contingency, we would be better off than we are today. A growing professional opinion says "Yes." In past and present disarmament plans, each side has not very skillfully arranged things so that its presumed strategic advantage, whether in missiles, tanks, aircraft carriers, bases, or military manpower, was retained in the first stages. Clearly no such strategic advantage will ever be agreed to by the other side, and this fact has contributed mightily to the arms stalemate. More realistic proposals must rest in legitimate considerations of strategic balance, but alongside these considerations ought to be the criterion of relative nonintrusiveness of inspection.

A new first stage would thus include as many measures as possible that could be verified with a satisfactory degree of confidence by external technical means – inviting the other side to witness agreed destruction, maintaining existing levels of attaché and tourist observation – all supplemented by such techniques of national intelligence-gathering as might continue during the disarmament process. But it would not include measures that could be verified only with high levels of penetration – as current proposals by both U.S. *and* the Soviets do. Nor would it leave to an admittedly utopian third stage (as both sets of proposals now do) many measures of inspection that could be taken with minimum intrusion. The first stage would not include *all* easily verified measures, but it would give far more weight to this criterion than in the past.

From such an approach it is possible to propose arms control measures that have a chance of being negotiated. Whether they comprise a package or a new first stage of Western proposals is less important than the general conclusion that significant disarmament might be achieved without conditions that make the goals of arms control so chimerical.

ENFORCEMENT AND VETO

Moving to another fundamental stumbling block, the crux of the arms control issue is often said to be enforcement — the punishment of the violator, presumably through the United Nations. The crux of enforcement is in turn said to be the question of the veto in the Security Council. It is apparent that under present political circumstances, or even with substantial disarmament, the most to be expected is retention of the great-power veto — whether called that or not — at the crucial strategic level, above all where enforcement is involved. Any other arrangement would surely be as unacceptable to the United States Senate and the people of France as to the Soviet Politburo and the suspicious ideologues of Peking.

Under any system, enforcement, in the sense of responses by one nation or group of nations to undesirable behavior on the part of other nations, invariably depends on the relative power of the parties, on the depth of feeling involved in the issues, and on the strength of will of those who like the system as it is. This is true now; it would also be true if arms were substantially reduced or controlled (short of utopian institutional arrangements that we are rejecting here as unrealistic). If these assumptions are valid, the question of a veto over enforcement turns out to be not particularly meaningful after all. If the Security Council is to be the final arbiter of violations, as most disarmament schemes seem to suggest, the built-in veto will remain. But the veto at the topmost political level does not *intrinsically* hamper a disarmament scheme any more or less than it has hampered a fairly workable form of collective defense in a nondisarmament environment. In a drastically disarmed world the purpose, resolution, and intelligence of the major governments would in the end surely determine the response of the community to violations.

Even under the present system, an effective majority of responsible powers has at its disposal instruments of coercion that could be fearfully effective if that majority chooses to react against a clear violation of a disarmament agreement. The will to act is always more important than the modalities; this central lesson of politics is the one indispensable component in political analysis that no computer, no random theory of numbers, no matrix of game strategies can ever reproduce. Given that will, there exist even now embryonic international legislative and judicial organs, a somewhat better developed executive power, and a sometimes influential framework of moral suasion and *ad hoc* political pressure, that can carry as much traffic as the principal nations are prepared to allow or encourage.

If there were substantial reduction of all types of armaments *but if the present political order continued,* would Western security be adversely affected? The arguments in the affirmative stem from the notion that aggressive victories are prevented solely by the inhibiting power of Western nuclear weapons. But in a less dangerously armed world it might have been possible to oppose Soviet and Chinese advances with considerably less restraint. It can be argued that Soviet and Chinese gains have taken place partly as a consequence of the nuclear stalemate. The case can be made that the chances of armed conflict would be no greater if the military balance were maintained at lower levels, and that the consequences for mankind of reduced levels of armed conflict would at least be tolerable.

If this hypothesis can reasonably be entertained, it becomes possible to visualize a comprehensive disarmament program without elaborate political arrangements for intrusion or enforcement, arrangements that are unattainable because politically unacceptable.

ADMINISTRATION

Given a continuation of the present political order, it becomes possible to focus on the political control of any technical administration of a disarmament agreement agreed to by the participating nations. The goal of such a body is *the accurate, reliable, and timely reporting and transmittal to the appropriate political authorities of information gathered.*

In achieving this end, the only place where a veto would be inadmissible would be in the field system which gathers and transmits facts. If the only way to verify compliance with a given measure is to witness it, it must be witnessed. National intelligence operations would complement and reinforce such information. In the drafting of the initial agreement, in the choice of personnel in top positions, in the political decisions about how to act, a veto would be acceptable, as it is today in the United Nations. Nor would a neutral administrator be necessary, as the West has insisted. Efficiency would certainly suffer under a troika or collegial administration, but so long as the raw information was collected and transmitted directly to the level of political judgment, the admittedly severe disadvantages of such a system would be outweighed. There is no inherent reason why a U.N. body operating under these rules could not be set up.

It may be that a precedent set in an arms-control agreement would be damaging and prejudicial to the integrity of the Secretary General of the United Nations. This is an issue of priority choices that can be decided only by Western political leadership. But such a decision would not need to be complicated by the conviction we have hitherto entertained that there could be *no* arms control or disarmament agreement without Soviet capitulation on the question of a single neutral administrator, or on what amounts to the surrender of the regime's total authority over its subjects. If this thesis is correct, the negotiating area can be defined with a good deal more precision than exists today.

REGIONAL ARMS CONTROL

The growing importance of the subject of regional arms control brings it increasingly before the United Nations. The regional approach to arms control has particular relevance to developing areas outside of Europe, where arms stabilization agreements could do much to reinforce economic and political efforts for development and improved living standards.[10]

The restricting of new-nation arms competition is a vital part of the great United States interest in reducing the capacity of secondary disputes to erupt into great-power war. It should not be forgotten that the more stable the strategic balance in great-

[10] See Lincoln P. Bloomfield and Amelia C. Leiss, "Arms Control and the Developing Countries," *World Politics,* October 1965. For a detailed study of the problem alluded to in this section and the reasoning underlying the recommendations, see the report prepared under the author's direction entitled *Regional Arms Control Arrangements for the Developing Countries — Latin America, Africa, and the Middle East* (Cambridge: Center for International Studies, M.I.T., 1964).

power relations, the greater may be the temptation for one of the superpowers to engage in competitive military assistance in areas adjacent to the zones of dominant influence of the other. Thus the potential for intensified arms competition may be growing in the developing areas, and vigorous arms-control policy may be necessary.

In considering arms control for these regions, one clearly must, as in planning great-power arms control, "design around" the obvious obstacles. There is of course no assurance that if obstacles did not exist, or if they magically disappeared, arms-control measures would be acceptable. Perhaps if no obstacles existed, arms-control measures might not be so important as they are now. But as it is, there are built-in dynamics to regional quarrels and threats which bode ill for the future unless steps are taken to control them. The very impetus to arm against a third party can itself engender a new and dangerous bilateral arms race — as witnessed by the case of India and Pakistan, where it made war possible.

In some instances, notably in the Middle East and Asia, any policy idea that depends on intraregional cooperation is obviously unrealistic. In other areas it is reasonable to urge local action. In all areas, including the Middle East and Asia, there are some measures the United States could profitably consider applying. Two overall policy steps stand out as essential. The first is *to take action, through seeking formal agreements first by nuclear powers and then by all other states, for the prevention of the further spread of nuclear, bacterial, chemical, and other weapons of mass destruction, including a ban on the manufacture, storing, or testing of weapons, and on the devices to launch them.*

If agreements were made along such lines, it would be necessary to provide adequate controls. If U.N. or some other international inspection could be agreed to, including such overflight and on-site surveillance as is required, United States security needs would be met. Realistically, this is unlikely, and considerable reliance will probably have to be placed on the unilateral capabilities of United States and other national intelligence. Whatever form inspection might take, its aim would be to detect with a reasonably high degree of confidence any development of significant strategic delivery capabilities before the increase could become an area threat, let alone a worldwide one. What the United States could not favor are prohibitions on unilateral overflight or outer-space surveillance in the absence of effective international machinery.

The principal difficulty about inspection lies in the relatively rapid quantitative spread of nuclear reactors for research or power production. It seems logical to apply the inspection and reporting standards and procedures of the International Atomic Energy Agency. The policy corollary for the United States Government is a determined effort to improve and enlarge the writ of the International Atomic Energy Agency (IAEA) along lines it has already embarked upon.

One can only speculate on the lengths to which the Soviet Union is in fact willing to go to stanch the potential spread of nuclear weapons technology. It abstained in the 1963 United Nations resolution on a Latin-American nuclear-free zone. In later years in the Eighteen-Nation Disarmament Committee (ENDC), however, it has expressed readiness to seek agreements to this end. Reportedly, Soviet agreements for assistance with research and power reactors contain provisions to prevent the diversion of radioactive products to unauthorized uses.

The second broad United States policy that ought to be applied consistently in all regions is *to seek formal or informal undertakings among suppliers of weapons to the developing countries that they will not provide any arms other than those legitimately required for internal security needs. This would bar the sale or transfer of weapons that are commonly understood to be sophisticated, offensive, or expensive, along the lines suggested in the first policy step.*

One thing that *can* be done is for the United Nations to revive the League of Nations' most useful practice of widely publicizing statistics and other facts about the arms trade. Communications have improved considerably since the interwar period, and there might be few better deterrents than continuous publicity about arms races.

The wisest course for regional arms-control measures would probably be a broad-spectrum approach in which no particular region is singled out and in which universally applicable principles and measures constitute the basis of United States policy. Perhaps the most important single reinforcement of regional arms contro' would be evidence that the great powers were pursuing with equal vigor measures of arms control applicable to themselves.

Global total disarmament remains a utopian objective. Even arms control that is universally applicable may be too much to hope for now. But the steps outlined here for regional arms control, some of which lie within the present capacity of a few nations to execute, are almost as urgent as measures of arms limitation among the great powers. Moreover, these proposals are the most feasible and practicable policy steps for this country to take now in the arms field. The fact that these steps *are* real and practical possibilities constitutes one more reason (and perhaps the most undervalued one of all) for the United States to settle now upon an overall arms-control and disarmament policy – upon a policy that conforms to the realities of the times, that reflects the urgent need for steps to reverse the present course of events, that sees the necessity of a believable position on less-than-total disarmament, and that relies on the wise use of the national power of the United States to lend confidence to a world still without trust.

The United States has a clear interest, along with most of mankind, in bringing the arms race under control. Since the general problem of disarmament and arms control depends on the political environment, and since preliminary decisions are bilateral in nature, the United Nations supplies an alternative means of negotiation, a way of involving and using the talents of other nations who share concern with the problem, a source of international pressure on the great powers, and an agency for implementing agreements reached.

To resolve the Nth country problem, the final negotiations must be multilateral. A further thought, to which I do not attach much value but nevertheless believe may have utility, is that given the built-in proclivity of the parties to seek advantage for themselves, it might be worth at least experimenting with having the small and medium powers in the United Nations draw up detailed, concrete disarmament proposals. Such proposals might be more objectively conceived and thus more likely to secure mutual agreement.

The United Nations is the appropriate agency for implementing an agreement, first because of the availability of neutrals, second because of the technical possibility of monitoring agreements from orbiting observation satellites in the not-too-distant future — satellites that for this purpose logically should operate under international auspices. The experience of the U.N.-related International Atomic Energy Agency with limited controls and safeguards in the peaceful uses of atomic energy might supply valuable pilot models toward more comprehensive agreements.

PART III The United Nations and the Superpowers

CHAPTER NINE

Changing Perceptions

CHAPTER TEN

Challenge and Cooperation in Space

CHAPTER NINE

Changing Perceptions

We now turn from military policy considerations to the realm of what might be called political security. Our analysis of U.S. policy objectives moves from the short run to the middle range of time and action. If we fail to meet military security objectives, it goes without saying that all else is in grave jeopardy. But assuming a comprehensive and versatile defense program, there is a good chance that with few exceptions the major battles will be fought in the realm of politics.

It must be emphasized at the very outset that the West, and particularly the United States, must overcome the tendency to believe that if Communist leaders temporarily rule out military means to achieve their goals, it follows that they are prepared to negotiate solutions in what we conceive to be rational terms. For they have tirelessly proclaimed to their followers that peace and war are interchangeable phases of the basic conflict.[1] The increasing sophistication of the Soviet leaders concerning the dangers of war in the nuclear age does not mean that the conflict itself has been abandoned. While prudent when it comes to the

[1] See Mao Tse-tung's *Collected Works* (New York: International Publishers, 1954).

survival of their regime, Chinese leaders, with a vastly less developed society, and in almost total isolation from the West, sound considerably less committed to a strategy of caution and low risks. Whatever his nationality, a dedicated Communist remains convinced that the core battle is being fought for the prize of history itself, that all else depends on its outcome.

Moreover, distinct from the dynamics of communism but now serving the Communist cause, both Russia and China have a driving sense of national destiny, and powerful national interests that cut across ideology. De Tocqueville prophetically stated one part of the situation we face today when he wrote a century ago:

> There are at present two great nations in the world, which started at different points, but seem to tend towards the same end. I allude to the Russians and Americans. The principal instrument of the [latter] is freedom; of the [former] servitude. Their starting-point is different and their courses are not the same; yet each of them seems marked out by the will of Heaven to sway the destinies of half the globe.[2]

And Henry Adams, fifty years later, spoke of the "inevitable struggle for the control of China which . . . must decide the control of the world." [3]

The United States possesses double political objectives — to ensure the survival and prosperity of our political and social values, and at the same time to find ways — and I use an oversimplified shorthand — of "liquidating the cold war" on better terms than those the Communists have in mind. It is with this double objective in mind that we inquire into the uses of the United Nations to achieve Western purposes in terms of what can conveniently be called political security.

Before considering the possible substance of U.S. planning, however, we must pause to consider two powerful conditioning factors: the basic view we hold of the nature and prospects of the Communist system, and the Communist view of the United Nations.

[2] Alexis de Tocqueville, *Democracy in America,* Volume I (New York: Knopf, 1945), p. 435.

[3] Henry Adams, *The Education of Henry Adams* (New York: Modern Library, 1931), p. 391.

THE U.S. VIEW OF COMMUNIST DEVELOPMENT

In recent years the formerly monolithic Communist movement has become polycentric. The Soviet Union, Yugoslavia, the other countries of Eastern Europe, and most distinctly China are all speaking in different voices. However, the first concern of American security policy remains the Soviet Union, and there are two general and broadly contrasting American views of what inner process Soviet communism is undergoing and how that process can be affected in constructive ways.

One point of view sees the struggle fixed and essentially unchanging. Its proponents warn us against being seduced by the illusion that the changes taking place are meaningful enough to justify altering our basic estimates of Soviet intentions.[4] The other and more widespread school of thought sees the Soviet system as in flux and moving toward a more acceptable international posture. This school urges us not to act as though Soviet communism were static, but to abandon the conditioned reflexes that the cold war has built into our responses to events in the Communist countries and be prepared to respond flexibly to its dynamics.

Those who fear that we may be taken in by superficial changes argue that Communist tactics characteristically make an virtue of necessity by using change to confuse and soften up the enemy while assimilating the changes into a renewed pattern of ideological strength. Thus Western strategy, unless it is to succumb to the disease of false optimism and wishful thinking, must sustain an attitude of unremitting skepticism toward apparent changes, and reject strategies that assume that such changes will significantly modify the profound hostility and implacable dedication of the Communist leadership.

There is much to commend this line of reasoning. The West in general, and Americans in particular, are at their most pitiful when they refuse to believe that the great dictators of the age — whether Lenin, Hitler, Stalin, Mao, Khrushchev, or the last

[4] A notable example is Robert Strausz-Hupé, William R. Kintner, and Stefan T. Possony, *A Forward Strategy for America* (New York: Harper, 1961).

two's successors — mean what they clearly say. It would be gross negligence to proceed upon any assumption other than that the Soviet and Chinese leaders today are still following the path defined by Lenin in 1920: "As soon as we are strong enough to strike down capitalism we shall seize it by the throat." Who is wise or prescient enough to guarantee that Khrushchev had something less harmful and more acceptable in mind when, thirty-six years later, he told the American Ambassador with a candor few world leaders permit themselves:

> When we win this competition we shall also re-educate you. We Bolsheviks are ravenous people. What we achieve through our struggle in the past is not sufficient for us. We want more — tomorrow.[5]

The continuing Chinese world view was clearly restated by Peking Defense Minister Lin Piao in September 1965 when he said that Mao's theory of encirclement of cities from the countryside

> is of outstanding and universal practical importance for the present revolutionary struggles of all the oppressed nations and peoples . . . if North America and Western Europe can be called "the cities of the world," then Asia, Africa and Latin America constitute the "rural area of the world." [6]

Communist leaders are entirely capable of using reforms, however genuine, to delude others into believing that communism has abandoned its *élan vital* along with some of its internal controls.

The prize exhibit for the theory of delusion was Mao Tsetung's "Let a hundred flowers bloom" campaign, when ostensible liberalization handily uncovered victim after victim for renewed persecution. But we cannot be at all sure about the inner sequence of motivation. Was the whole affair deliberately planned, or did the untoward reaction frighten Chinese leaders into quick retreat? The same question remains unanswered regarding some of the events of the "thaw" of the mid-1950s that led to revolutionary disorders in Poland and particularly in Hungary. Were

[5] Quoted in *New York Times*, April 22, 1958.
[6] Published in all major Chinese Communist newspapers September 3, 1965.

the Soviet withdrawal and the October 30, 1956, public statement on a more liberal satellite policy elements in a Machiavellian plot? Or was the trend suddenly and brutally reversed by the unanticipated reactions, accompanied by internal convulsions in the Soviet leadership? The same sort of fundamental question can be asked about Soviet disarmament policy. To what extent did limited arms-control agreements in the 1960s reflect a strategy of genuine détente? To what extent were both arms control and détente tactical? Or did tactics become strategy? [7] Answers to these questions would go a long way toward illuminating the interpretation of "liberalizing" trends in the Communist states.

In general nothing could be more fatuous than our public expectations that one or more effort is all it would take to "break the deadlock," or "eliminate tensions," or, put most naïvely, "bring peace."

But the advocates of "hold fast," despite the value of their advice as a necessary corrective to wishful thinking, are not entirely persuasive. Although they quite rightly warn us against entertaining false hopes for basic changes in the nature of Soviet communism, by accepting at face value the Communist pretentions to consistency and to a fixed destiny, they themselves fall into the trap of historical absolutism which has invalidated so much Communist doctrine.

Evidence of changes in the Soviet Union is everywhere. The very foundation of security for the Soviet state — insulation and isolation from the outside world — has been breached in ways unthinkable a decade ago. Interpretations of this evidence may of course differ. The unprecedented exposure of Soviet leaders to America, and of the Soviet people to Americans, may simply reflect new confidence in Soviet power and in Russian immunity to Western influence.

The signs and portents today are even more ambiguous than usual. Evidence for the two competing theories is seen in the same events, both by those who believe Soviet communism is un-

[7] This issue is investigated in detail in *Khrushchev and the Arms Race — Soviet Interests in Arms Control and Disarmament: 1594–1964* by Lincoln P. Bloomfield, Walter Clemens, Jr., and Franklyn Griffiths (Cambridge: M.I.T. Press, 1966).

changed in its strategic goal of destroying our society, regardless of tactical fluctuations, and by those who believe that the conservative implications of the Soviet Union as a modern, increasingly well-to-do society represent a greater reality than an ideology that may have become attenuated and in important ways irrelevant. There is no responsible basis for policy other than considering both theories (nor anything more irresponsible than committing everything to one of them). Given the ambiguity of the evidence, the American interest will be best served by making two sets of assumptions: first, that the Soviet Union *is* changing in irreversible ways, that the high mass-consumption society it is becoming will grow conservative about its own goals, that the thrust is draining out of the ideology; and, second, the equally compelling assumptions that, just as soon as new strategic opportunities open up, renewed life and meaning will be injected into the communist ideology of unlimited ends harnessed to national power goals, and the tactical zig will become the tactical zag.

The acknowledgment of uncertainty furnishes an entirely proper basis for policies directed to normalization of relations with the Soviet Union, such as increased trade and a steady flow of individuals through tourism and exchange programs. The validity of the latter rests not on the sentimental hope that personal contact will somehow dissolve profound political differences at the governmental and societal levels, but on the deep breach it represents in the isolationism of the Soviet Union and the chance it offers to correct in some key Soviet minds dangerously inaccurate estimates of Western morale and capabilities. The great hazard of the exchange program is not that Americans will be corrupted by Communist ideas, but that it will lead to faulty reasoning and inadequate policies. One of the grossest errors on the part of top-level Western statesmanship in the 1950s was to conclude from flimsy evidence that the Soviet system was on the verge of collapse, from which it was only a short step to the conclusion that the *coup de grâce* could be administered by purely verbal blows. Events soon revealed the fraudulence of this comforting view.

But we do not have to insist on the immediate collapse of the Soviet system in order to perceive changes of an evolutionary nature. The appropriate Western posture would combine two strands: open-mindedness to the notion that communism, like all other political movements, is subject to non-Marxian laws of growth, development, maturation, decline, and ultimate transformation; and the maintenance during this process of strong military and political defenses along with a purposeful policy designed to encourage the process of peaceful change.

The overall strategy in such a posture involves four difficult but vital elements. To do more than hold our own in the political struggle, we must be less fastidious than we have been about exploiting the vulnerabilities in the Soviet system; we must cease to allow political battles to be waged only on our own home grounds while accepting the Communist version of its own privileged political sanctuary. Second, we must continue to avoid sharpening the struggle by gratuitous provocation or by unrealistic cold war aims of our own. Third, we must encourage the process of change by acting on the assumption that Communists, no less than capitalists, are creatures of history and subject to non-Marxian laws of historical development. We must prepare for transformations in the Communist system that today we cannot even begin to predict. Fourth, our objective in liquidating the cold war must be spelled out in better and more universally acceptable terms than those the Communists would impose.

When we consider Communist China in this context we see that here again there are two ways of approaching the problem. One is to view the Chinese Communists as potentially more of a threat to the West than Stalinist Russia was in the late 1940s, and to deal with the problem in the same way. The other approach is to contain Chinese power but to increase contacts, reduce Chinese isolation, and generally broaden Chinese perceptions of the rest of the world.

Until now the problem of U.S. political strategy as it concerns the United Nations has been limited to Western-Soviet relationships. China has expressed increasing scorn of the United Nations and its works, which culminated in the mid-1960s with threats to set up a rival institution. Under those circumstances it was not particularly difficult to keep China out of the United Nations. However, China as a nuclear power became a new quantity in the opinion of much of the world. Pressure to bring Peking into international forums began to grow rapidly. Given the prospect of the United States having to confront both the Soviet Union and China in the United Nations, it is important to understand their views of the organization.

COMMUNIST VIEWS OF THE UNITED NATIONS

For the Soviet Union the United Nations has been another arena in which to press the struggle. The dramatic increase in membership in the 1950s and 1960s offered the Soviet leadership opportunities for reducing American power and prestige in the organization. It also provided them opportunities, at whatever cost to responsible statesmanship, for identifying with the extremists of the anticolonial cause – the issue which above all others dominated the mid-1950s to mid-1960s in the United Nations.

Beginning roughly with the flight of Sputnik I in October 1957, Soviet leadership made no secret of its revised assessment of the world equation of power and influence based on spectacular Soviet advances in rocketry and missilry. This strategic reappraisal carried with it the Soviet demand that diplomatic arrangements henceforth reflect the new equation. Deadlocks on outer space and disarmament were resolved only when the composition of the appropriate committees was adjusted accordingly.

The U.N. Congo operation supplied the requisite opportunity as well as the conclusive reason for the Soviets to demand the extension of the principle of parity to the office of the Secretary General – who had since 1955 been virtually an independent diplomatic power in the Middle East. Soviet pressure accelerated during and after the Suez crisis (when the United States, for one, was delighted to believe that important elements of policy could be left to Mr. Hammarskjöld). Perhaps the event that tipped the scale was not the Congo, but Laos in its earlier international incarnation, *i.e.,* in 1959 when the Secretary General followed up the efforts of a Security Council subcommittee by himself sending and keeping on the scene a United Nations presence in the form of successive high-ranking Secretariat officials.

By the interior logic of Soviet doctrine, as the Secretary General became more and more a political force in world politics, it was inevitable that the institution his office represented would require revision to reflect the realities of world power. The matter reached a head when, in the Congo, Mr. Hammarskjöld for the first time actually thwarted an important Soviet Union policy objective. The Russians found they could no longer tolerate the position of independent strength reached by the Secretary General. The violent death of Congolese Premier Patrice Lumumba supplied the trigger for activating a Soviet policy which undoubtedly reached deeply into ideological depths.

There was of course, nothing new in former Soviet Premier Khrushchev's assertion to Walter Lippmann that, while there may be neutral countries, there are no neutral men, and that he would never entrust the security of the Soviet Union to any foreigner.[8] Maxim Litvinov used to say that only an angel could be neutral and there were no angels. That the security of Russia should be placed in the hands of anyone but Russians has always been unthinkable. Thus the historical background places in a rather clearer light the Soviet attack on the Secretary General and the subsequent Western assertion that the Russians want to destroy the United Nations. It also gives a more sophisticated meaning to the Khrushchev statement at that time that for the United Nations to be an effective medium for settling international disputes, "treatment with very good medicine" must be undergone so that it would not become a "weapon for imposing the will of one state over another." [9] Finally, this ideological background suggests that American diplomacy faces the task of a battle for control, which in many ways is harder and more complex than a defense of the United Nations against its outright destruction.

The Soviets have never pretended — or expected — that they could achieve their objectives all at once. In the years when the votes were 55 to 5 — a situation Americans would have enormous difficulty in adjusting to under reversed circumstances — Soviet representatives managed to rationalize their defeats into victories, or at least publicly pretended they did not matter. In more recent years departing Soviet representatives have tended to be positively euphoric as to the outcome on some U.N. bat-

[8] *New York Herald Tribune,* April 17, 1961.
[9] Speech at Yerevan, May 6, 1961; *New York Times,* May 7, 1961.

tles they lost. They have seemed to be saying that if the campaign to convert the organization to the Soviet image does not succeed this year, next year will do, or the next. Thus speaks a state with a plan. We can conclude from all this that the Soviet image of the United Nations is probably undergoing a process of change, based largely on the crucial place of the underdeveloped and neutralist nations in the United Nations in a period when Soviet strategy has shifted to political and economic warfare in the "gray areas" of the world. This is undoubtedly the paramount Soviet interest in the United Nations today.

When it comes to Peking's attitudes, however, the picture is somewhat blurred. For one thing, Peking's relations so far with the United Nations have been minimal and generally antagonistic on both sides. Direct communication between the two has been rare. The Communist regime initially acted as all other successful revolutionary regimes do and in November 1949 repudiated the U.N. delegation still representing China, soon sending the Secretary General credentials for a Chinese Communist delegation to the 5th Assembly. The delegation was not accredited, and China's attitudes have been increasingly bitter ever since. The whole situation became profoundly exacerbated when Chinese troops entered the Korean War. Chinese representatives have periodically been invited to attend certain U.N. debates, but have accepted only once (in 1950 when the Security Council took up Peking's complaint of "armed invasion of the island of Taiwan"). Other invitations were extended in connection with the Korean prisoner-of-war issue (which in fact took the Secretary General to China in January 1955) and with the dispute the same year over the offshore islands. In rejecting these invitations Peking declared that all decisions taken by the United Nations would be considered "null and void."

There are grounds for believing that Peking could have been seated before now if its attitude had been more conciliatory. But on the specific issues that represent concrete obstacles to a seat for Peking, Chinese responses have become increasingly uncompromising and imperious. The bill of particulars has been presented by Foreign Minister Chen Yi:

> The United Nations must rectify its mistakes and undergo a thorough reorganization and reform. It must admit and correct all

its past mistakes. Among other things it should cancel its resolution condemning China and the Democratic People's Republic of Korea as aggressors and adopt a resolution condemning the United States as aggressor; the U.N. Charter must be reviewed and revised jointly by all countries, big and small.[10]

As for Taiwan, or any version of a "two Chinas" solution,

China will not participate in any international conferences, organization or undertaking in which representatives of the Taiwan local authorities are participating, no matter by what name they call themselves.[11]

China will never enter into any relations with the United Nations and any conference connected with it before restoration of her legitimate rights in the United Nations and the expulsion of the Chiang Kai-shek clique from the organization.[12]

When in January 1965, Indonesia became the United Nations' first temporary dropout, Peking applauded, characterizing the United Nations as a U.S. tool for supporting "reactionary," "imperialist" groups. Unless the United Nations were drastically reorganized, said Premier Chou En-lai,

A revolutionary United Nations may well be set up so that rival dramas may be staged in competition with that body which calls itself the United Nations but which, being under the manipulation of United States imperialism, is capable only of making mischief and can do nothing good.[13]

An intriguing and perplexing question is how seriously to take Peking's belligerent assertions. Some apparently consider that the polemics of Chinese leaders are to be fully believed and that it would be the height of folly not to assume they mean precisely what they say.[14] At the other extreme are those who either ignore their statements or dismiss them as propaganda.

[10] Press Conference, September 29, 1965, New China News Agency.

[11] Quoted in *Intercom,* "The China Problem," Vol. 7, No. 1, Foreign Policy Association, January-February 1965, p. 25.

[12] Foreign Ministry Statement, December 1, 1965, *New York Times,* December 2, 1965.

[13] *Ibid.,* January 26, 1965. Indonesia resumed its membership in 1966.

[14] See *The Economist,* August 20, 1966, pp. 709–710, quoted approvingly by President Johnson in speech August 30, 1966, *New York Times,* August 31, 1966.

It seems wisest to take the statements very seriously indeed, but also to understand the psychology involved. The Chinese Communists are Asians whose race was historically given to feelings of superiority but was humiliatingly dealt with by lesser, *i.e.,* Western, breeds (as anyone who lived in pre-1949 China can attest). Since taking power they have been treated as pariahs. They now behave in a way extraordinarily similar to the way others have when excluded from clubs. "I didn't want to join your miserable club anyway," or "I'll form my own club," or "If you want me back you'll have to crawl" seem somehow more natural to the circumstances than "I'm sorry, you were right all along, I'm grateful you finally will let me in, and I promise to behave on your terms." Some U.S. officials refer to this interpretation of Chinese psychology as a "neurosis" theory, rejecting it because they believe it rests on the assumption — which I do not share — that membership will "reform" Peking.[15] The neurosis can, I think, be readily demonstrated, however cloudy the prognosis for its cure.

A more tangible explanation is found in Peking's own private admission that if China joined the U.N. "we cannot have a majority in voting; formally the difficult situation may be moderated to some extent, but the struggle that arises will be more violent and we shall lose our present freedom of action." [16]

On balance, it probably ought to be assumed that China may not in reality be posing insuperable obstacles to taking its "rightful" seat if offered, although it may in face-saving fashion arrange a humiliating and anxious wait before showing up. If the scenario unfolds as most predict, the General Assembly will be the first to vote Peking in. It may or may not have worked out a formula for keeping Taiwan in. For some years it seemed many members were not concerned about a place for Taiwan, perhaps underestimating the strength of American feelings in the matter. Peking will doubtless make Taiwan's complete ouster a condition for taking its seat; the present representatives of the

[15] See speech by Assistant Secretary of State William P. Bundy, Feb. 12, 1966, Dept. of State Publication 8049, p. 71.

[16] *The Politics of the Chinese Red Army — A Translation of the Bulletin of Activities of the People's Liberation Army,* Ed. J. Chester Cheng (Hoover Institute on War, Revolution, and Peace, 1966), p. 480.

Republic of China could be expected to insist on remaining. There being no provisions for expulsion, one can anticipate great confusion, unpleasantness, and pressures for the creation of a committee to find ways out of the parliamentary labyrinth. As for the United States, its firm treaty commitment to Taiwan may well lead it ultimately to favor a "Two-China" solution as best protecting the continued status of Taiwan in the United Nations should Peking be seated.

It can also be assumed that Peking would insist on all the perquisites of membership including the Chinese seat in the Security Council before deigning to arrive. These two conditions could keep the mainland Chinese out for a matter of years. But, like the Soviets in August 1950, Peking may decide that exigent political interests, above all the chance for intimate contact with Afro-Asians and with gut issues affecting them, override other considerations.

To return, then, to U.S. political strategy, several observations can be made. First, U.S. planning must embrace a realistic view of the possibilities for change in Soviet communism, accepting both the likelihood of a continuation of the cold war and the inevitable working of the laws of historical evolution. Second, in view of the current Soviet view of the United Nations, the United States faces the tactical task in the United Nations of recapturing from the Soviets the role of champion of the virtues prized by a growing majority of nations. In this sense continued United Nations membership offers both a danger and an opportunity to develop a more constructive and politically profitable worldwide image of the United States and its values. With China a member, the task will be complicated further by the racial leadership China will doubtless seek to exert. However, the competition between the Soviet Union and China will offer opportunities to the West, and on balance there is no reason to assume that the United States cannot profit from the challenge.

Assuming a continued period of "competitive coexistence" (which, in the words of its author, is an "economic, political and ideological struggle, but not military," [17]) we must consider what

[17] Premier Khrushchev in a speech at Novosibirsk, October 10, 1959, reported in *New York Times,* October 14, 1959.

influence might be exerted by the United Nations that would advance the U.S. interest in this struggle.

THE U.N. INFLUENCE ON COMMUNISM

The assumption is sometimes made that the United Nations, by exposing the Communist mentality, whether European or Asian, to the values of the West, can help to modify its intransigent and dogmatic hostility. Some important possibilities exist under this heading, but they need to be separated from the common misconceptions that sometimes cling to them.

There is a temptation, for example, to take too literally the use of words such as "democratic" and "parliamentary" in referring to the processes that take place in the U.N. bodies. In the absence of a genuine constitutional order, the "democratic" process in international relations is so qualified as to be highly misleading. Likewise, the notion of the United Nations as a "parliament," while apposite in a limited sense, tends to convey a homely image of a legislative body in which individual members act out of both interest and persuasion. The fact is that U.N. bodies have little if any genuine legislative powers; and nothing could be more fallacious than the widespread impression that parliamentary diplomacy in the United Nations has the primary function of persuading the individual delegates to adopt or reject certain positions.

It is true that on certain minor issues, or in the case of some smaller countries where delegates have been given full discretion or are completely uninstructed, persuasion *can* have a decisive effect on the individual delegate, resulting in a policy decision on his part that can be directly attributed to the debate itself. This has been known to happen within the United States delegation on some occasions. But in general, and particularly in dealing with delegates of the Soviet Union, there is little or no connection between the delegates' personal roles in the United Nations and the policies of their governments. This is not to say that individuals are not influenced by what happens within the organization; they may be influenced profoundly. But personal reactions are generally, and specifically in the case of Communist delegates, unrelated either to basic governmental policy or to the development of genuine understanding between the countries concerned.

It is possible to conceive of a hypothetical situation in which a delegate from Israel and a delegate from an Arab state are so mutually stirred by the atmosphere of a debate and the logic of arguments for reconciliation that in a transcendent moment they come to look harmoniously and sympathetically at the need for resolving their differences. But even if this unlikely event happens, there is little evidence from the diplomatic process as we know it at the United Nations — and elsewhere — that any change at all could be anticipated in the policies of the respective governments. It is far more likely, given the situation in the area, that the Arab government in question would repudiate its representative as a turncoat and traitor. If he happened to be a man of great influence at home, other individuals might become influenced by his views. But however personally moved by logic or by the impulse to agree, a delegate representing a strong and self-disciplined government cannot normally be expected to commit his country to a course it is otherwise unwilling to take, or for which its public opinion is unprepared.

This truth, deplorable as it may be to the idealist, suggests that the proper target of U.N. influence is not the individual diplomat but public opinion in his country. In turn, world public opinion being a highly potent element in foreign policy today and for the foreseeable future, the most logical way to provide a genuine political foundation for international agreement would be to present the facts, neutrally and "internationally" interpreted, to all the peoples of the world. It is unlikely that many governments involved in major international controversies would agree to have such an impartial — and potentially subversive — presentation directed to their people. But the United States, in the interest of promoting more rational international behavior, ought to devote serious thought to ways of encouraging greater propagation of neutrally oriented facts, looking toward the day when public opinion, even in authoritarian countries, will demand as its right the privilege of access to unbiased information on international subjects.

The entire process may be accelerated by the foreseeable development of communication satellites capable of direct FM or television transmission simultaneously in several languages to homes around the entire globe. U.S. planning should be concentrating on how to ensure that these potential propaganda and educational weapons do not become additional weapons of hostile propaganda. Careful judgments will have to be made to balance the complete freedom of the airwaves, which we would generally prefer, against the dangers of misuse. The United Nations and its technical specialized agencies have an important role to play in achieving this balance.

Another potentially deceptive and illusory aspect of the United Nations has to do with the passing of resolutions. The increasing variety of unanimously passed U.N. resolutions – on issues ranging from South Africa to the effects of atomic radiation and "general and complete disarmament" – can lead to highly misleading conclusions about the common ground that actually exists. Highly dilute resolutions on controversial subjects, however unanimously passed, do not necessarily have significant influence on the course of East-West relations. Of greater potential significance may be the precedent established by the U.N. Conference on Trade and Development and its Executive Board in 1965. An agreed set of conciliation procedures is to be invoked, if need be, before ever a vote is taken on nonprocedural matters.

Dismissing the hopeful but generally misleading notion of the United Nations as a pervasive, benign force that can alter Communist purposes simply because it exists and because the Communist states partake in its processes, there still remains the simple but important fact that the United Nations is a place where the two opposing sides can keep contact. The famous corridor conversations between Ambassadors Jessup and Malik in February 1948, which led to negotiations on lifting the Berlin blockade, are frequently cited as evidence of the value of continuous contact. Indeed, during the airlift, contact had been informally maintained in one or another U.N. agency, providing a place where one side or the other could "bail out" if necessary. Again, during the Cuban missile crisis of 1962, the Secretary General proved to be extraordinarily useful as a third party to assist in disengaging the principals. These episodes and others have demonstrated the value of casually rubbing elbows at times when such unpublicized contacts would be next to impossible in more conventional diplomatic settings. Corridor conversations in New York are not featured in sensational headlines in the same fashion as the arrival of the Soviet Ambassador at the State Department at the height of an international crisis.

The late Secretary General Hammarskjöld went considerably beyond this in his evaluation of the effect of the United Nations on the structure of international conduct. He saw it as a genuine bridge:

> It is because world community does not exist at a time when world interdependence has become a reality that world organization has become a necessity as a bridge which may help us to pass safely over this period of transition. . . . A more effective and increasing use of the United Nations as a diplomatic instrument, in which the functions of debate and vote are used more frequently to further a diplomacy of reconciliation . . . than merely to score propaganda points, or to defend against them, offers the best hope . . . for a peaceful evolution . . . in the relationships of the West with the communist countries.[18]

The direct influence that the United Nations can have on the Soviet attitude does not significantly alter the pattern of Communist hostility. But the United Nations provides a locus where aspects of the superpower relationships can be continuously discussed and even negotiated.

Taking the Soviet estimate of the United Nations at its face value — the only prudent course — one must assume that the Kremlin will continue to remain far less influenced by the processes of the United Nations than by its own strategic decisions — decisions based on evidence regarding power relationships, internal stresses, and the like. A United Nations consensus condemning Soviet actions, as in Hungary in 1956, can embarrass the Soviet Union. But there is no reason for believing that the United Nations, either through a general influence on the tone of international morality or through actions which under present arrangements can be only hortatory, can have a significant effect of itself on the direction and quality of Soviet policy.

Nevertheless, the United Nations has a value that is particularly great at times of tension for bringing Communist and

[18] Address to members of both Houses of Parliament, London, April 2, 1958, *United Nations Review,* May 1958, pp. 6–7.

Western diplomats into continued casual contact, thus furnishing an important supplement to more traditional diplomatic channels. Moreover, the United Nations plays a politically crucial role in offering constructive alternatives for international behavior to the Soviet Union, and perhaps eventually to Communist China. If mutual deterrence continues and if the competition for power is to continue to be "peaceful" and to involve primarily influence in new nations, the influence of the United Nations assumes increasing importance. The United Nations may be a marginal diplomatic instrument to the great powers. But to the small and weak it is a window to the world and a hope for the future.

The usefulness of the United Nations in its possible effect on communism cannot be measured simply in terms of direct influence. Since the only real basis for international harmony lies in the realm of common interests, it is worthwhile to ask whether in the period ahead the United Nations can promote and institutionalize common interests among the great antagonists. It sometimes appears that the only common interest of the two superpowers regarding the existence of the United Nations is the possibility of using it as a weapon in their political propaganda warfare. But this is not the whole story.

Even though the Soviet Union acknowledges no common interest in the formation of a world community based on Western "bourgeois" values, it has come to find a succession of partial and, to it, temporary common interests of a specific nature. This is a step-by-step process as one or another topic opens up to common treatment by both sides. Perhaps the most significant has been the 1963 limited test-ban treaty, and the pledge the same year against weapons of mass destruction in space. Frequently, as with the Atoms for Peace Program, the initial program for the peaceful uses of outer space, and some of the specialized agency activities, the Soviets have not acted until the international program was well under way. Experience argues powerfully for the possibility of creating areas of common interest, even if limited, by moving ahead with international machinery and institutions that do not wholly depend on Soviet collaboration, without waiting for Soviet participation. In this way perhaps more than any other, the United Nations is, as Arnold Toynbee wrote in its very earliest years, "a political machine for putting into effect the maximum possible amount of cooperation between the United States and the Soviet Union." [19]

What are some of the specific common interests that can be anticipated and planned for? There is a self-evident interest in further curbing the possibility of a catastrophic surprise attack by either side, in taking the final steps to eliminate the hazards arising out of nuclear testing, and, conceivably, in reducing significantly the general level of armaments. A common interest may also exist in reducing the potential military dangers that could develop from outer-space technology, although here possible advantages — military, propaganda, and political — militate against the possibility of agreements on other than relatively low-level functional cooperation. The Soviet Union, at least for the present, may continue to object to the notion of U.N. peacekeeping as setting a dangerous precedent for intervention as well as detracting from Soviet controls in the United Nations via the Security Council. But, since there is a Soviet interest in avoiding unwanted involvement in small wars — an interest graphically demonstrated during the resumed Kashmir war of 1965 — the United States should seek to create such forms of international machinery on the assumption that the Soviets may well come to acknowledge their interest in participation.

One of the common interests we can reasonably postulate is the interest in being "taken off the hook" by the United Nations, in the sense that the French, British, and Israelis were in 1956 in Egypt, the Americans (and Russians) in Korea, the Americans and British in Lebanon and Jordan in 1958, the NATO powers in Cyprus, and the Soviets on numerous occasions, most notably in Cuba in 1962. The essence of this process was aptly described by Secretary General Hammarskjöld when he referred to his efforts in "denaturing" the Syrian-Turkish crisis (manufactured — and then repudiated — by the Soviets in the fall of 1947) as "Operation Parachute." The object was to let everyone down softly and safely.

There is a school of thought that, accepting the political struggle as inevitable, sees the technical and nonpolitical, *i.e.*, "func-

[19] Arnold Toynbee, "The International Outlook," XXIII *International Affairs* (1947), p. 469.

tional," areas of collaboration as the proper foci of concentration in the task of "building bridges" with the Soviet Union. Active common interests have been found in limited areas of everyday contact, such as safety at sea and in the air, control of epidemics, and development of agricultural and reforestation techniques. It is argued that so long as the ideological battle is unsolvable, efforts should be focused on new areas of practical common interest that reflect the reality of interdependence and provide a basis for creating limited communities of interest and action.

There is much to respect in this point of view. New technologies may overtake political arrangements even more dramatically in the next decade. The field of science contains highly promising possibilities for cooperation between the scientific communities, and perhaps between the governments as a consequence. The Soviet attitude has been "softer" in the scientific field than in any other field in which Americans have dealt with them. Based on the extraordinary success of the International Geophysical Year in transcending political barriers and creating bonds of collaboration at the scientific level, a strong sentiment has developed for bypassing political obstacles by increased scientific collaboration.

But this approach, promising as it is, has obvious limits. The effect of scientific collaboration on Soviet political decision-making has to be measured in terms of the relative place of the Soviet scientific community and intelligentsia in the Soviet power hierarchy. A strategic choice made at the apex of political power can wash out all the bridges built at the professional and technical levels, as tragic experiences with German scientists prior to World War II showed. So long as the political atmosphere is poisoned by ideological hostility, the so-called functional areas are of secondary importance in the larger strategic scheme. Until Soviet doctrine realizes a common interest in accepting the legitimacy of other societies, such collaboration will take place in a political climate whose essential danger to world peace and stability remains unbounded.

But recognition of this condition does not diminish the value of continuing to offer the Soviets alternative courses of political action – courses that one day may appear realistic and attractive to them. With or without them, we should continue working to institutionalize areas of common action and to create an international community that can compete successfully with the barren Soviet variety. We have already led the way in nonpolitical programs such as health and technical assistance, which the Soviets, for many reasons, ultimately have come to join. It is in our interest to urge greater experiments with multilateralism among those disposed to cooperate, and in this area of actions there is no substitute for the good offices of the United Nations.

What can or should the United Nations – that is, an effective majority of its members – do to exploit vulnerabilities in the Soviet system as they may appear?

The United Nations can and should focus world attention on iniquities and injustices in the Communist empire, with emphasis on the contrast between Communist pretensions and realities. As the vestiges of Western European colonialism disappear in Asia and Africa and the Middle East, and as new arrangements are worked out between the European nations and their former possessions, such vigor as the idea of self-determination still possesses may well be focused on violations still taking place in Eastern Europe. The embarrassment to which our Western European friends were subjected in the United Nations – in part from us – probably accelerated their withdrawal from former colonial areas. The Communists have not in the past been as vulnerable to such embarrassment, but potentially they are prime targets.

Communist vulnerability arises in the first instance from the hypocrisy of its ideological pretensions. Bukharin wrote:

> We do not speak of the right of self-determination of nations (i.e., of their bourgeoisie and their workmen) but only of the right of the working classes.[20]

Communist literature contains ample evidence that its strategy includes the exploitative uses of the colonial movement. So far it has not been profitable for the United States to take the lead in emphasizing this discrepancy in the course of U.N. debates on colonial problems. Of course some neutralist countries frankly do not believe the Western portrayal of Soviet policy, and they have

[20] N. I. Bukharin, *The ABC of Communism,* Part 59, "Communism and Nationality."

sometimes been able to contrast Soviet action on racial matters with the slights and abuses traditionally practiced by the West. And there has been little firsthand contact with the imperialistic side of Communist rule. At present, pointing in the United Nations to the Soviet position in Eastern Europe or to the Chinese position in Tibet, for example, either bores those who care only about the imperialism they know or creates resentment on the part of others for using the United Nations to sustain or sharpen international tension.

Nevertheless, the Soviet Union and Communist China are often imperialistic in their foreign policies – in the Eastern European satellites, in the Baltic states, with the Moslem minorities in Russia and China, in North Korea and North Vietnam, in Outer Mongolia, in Cuba, and in Tibet. The experience of Asian states with Chinese imperialism in Tibet and Laos, plus Indian concern for her northern borders, may open doors for a new international focus on the Communist problem. If the United States cannot suitably act as the sponsor of comparisons between Communist words and action, there are some indications that Asian or African states may be encouraged to take such an initiative themselves, particularly if disillusionment with Communist aid practices should grow. Future insistence by world opinion on the right of self-determination for Tibetans, East Germans, Poles, Czechs, Albanians, and perhaps even for Uzbeks, Khirgiz, Armenians, and other Central Asian Moslem and Christian minorities, might have an effect on Soviet planning and thinking that we are unable to predict today.

Western strategy can and should use the United Nations for purposes of embarrassing and if possible restraining the Communists when situations like those in Hungary and Tibet arise. To many, the touchstone of the value of the United Nations was "its" failure to redress the Soviet suppression of the Hungarian revolt in the fall of 1956. In fact, the capacity of the United Nations for action was directly dependent upon United States policy.

The lesson of Hungary was that without great-power initiative or at least acquiescence, the United Nations is impotent as an agency for significant political action. Certainly on matters involving challenges to Soviet power, it is nothing without the

United States; in making its "hands-off" decision, the United States had effectively removed any chance that the United Nations would take effective action in Hungary.

In the absence of American willingness to go beyond purely verbal protests, the United Nations probably did all it could in Hungary. To the extent that its resolutions of condemnation impressed people in areas where the facts are not readily come by, the United Nations even rendered a valuable service. Embarrassing the Soviet leadership was politically significant despite its lack of effect on their actions. Conceivably it may have sensitized a good many nations against Soviet propaganda on the workers' paradise.

But the conclusion from this tragic episode is a sobering one. We are by no means prepared to stand still for new Communist aggression. But until and unless we are prepared to crush the Soviet Union or China, as the case may be, in order to alter the present territorial *status quo,* we are essentially onlookers, confined to using moral and political weapons regarding what the Communist states do behind the truce lines. The larger dilemma remains: How can the United States and the West sustain the hope of those people under totalitarian rule for eventual freedom and self-determination and at the same time work toward greater international stability? How can vulnerabilities in both the Soviet and Chinese empires be exploited without, as it were, letting all the wild animals out of the cage? The hope for the future rests on a combination of dynamic processes, aided where possible from within the United Nations, leading to evolutions that we cannot now foresee but that we can consistently help to materialize.

CHAPTER TEN

Challenge and Cooperation in Space

Few areas of competitive activity so dramatize the contemporary struggle among nations for power and prestige as does outer space. This has been the case in the genesis of the space programs, in every stage of their technical growth, and in their great political meaning. To be sure, the first earth-satellite experiments were conducted under the banner of the International Geophysical Year. But the booster rockets that made it possible for the Soviet Union to be spectacularly first were originally developed to hurl an intercontinental ballistic missile across vast distances on earth. In the late 1960s space, still to all practical intents the monopoly of the two superpowers, preempts a growing portion of the budgets and specific efforts of both countries. The United States spends about 7½ percent of its national budget on space, more than on any cluster of domestic programs. Even more startling evidence of the steadily increasing commitment to the space race is the fact that almost all the engineers and scientists entering research in the United States are absorbed into space-related activities.

President Kennedy in May 1961 defined the goal of the United States as "landing a man on the moon and returning him safely to earth" during this decade. The time has arrived, he said, "for this nation to take a clearly leading role in space achievement, which, in many ways, may hold the key to our future on earth." [1] President Johnson has described his goal as that of making the United States the world's number-one spacefaring nation.

As for the Soviet Union, although former Premier Khrushchev denied in 1963 that his country was in a race to the moon, it is noteworthy that the combined Soviet military and space budget continues to climb, that the Soviets did not respond to the United States offer of a jointly planned moon shot, and that Soviet space technology has become increasingly sophisticated and complex, specifically in the techniques of maneuver and rendezvous in space, which have potential military significance. The heroic welcome for Soviet cosmonauts and their treatment as new folk heroes, the unqualifiedly military complexion of the Soviet Union's space program, the payload of the Soviet Union's pioneering hard moon landing in September 1959 [2] and their success in reaching Venus in 1966, all indicate the high regard in which the Soviets hold their space effort.

As Western Europe resumes its place on the world scene as a potent mover of events, it too enters the space race. The European Launcher Development Organization (ELDO) and the European Space Research Organization (ESRO), Europe's joint space agencies, are now paced by Eurospace, a combination of more than a hundred European commercial firms seeking significant shares in the lucrative space-equipment business. While flirting with the notion of an independent, competitive satellite communications organization of their own, the European countries have now made satisfactory arrangements with the United States Communications Satellite Corporation (Comsat), the United States' quasi-private instrument for space communications. But substantial space programs are under way in Europe, as much, one surmises, for prestige reasons as for any other.

A possible future significance of space, which we overlook at our potential peril, is as a new *place d'armes,* a sort of strategic suburb of earth to which the cold war has already expanded and

[1] *New York Times,* May 26, 1961.

[2] It consisted of multiple metal fragments bearing the hammer-and-sickle emblem and etched with the Cyrillic characters "CCCP," which scattered on impact, plus a foot-long Soviet flag.

from which, as visualized by at least some military strategists, a hot war could be fought. Both superpowers agreed in a 1963 United Nations resolution to abstain from placing nuclear weapons in orbit around the earth.[3] But both are also reportedly at work developing, among other things, manned space platforms, a fundamental first step in establishing a controllable and potentially versatile military presence in space. Information about military technology in space is highly classified, but whether through genuine fear of United States progress or as a smoke screen for their own militarization of space the Soviets have at times made such significant statements as this one:

> The Soviet Union, which is resolutely opposed to the utilization of outer space for military purposes, cannot ignore all these preparations of the American imperialists and is forced to adopt corresponding measures in order to safeguard its security against an attack through outer space. It is no secret that the technical basis for the launching of earth satellites and spaceships is the ballistic missile and its guidance system. Such complex, perfected technical equipment . . . is in the possession of the Soviet Union.[4]

If we allow our imaginations to wander, then, to the darkest prospects for the future, we can envisage the day, not too far off, when the great powers have positioned secretly launched weapons systems in outer space. The consequences would surely be that each power would try fiercely to preempt the other's satellites, tension on earth would be greatly heightened, hostile action would be threatened on the ground – in short, all the direst consequences of an all-out struggle for prestige, power and ever more exclusive sovereignty and secrecy in heaven as it is on earth. This, then, would be outer space as one more arena for virulent forms of nationalism, powerfully reinforced by the clash of ideologies. From all this can come only increased hostility, growing suspicions, ever greater militarism, and, perhaps in the end,

[3] General Assembly Resolution 1884 (XVIII), October 17, 1963.

[4] V. Larionov, "Kosmos i strategiya," *Krasnaya Zvezda,* March 21, 1963, p. 3. See also V. D. Sokolovskii, *Soviet Military Strategy,* translated and edited by Herbert S. Dinerstein and others (Englewood Cliffs, N.J.: Prentice-Hall, 1963), p. 427. Retired United States Air Force Chief of Staff Curtis E. LeMay has written that "many of the techniques the Soviet Union has developed so far point strongly toward a military space effort" (*New York Times,* March 26, 1965).

World War III. The optimists who see competition in space as a desirable kind of surrogate for conflict on earth must be mistaken as long as one of the superpowers remains devoted, however qualifiedly, to the downfall of the other.

There is another side to the space race, which is the reverse of the first in spirit and outlook and grows out of technological – but not necessarily political – reality. If anything makes nonsense of national boundaries, however useful and meaningful they may be in other ways, it is the earth satellite, orbiting every 90 minutes or so over different countries, passing over their boundaries without passports, travel documents, customs inspection, or even permission. Still more mocking of the narrow provincial spirit on earth is the flight outward to the moon, to Mars, to deep space. One of the favorite dialogues in contemporary science fiction has to do with the perspective by which observers viewing earth from a great distance see the exclusive barriers erected by men and their petty earthly quarrels. From this perspective one is, at least in theory, entitled to deduce the self-evident norm of internationalism – at a minimum cooperation, at a maximum integration.

Both aspects of space – as an arena for the conflict of national ambitions and as a nation-transcending challenge to the skills and knowledge of mankind – both these "faces of space" represent reality. Neither alone explains the full nature of the political problems involved in space cooperation or indicates with any reliability the avenues of policy that are actually open to the responsible countries with space potential. And neither alone completely describes the prospects we can legitimately envisage when we ask ourselves whether there is to be real cooperation – or real conflict – in space in the time ahead.

TECHNOLOGICAL ADVANCE AND POLITICAL CONFLICT

There is thus a high degree of political content superimposed on "neutral" technology. One of the enduring clichés of the Space Age speaks of the gap between man's technical progress and his failure to devise political arrangements for mastering that progress to the benefit and enrichment of mankind rather than for his possibly accelerated destruction. In 1961 the United States Representative to the United Nations may have been too pessimistic when he conceded:

> Unhappily this astounding progress in space science has not been matched by comparable progress in international cooperation. In the race of history, social invention continues to lag behind scientific invention.[5]

But the late Ambassador Adlai Stevenson may have been overly sanguine when two years later he said:

> In outer space . . . our sense of social responsibility and our capacity for social invention are not doing too badly in response to the challenge laid down by the inventions of our scientists.[6]

The truth of the matter is that while the growth of technology tends to proceed along a fairly uniform curve – though sometimes at an exponential rate – the political curve is characteristically irregular, faltering, sometimes cyclical, and not at all predictable. The capacity for political invention is irregular because it is a function of the changing dynamics of international political life.

Specifically, it is not possible to chart with any depth of understanding the progress of international cooperation on outer space without specific reference to the state of Soviet–United States relations at any given time. Mr. Stevenson's 1961 statement was made in a frosty atmosphere, engendered, after a period of relative thaw, by a renewed Soviet hard line, exemplified in intensified threats to Berlin culminating in the erection of the Wall, the stealthily prepared breach of the three-year moratorium on nuclear testing, and the boasts of terror weapons that accompanied it. Stevenson's 1963 statement surely reflected the warming trend as, after the 1962 Cuban missile adventure had failed, reality at least temporarily returned to Soviet strategic thinking, and détente, reinforced by the steadily mounting costs of space and defense, was again in the air. If 1963 was a vintage year in terms of limited agreements about both arms and space, it was because both the United States President and the Soviet Premier had committed themselves to policies of relative restraint in interna-

[5] Statement in the First (Political and Security) Committee, United States Delegation to the General Assembly, Press Release 3875, December 4, 1961.

[6] Department of State *Bulletin,* December 30, 1963, p. 1011.

tional relations. Strategically supported by mutual deterrence, both sides found it politically possible, at least at the time, to fend off pressures for more bellicose policies. The 1966 negotiations on an international treaty on the law of space had to contend with the backlash of the Vietnam war – but succeeded.

Political progress can thus lag behind technological progress and be unaffected by apparent moral and intellectual imperatives that people believe they discern in the march of science. But advancing technology can also carry social invention along with it at a surprising clip, given the will and the propitious congruence of political and strategic forces. The key variable may be the pressure of technology on politics, but its operational force depends on the drawing of relevant political conclusions – not always a self-evident process.

What *is* unmistakable is the pace of technology. Progress in space communications is perhaps best known. United States satellites have brought space into the homes of millions of television viewers. The synchronous satellite, with its capacity to appear to hover over the equator and thus remain stationary in relation to its earthly audiences, has the potential to revolutionize communications, education, and propaganda. The Early Bird satellites, launched in April 1965 with telephone and television channels, were the forerunners of an operational system providing telephone, telegraphy, high-speed data, facsimile, and television communications services on a global and nondiscriminatory basis. The Soviets for their part launched a communications satellite, Molniya I, in late April 1965, and European countries, notably France, have spoken of a European system.

It will be some time before one can make the predicted ten-cent overseas phone call via satellites. But satellites can soon link together countries in Africa that have traditionally been "wired" directly to European capitals, and can permit such countries as Brazil to bypass some stages of conventional internal wired communications by linking remote areas within the country through the use of a few ground stations and satellites. The British writer Arthur C. Clarke, no mean prophet of the Space Age so far, has written:

> It may be no exaggeration to say that priority in establishing the satellite communication system may determine whether, fifty years

> from now, Russian or English is the main language of mankind. The TV satellite is mightier than the ICBM, and intercontinental TV may indeed be the ultimate weapon.[7]

Satellite science is teaching men more than they ever dreamed about the nature of space, solar "weather," conditions on the surfaces of the planets, and the real visage of the planet Earth. But even here there are important military implications. The Secor system, like the earlier Anna and Transit, not only aids scientists in determining the exact size and shape of the earth but also helps to pinpoint targets by improving the exact navigation of Polaris and other weapons-delivery systems. The Soviet Union and the United States are making faster progress toward reaching the moon than toward making arrangements to coordinate their findings or to ensure against hostile acts from emplacements in near space or on celestial bodies such as the moon. If life exists on Mars or on Jupiter, there is only an informal indication that the first men to reach these planets will not fatally contaminate it – or that we as a society of nations are spiritually and socially prepared to apply the Golden Rule to "them" any more than we apply it to each other.

Some tangible steps have been taken, inside and outside the United Nations, in the direction of cooperation. However, any judgment of these efforts, especially in terms of the performance of the United Nations and its related agencies, is handicapped by the lack of appropriate criteria.

If we take as our prime criterion the "internationalization" of all outer-space activities, we shall certainly stack the deck against an intelligible finding; for the objective of keeping space immune from conflict appears unrealistic unless one can also eliminate the political warfare that underlies it. As long as the cold war continues, space will represent a race for prestige and for strategic superiority. The time may be coming when political conflict on earth will have abated to the point where space can be labeled as truly out of bounds. The 1966 Space Treaty goes a long way in this direction. But a truly effective ban against the military use of space may require successful action in the realms of dis-

[7] Arthur C. Clarke, *Profiles of the Future* (New York: Harper & Row, 1962), p. 190.

armament, inspection, verification, sanctions, and enforcement measures — elusive goals not limited to the context of space.

What then *can* legitimately be set forth as reasonable and realistic desiderata for international cooperation in space, enabling us to evaluate the role and prospects of the available means of such cooperation, notably the United Nations? First, assuming a continuing political conflict between leading nations, it is both desirable and reasonable to seek to achieve a maximum of cooperation in every aspect of space activity, while not expecting the conflict to cease or the leading nations to abandon prestige or power as fundamental goals.

Second, given the unlikelihood of enforceable international law under present international political circumstances, we should expect a maximum effort to draw up practical functional rules of conduct in and concerning space, rules that are clearly in the interest of all to have established and obeyed. To the extent possible, the quest should also be pressed to establish broad principles of national conduct that can become "law" through custom or international covenant.

Third, we can legitimately ask for the creation of the appropriate international machinery to do those jobs which nations agree to delegate to it, and, in addition, for the optimum utilization of existing international organizational machinery.

Fourth — a special exception to the highly constrained political framework we have postulated here — it is in our own and in the common interest to seek a maximum of arms control in the realm of space. Hopefully, we should find movement toward this goal easier than the attainment of arms control on earth because space is as yet unmilitarized. Nonetheless, as pointed out in Chapter Eight, negotiations on space take place within the larger reality that inhibits agreements involving significant inspections of sensitive military installations — especially if the proposed inspections include undeclared facilities or are to be made at random on the territory of states.

UNITED NATIONS EFFORTS

Bearing in mind the counterpoint supplied to the theme of international cooperation by the continuing great-power struggle, we can look at the record of United Nations activity for some provisional answers to the questions raised.

The United Nations has not been slow to take up its duties regarding the new dimension of space, although at first there was little real sense of what those duties in fact were. The 13th General Assembly on December 13, 1958, established an eighteen-member Ad Hoc Committee on the Peaceful Uses of Outer Space. The composition of the Committee not surprisingly emphasized the countries most likely to be involved in space; the Soviet Union, perhaps also not surprisingly, boycotted its activities.

The Committee's consideration of the subject was rather cautious and conservative, inhibited both by the absence of several members and, some felt, by a lack of positive direction on the part of the United States. The final report, adopted on June 25, 1959, by the thirteen states that remained, nonetheless represented the first concerted intergovernmental assault at the political level on outer space as an international problem area.[8]

The Committee ruled out at the start any comprehensive legal code that would impose a rigid framework on a subject not yet well understood. Instead, in response to the Assembly's request for a report on "the nature of legal problems which may arise in the carrying out of programmes to explore outer space," the Committee identified the following as questions calling for "priority" treatment: (1) freedom of exploration and use in outer space; (2) liability for injury or damage caused by space vehicles; (3) allocation of radio frequencies; (4) avoidance of interference between space vehicles and aircraft; (5) identification and registration of space vehicles and coordination of launchings; and (6) consideration of legal problems involved in the reentry and landing of space vehicles.

The Committee designated as a "nonpriority" question the favorite of international lawyers up to that time – the matter of where outer space begins and sovereign airspace ends. Discerning "no consensus" here, the Committee believed that an international agreement would be "premature," but it did suggest that a range might be set with the "boundary" neither so low as to interfere with existing aviation nor so high as to impede explora-

[8] U.N. Document A/4141.

tion.[9] As other nonpriority questions the Committee listed protection of public health and safety, safeguards against contamination (which has more recently become a genuine priority item for biologists), questions relating to exploration of celestial bodies, and avoidance of interference among space vehicles. Many of these items in both categories, became the subject of later action.

The Committee reported that it saw the need for international agreements on a range of practical functional questions. These included the use of radio frequencies in space, termination of radio transmission at the end of a satellite's useful life, destruction of spent satellites, reentry and recovery of manned vehicles, return of equipment, identification of origin, and the contamination problem. And the Committee was particularly cautious in approaching the question of new institutional machinery or international controls.

The fall of 1961 was a high point. On the basis of proposals outlined by President Kennedy in his speech to the Assembly on September 25, 1961, the Assembly passed a resolution that established basic principles of conduct in space that stand today as the closest thing to common law on the subject. One preambular clause is worth quoting:

> Believing that the exploration and use of outer space should be only for the betterment of mankind and to the benefit of States irrespective of the stage of their economic or scientific development. . . .[10]

The resolution recommended to states for their "guidance" the principles that international law, including the U.N. Charter, applied to outer space and to the celestial bodies, and that the latter were free for exploration and use by all in conformity with international law and not subject to national appropriation. The resolution called on the Secretary General to set up a public registry of launchings; it encouraged the plans of the International Telecommunication Union (ITU) to foster the development of global communication-satellite systems, and similarly the efforts

[9] The question was newly raised by a Soviet writer in *Nedelia,* the weekly supplement of *Izvestia,* March 20, 1965.

[10] General Assembly Resolution 1721 (XVI), December 20, 1961.

of the World Meteorological Organization (WMO) with respect to weather-satellite activities; finally, it increased the Committee's membership to twenty-eight.

In March of the following year a dialogue began between the leaders of the two space powers that ultimately yielded some modest steps toward direct cooperation. In a letter to Premier Khrushchev, President Kennedy suggested a number of joint activities, including establishment of an early operational weather-satellite system and of radio tracking stations on each other's territories, cooperation in mapping the earth's magnetic fields, testing of communications by satellites, and exchange of information on space medicine and on manned and unmanned space explorations. Premier Khrushchev replied favorably on all but the tracking-stations proposal.

The same month, a newly reconstituted U.N. Committee on the Peaceful Uses of Outer Space met, this time with all in attendance. In its legal subcommittee ideology and political conflict caused disagreements, some of which persist to the present time. The major points of disagreement were five: (1) the unspecified Soviet desire to prohibit "war propaganda" in space which quickly brought up two unresolvable issues – the question of what constitutes "peaceful uses" of space and the question of disarmament itself; (2) the Soviet desire for prior agreement (*i.e.*, a veto) on any measure that might affect another country's use of space; (3) the Soviet insistence that "states" be the only agents in space – an attack on the evolving Comsat concept in the United States; (4) the Soviet desire to condemn what it called "intelligence-gathering" from space (clearly aimed at the United States reconnaissance satellites); and (5) the nature of the principles governing the use of space and the form of instruments to be used in setting them forth.

Although the Committee was to wrestle with the substantive issues for the next two years, an institutional development of high potential significance emerged in the voting procedures agreed to in the Committee. This provided for preliminary informal consultations among all participants until unanimous agreement on a given issue was reached. Thereafter the consensus of the Committee was recorded by acclamation and without voting. (The potential utility of such a "sense-of-the-meeting" substitute for formal voting was demonstrated in an ironic fashion several years later, when, in the face of the threat of confrontation over Article 19, the deadlocked 19th Assembly resorted to informal polling followed by "voteless" voting by acclamation in order to accomplish its minimum business.)

The counterpoint of superpower relationships accompanied the Committee's work externally as well as dominating it from within. Continuing talks began between two leading government scientists, the Deputy Administrator of the United States National Aeronautics and Space Administration (NASA), the late Dr. Hugh Dryden, and Anatoly A. Blagonravov, Chairman of the Space Commission of the Soviet Academy of Sciences. This period also saw the uncommonly heated United States Senate debate leading to establishment of Comsat. And in July 1962 the age of space communications commenced in fact with the orbiting of the first active repeater satellite – Telstar I. Finally, the Cuban missile crisis in the fall of 1962 can be seen as a turning point in Soviet–United States relations, followed as it was by a renewed thaw.

On August 22, 1963, the United States and the Soviet Union reported to the United Nations a number of agreements on co-operative space ventures.[11] These included a coordinated weather-satellite program, joint experiments with communications using a passive reflector satellite (Echo II), and joint contributions of satellite data to the World Magnetic Survey to be conducted in 1965. Their memorandum also announced the scheduled establishment by early 1964 of a full-time telecommunications link between Washington and Moscow for transmission of cloud photographs and other data from experimental meteorological satellites operated by each country.

In October and November 1963, an event of great importance for the development of space communications took place. The International Telecommunication Union (ITU) Extraordinary Administrative Radio Conference, called to make allocations of radio frequencies for space communications, increased the proportion of the table of frequency allocations available for outer space from about 1 percent (1959) to about 15 percent. This represented a surprisingly large allocation to communication satellites of 2,725 megacycles (2,000 of which were contained in the

[11] U.N. Document A/5482.

United States proposal), sufficient through the late 1970s, when, it is estimated, two-thirds of the world's communications will be via satellite. The allocation is sufficient to handle 500 television programs or 300,000 telephone calls simultaneously. The Conference cleared the frequencies necessary for meteorological and navigation satellite communications and (of particular interest to radio astronomers listening for signs of intelligence in space) the crucial "hydrogen band" after the Soviets dropped their reservations.

Another milestone in the same period was the General Assembly resolution of October 17, 1963, welcoming expressions by the United States and the Soviet Union of their intention not to station in outer space any objects carrying nuclear weapons or other kinds of weapons of mass destruction and calling on all states to refrain from stationing such weapons in outer space.[12] Although the unofficial agreement did not provide for inspection, it nevertheless was of high potential significance since technological progress could eventually be expected to permit unilateral rendezvous and "eyeball" investigations for violations.

Shortly thereafter, in November, the U.N. Committee agreed on a draft "Declaration of Legal Principles Governing the Activities of States in the Exploration and Use of Outer Space." This incorporated the principles previously approved by the Assembly in December 1961. On the points of previous major disagreement it asserted that an earlier Assembly resolution condemning propaganda threatening peace was applicable to space; it urged states to undertake "appropriate international consultation" when they had reason to believe their activities might cause potentially harmful interference with the activities of other states; it agreed that states should bear international responsibility for national activities in space, whether by governmental or nongovernmental agencies; and it stated that states should regard astronauts as "envoys of mankind in outer space," and should give them all possible assistance. The Declaration made no mention of the espionage issue.[13]

[12] General Assembly Resolution 1884 (XVIII).

[13] These principles were embodied in General Assembly Resolutions 1962 and 1963 (XVIII), December 13, 1963.

A further step in international cooperation in space took place in January 1964, when a group of six scientists visited the Thumba International Equatorial Sounding Rocket Launching Facility, a cooperative enterprise of India, France, and the United States. The group unanimously recommended that the facility be given U.N. sponsorship.

On July 23, 1964, culminating a surprisingly successful conference in Washington called by the United States to bring other nations into the Comsat enterprise, eighteen nations and the Vatican completed agreements on the international ownership and management of the global communications satellite system being developed by the United States. The Soviet Union and its allies criticized the agreements as inconsistent with the agreed principles that satellite communications should be available to the world on a global and nondiscriminatory basis and that states bear international responsibility for activities in outer space. The Soviet Union said that the agreements bypassed the United Nations and ITU, that they were drafted with monetary profit as an objective, and that the provision for weighted voting in the agreements was incompatible with the principle of sovereign equality. In reply the United States said that the agreements remained open for signature or accession by any state member of ITU, that all states would have access to the system whether or not they became parties to the agreements, and that only governments could sign and accede. Although voting was to be weighted according to the proportionate investment of each signatory, a provision was made that in enumerated major decisions significance was also to be given to the number of states assenting. Some fifty states have now joined the new "INTELSAT."

In the spring of 1966 the United States and the Soviet Union made parallel proposals for a formal treaty on the legal principles that ought to govern space exploration. In detail both proposals largely formalized the provisions of the earlier 1961 and 1963 U.N. resolutions and declarations on the subject. In addition several key provisions were agreed upon barring from space activities essentially military in nature. The treaty concluded in the General Assembly in the fall of 1966 can stand as a milestone in the quest for arms control and a rule of law.

Two of the U.N. family of specialized agencies, ITU and WMO (World Meteorological Organization), have been the most involved in the actual control of space activities. ITU is responsible for the international coordination and rational use of all forms of telecommunication by land, submarine cable, and radio; all its constituent bodies have in the normal course of their activities a role to play in the field of space communications. Mention has been made of the 1963 Extraordinary Administrative Radio Conference, which allocated radio frequency bands for space communication purposes. The Conference decided that the same distress signals used by ships and aircraft should also be used by spacecraft, and set aside the frequency of 20,000 kilocycles for this purpose.

WMO has necessarily become involved in space-related activities and has been mentioned in virtually all the General Assembly's resolutions on space. Its tasks have included the application of meteorology to weather prediction, the development of international atmospheric observation and telecommunication networks, and the promotion of research. It has also aided new or developing countries in their efforts to establish or improve meteorological services, to promote research, and to create training institutes.

The Fourth World Meteorological Congress, held in Geneva in April 1963, created a high-level WMO advisory committee to consider principal research problems in the atmospheric sciences, ways of promoting meteorology, and methods of ensuring the availability of data. The Congress endorsed the concept of a World Weather Watch aimed ultimately at integrating national and international meteorological activities; it initially designated Moscow and Washington as world centers for data processing and envisaged a future third center in the Southern Hemisphere. In general WMO has admirably fulfilled its new responsibilities, showing a capacity to adapt and create, as well as successfully involving the most disparate countries in the World Weather Watch.

Other U.N. agencies are participating in space-related activities in lesser ways. UNESCO has sponsored scientific meetings relating to space, and has supported studies of the prospects offered by space communication for increasing the range and scope of mass media and for promoting a free flow of information, the spread of education, and a wider cultural exchange. The World Health Organization (WHO) is in the process of defining its tasks in the study of cosmic biology, genetics and radiation, the physiology and psychology of man in space, and environmental contamination from the transfer of chemical and biological agents to and from the earth. The International Civil Aviation Organization (ICAO) made a recommendation to the ITU Conference on telecommunication support for the operation of spacecraft and the use of earth satellites for communicating with aircraft. And the International Atomic Energy Agency (IAEA) has been concerned with the use of nuclear power for propulsion.

International cooperation is not exclusively an intergovernmental responsibility, and there has been a substantial division of labor between the U.N. system and other organizations. A nongovernmental organization, the International Council of Scientific Unions, has probably overseen more tangible cooperation than any other single international body. COSPAR, its Committee on Space Research which was established in October 1958 to continue the international cooperation in space research undertaken during the International Geophysical Year, is an interdisciplinary scientific committee with the objective of furthering international scientific investigation using rockets or rocket-propelled vehicles. Much of the impetus to scientific learning through space exploration grew out of the International Geophysical Year, and through COSPAR the IGY pattern of cooperation has been extended. COSPAR has not been immune from cold-war rivalries and incorporates in its procedures what some scientists deplore as a sort of great-power veto. In the main, however, it has proceeded effectively in bringing together scientists from the countries most concerned with space to work on problems of astrophysics, the atmospheric sciences, the life sciences, and other categories of scientific research.

How then can we sum up this record in terms of our desiderata? Are our embryonic efforts toward space cooperation unable to halt the trend, discerned by Erich Fromm, "toward a world of impotent men directed by virile machines"? Or are those involved succeeding, in the words of Dean Rusk, in "occupying the horizons of their responsibilities"?

First, one emerges with a strong sense that, within the formidable constraints imposed by the cold war, the amount of actual cooperation that has been achieved through a combination of United Nations, specialized-agency, nongovernmental, and bilateral relationships has for the moment probably been about as great as the traffic will bear.

Second, some rule-making has been undertaken, both at the level of general principles and in terms of detailed regulations, particularly in the highly practical matters of ownership of satellites, responsibility for damages incurred, and rescue and return of both astronauts and their vehicles. Rules are most precise and binding with respect to the allocation of radio frequencies. One must continue to remember that the amount of agreed law will necessarily follow consensus on political objectives, and will suffer in effectiveness from the lack of procedures for punishing violations. But it was not wholly without meaning that soon after the space walk of Soviet cosmonaut Colonel A. Leonov, a Soviet commentator wrote that the sortie posed "for the first time" problems of citizenship, legal status, and ownership; he concluded that "it is time to begin to settle these." [14] The treaty soon followed.

Third, maximum use has undoubtedly been made of the existing specialized agencies, particularly recently as they have sought to adjust to new and unforeseen responsibilities. One need only visit the computer room of ITU in Geneva to sense the strides that ITU and other "old-line" agencies have taken in this regard. Likewise, the U.N.'s administrative structure has been adapted to service both the specialized agencies in their space-related activities and the General Assembly's Committee on the Peaceful Uses of Outer Space. A small unit, the outer-space-affairs group exists in the Secretariat to assist the Committee; in addition there are an interdepartmental working party on space (which has reportedly not been very effective) and a special interagency working group under the Administrative Committee on Coordination

[14] *Nedelia,* March 20, 1965.

(ACC) for consultation and correlation on space matters between the United Nations and the specialized agencies; the latter has now gotten off the ground and is reported to be working well.

UNFINISHED BUSINESS

How else can the United States legitimately take the lead in the forum of the United Nations in seeking to widen the area of cooperation in space and to set space aside from the area of confrontation on earth?

There is ample opportunity for the exercise of imagination and energy in helping to steer the Space Age into constructive channels. One interesting suggestion made by two staff members of the Massachusetts Institute of Technology combines scientific, technical, and political desiderata in a recommendation for an international space launching facility. It would be located in the Australian-administered trust territory of New Guinea (New Ireland is the site recommended) and would provide additional needed launching facilities, proximity to the equator, accessibility to sea transport for heavy booster rockets, and a relatively uniform climate – all in an area politically free of historical great-power vested interests.[15] This proposal deserves further study.

I have described the successful negotiations in 1966 leading to a treaty embodying most of the ground rules already agreed to concerning outer space, plus a few innovations such as prohibiting military activity on the moon.[16] The treaty is of course not enforceable. But by the form it took, it elevated some of the "common law" on space to the more formal level of statute law.

But several policy areas of extraordinary future importance were not dealt with in the treaty proposal, nor indeed have been dealt with anywhere. The first arises out of the likelihood that early in the 1970s direct television broadcasts into the home via satellite will become technically feasible. The implications for this are portentous indeed, whether for good – widespread education, the end of illiteracy, the free dissemination of news – or

[15] Joel B. Searcy and Philip K. Chapman, *A Proposal for a New Space Launching Facility* (Lexington, Mass., April 1964, multilithed).

[16] *New York Times,* Dec. 9, 1966.

evil — war propaganda, race hatred on a mass scale, indoctrination. (Between the two extremes is perhaps the escalation of deodorant commercials to an audience of billions in Swahili, Hindi, or Mandarin.) The main point is that governments and networks would lose their capacity to stand between their people and the satellite-reflected programs, unless they deliberately jammed the airwaves.

Some international analogy to the Federal Communications Commission and the laws under which it operates seems essential if this revolutionary development is to be met in an orderly way that maximizes both freedom of information and essential standards of political behavior. New concepts of international supervision need to accompany new machinery if this promising technology is not to degenerate into the worst rather than the best of which it is capable.

The need for an improved international regime in outer space, one that goes beyond present proposals, is underscored by the intensive development by the two superpowers of manned orbital capabilities — man in space with the future ability to detect, intercept, inspect, and possibly destroy another space object he believes to be hostile.

In the realm of arms control in space, some modest steps have been taken through the ban on weapons tests in outer space and the agreement not to orbit nuclear weapons. The latter particularly is handicapped by lack of inspection and verification procedures; as has been emphasized throughout, arms control in space suffers from its intimate connection to earthbound arms control. It may, however, offer some special prospects growing out of the relative newness of outer space and the consequent common interest in demilitarizing it, much as Antarctica was demilitarized and in effect internationalized by the 1959 Antarctic Treaty; and as the 1966 Treaty sought to do for space.

It is possible that even without formal international agreements the technology of rendezvous and inspection by satellite will proceed unilaterally to the point where technical means will be at hand *de facto* for a scheme of international verification, unplanned though it may be. The Soviet Union's revelation, after years of Soviet denunciation of the United States reconnaissance-satellite program as "espionage," that it too had a "spy in the sky"[17] conveyed important implications for moving toward the more open world that many feel is the precondition to reliable arms-control agreements. The further suggestion that this sort of space observation could be legitimatized as a substitute for unilateral aircraft flights through sovereign airspace[18] makes it seem more possible than before to envisage serious negotiations, in the first instance between the space superpowers, about a regime of international cooperation in space dealing with the paramount questions of security and prevention of surprise attack. We ought to be considering ways to internationalize, under appropriate regulation and arrangements, the capacity to police space, and to seek agreement on it before a dangerous competition develops between two, three, perhaps four or five self-styled space police forces. Such agreements, either concerning space itself or using space as a means of bypassing the inspection deadlock on the ground, could justify everything nations have invested so far in the Space Age.

Finally, there has been a great disinclination to try to fix international rules defining outer space in relation to airspace. One difficulty in establishing such rules is that the airspace does not really end, scientifically speaking, for the thousands of miles out where molecules of "air" can still be found. Moreover, the fast-developing technology of spacecraft increasingly blurs the distinction between winged and rocket-powered craft. Lastly, military men have a natural proclivity to favor a rule enabling them to fly as low as possible over another's territory while keeping him as high up as possible over their own! Naturally this requirement makes the task of rule-making difficult if not impossible.

The kind of orderly space regime we seek would be advanced by establishment of a rule that national airspace terminates at a fixed limit. The most reasonable suggestions made so far would place the line somewhere between 70 and 100 kilometers — the lowest point reached by an unpowered earth satellite on one orbit. The space beyond, with the possible exception of a con-

[17] Interview of former Premier Khrushchev by former United States Senator William H. Benton, reported in *New York Times*, May 30, 1964.

[18] *Ibid.* According to Drew Middleton, Mr. Khrushchev suggested that space photography had eliminated the necessity for reconnaissance flights over Cuba.

tiguous zone of another 200 to 300 kilometers, by analogy to the laws of the seas, should be considered *res communis,* including all planetary bodies.

Prudence may well dictate a step-by-step approach so long as it augurs continued Soviet cooperation. The danger in such an approach is that, because of Soviet and American pragmatism and conservatism in formulating an international space doctrine, technical events rather than political forethought will continue to decide the possibilities and limits of a regime for outer space.

Outer space is a prime example of how our interest — and the common interest — would be served by *not* waiting until all the technical end-products are in service, until all the potential uses are made of communications satellites, and until the capacity is perfected for inspection, intercept, and destruction of space objects. We need to anticipate technological consequences by purposeful American policy planning. We need to work now to set specifications for space systems in terms of multinational operation or of utility for inspecting arms-control agreements.

With a clearly enunciated goal of developing greater international tranquillity and a more rational world order, a political strategy can be developed to strive toward an effective and rational international regime in space without waiting for the world of nation-states somehow to dissolve into something else. The opportunity exists here for the United Nations to perform at its most constructive level.

PART IV Toward a More Stable World

CHAPTER ELEVEN
The Settlement of International Disputes

CHAPTER TWELVE
Peaceful Change

CHAPTER THIRTEEN
The Developing Countries

CHAPTER FOURTEEN
Colonialism and Human Rights

CHAPTER ELEVEN

The Settlement of International Disputes

The issues dealt with so far — military and political security in the target context of the basic Communist-Western conflict — have represented overriding priorities for American foreign policy in the postwar years. Policy planning has tended to make all else subordinate, justifiable only insofar as it contributed to American objectives under these two headings. Yet even if the United States were to achieve all its objectives regarding military and political security, the overall national interest would remain only partly served.

American interests have become tied to the politics of every region, the economy of every nation, the social health of every people. They are particularly challenged by the unfolding development of new countries, new centers of population, new coalitions of political influence. The goals of American grand strategy are shaped as much by that set of problems as by the cold war. For the American objective of securing a more stable world and a more reliable and predictable world order is the natural, logical, and rational response of a rich, powerful, and stable nation to a political environment characterized by chronic instability and a highly impermanent equilibrium.

There are, therefore, real and exigent issues with which American policy must deal that are quite apart from the specific issues of the cold war. One crucial issue is the maintenance of unity within the non-Communist states in the face of Communist threats; another is the acquisition by the peoples in the "discontented areas" of a genuine stake in an international system that, while responsive to their particular needs and wants, is at the same time characterized by the values we prize. Such issues, which must be dealt with if American strategy is to be successful, would be difficult regardless of the cold war. They acquire particular urgency at least in part because of that overshadowing conflict.

Within this general range of issues lie the deep-seated conflicts between the non-Communist nations about colonial, racial, and human-rights problems; the aspirations of the newly articulate masses for the tangible economic and social benefits of political freedom; the hopes for a peaceful evolution of world society toward a true community. The bulk of these issues fall in the North-South conflict — the generalized tensions arising in the underdeveloped, anticolonial, and often neutralist areas of Asia, the Middle East, and Africa, and, increasingly, Latin America. It is these that are our present concern.

Within the non-Communist states one of the principal problems has to do with disputes and internal instability that sometimes lead to violence. The heart of the problem today is that if such violence is unqualifiedly suppressed it can lead to even greater difficulties later; yet if not suppressed, it may involve the great powers in a war of unpredictable dimensions. One way or another, therefore, the peaceful settlement of international disputes occupies a high place in our catalog of U.S. objectives. High priority is attached to ways of minimizing resort to violence, to devising better preventive measures in advance of such explosions, and to institutionalizing such measures as prove effective in order to construct a more durable international regime within which we can perfect our own society.

Three factors have inhibited genuine steps in the direction of peaceful settlement of disputes. First, our interest in order and stability was for a long time matched by an equally active interest on the part of the Soviet Union in fostering disorder and instability on which revolutionary forces could batten. It was not until the Suez crisis in 1956, the Cyprus conflict in 1963, and, most dramatically, the renewed Indo-Pakistani fighting in the fall of 1965 that the Soviets began to show both genuine concern about such situations and support for U.N. efforts to pacify them. The Chinese Communists for their part have characteristically worked to exacerbate and worsen situations of conflict, such as Vietnam, in the name of the strategy of encirclement and ultimate destruction of the non-Communist world centers.

Second, and regardless of cold-war considerations, disputes in the non-Communist states have often contained elements of at least temporary irreconcilability (Palestine, Kashmir, Cyprus) that sometimes can not be overcome by the most meticulously evenhanded justice; hardly ever can they be resolved by reversion to the *status quo ante*. The problem of pacific settlement thus invariably becomes the problem of peaceful change.

Third, one of the most historically popular means for settling an international dispute definitely — a military decision — is, despite frequent lapses, not really any longer acceptable or tolerable. This is not necessarily because of a new degree of civilized virtue, but because of the drastically altered nature of general war and the consequent universal unwillingness to look tolerantly on local situations carrying the potential of dangerously involving the great powers and their disproportionately destructive military capacity.

This dilemma underscores the vital necessity of developing more reliable means of preventing local disputes from reaching a point where East-West diplomacy could intervene with the military power which our strategy most seeks to avoid invoking. So far as the United Nations is concerned, it is here above all that the organization has taken significant action, and it is therefore here that its present and future potential is most clearly measurable.

The decisive consideration in U.N. action to settle disputes has been not the veto, as some believe, but the climate of international relations — in particular the power and will of a U.N. majority to stand back of its determination that force shall not be used in the settlement of disputes. A revision in the veto power could well follow a fundamental alteration in East-West relations accompanied by revisions in the present concept of national sovereignty. But here we are more concerned with the areas of action in which, in the years immediately ahead, more effective use might be made of the existing machinery of the United Nations to advance the larger objective.

THE UNITED NATIONS AS NEUTRAL GROUND

It might seem obvious that, of all the available or foreseeable diplomatic agencies, the United Nations is best qualified to furnish the needful neutral ground or third party in international disputes. There is, however, by no means general agreement with this proposition.

The view of the United Nations as a prime agency for the resolution of political disputes is not shared widely even within the Western alliance, primarily because the agenda of conflicts has in the past been heavily weighted with quarrels between colonial metropoles in Western Europe and rebelling or newly independent territories. At least half of the pacific-settlement issues before the United Nations have been of this variety, including Indonesia, Suez, and Algeria, to mention only a few of the major cases. Moreover, with the transfer of focus from the Security Council to the General Assembly, Western nations have become even more reluctant to subject matters affecting their vital interests to a body that more and more sympathizes with the anticolonial side in any argument, whatever the particular merits or complications. As the "swirling majorities" of underdeveloped, anticolonial countries grew, Western confidence diminished.

Thus France tended in the late 1950s to base her opinion of, and plans about, the United Nations exclusively on the attitude the organization took with respect to Algeria. The common French reaction to debate in the United Nations, not just on Algeria but earlier on Tunisia and Morocco as well, was one of profound annoyance, leading to a French walkout in the 1955 Assembly and French nonparticipation in the debates on Algeria in subsequent Assembly sessions. Much the same could be said of the Belgian view prior to the explosion in the Congo in 1960 and the Dutch attitude toward U.N. insistence on handing West New Guinea to Indonesia. In 1965 it was only when all other alternatives looked barren that the British turned to the United Nations to deal with the racist Rhodesian independence action.

Western European diplomats and politicians are skeptical of the usefulness of the United Nations on other grounds as well. They tend to assume, often with reason, that public debates in the United Nations have an incendiary effect on the local situation. If they place any value on the United Nations in such cases, it is usually on whatever facilities it offers for quiet diplomacy. The permanent head of the British Foreign Office wrote after his retirement:

> It is now generally recognized that the fashion in open diplomacy launched by President Wilson at Versailles in 1919 was ill-conceived and disastrous. Yet we still cling to it and in our hours of stress continue to clamor for the worthless panaceas of summit conferences and General Assemblies of the United Nations. Later generations will marvel at the obstinacy with which we refused to give ourselves the best chance of negotiating any international agreement.[1]

Sir Harold Nicolson has often articulated this theme:

> These conferences do little to satisfy the vague desire for what is called "open diplomacy"; but they do much to diminish the utility of professional diplomatists and, in that they entail much publicity, many rumors, and wide speculation, — in that they tempt politicians to achieve quick, spectacular and often fictitious results, — they tend to promote rather than allay suspicion, and to create those very states of uncertainty which it is the purpose of good diplomatic method to prevent. . . . Such negotiation as may occur in New York is not conducted within the walls of the tall building by the East River; it is carried out elsewhere, in accordance with those principles of courtesy, confidence and discretion which must forever remain the only principles conducive to the peaceful settlement of disputes.[2]

Certain American diplomats, notably George Kennan, have been similarly moved by what seemed to them a deterioration of the value of the trained diplomat.

These critics are to a degree correct; the objectives of diplomacy would often be better served by privacy and quiet rather than by publicity and the clamor of the crowd. But, like the loca-

[1] Sir Ivone Kirkpatrick, "As a Diplomat Sees the Art of Diplomacy," *New York Times Magazine,* March 22, 1959, p. 13.

[2] Harold Nicolson, *The Evolution of Diplomatic Method* (London: Constable, 1954), pp. 89, 91.

tion of the United Nations in New York (which for the same reasons could be considerably improved if moved to Bermuda, Geneva, or Majorca), the new tradition of public international debate cannot and will not be done away with. Like the American Congress the United Nations does much of its work in the smaller sessions, the cloakrooms, the private offices. But, also like the Congress, it has a public function as well, which the membership, for varying reasons, cherishes and would not readily see tampered with.

In retrospect it was perhaps a mistake to provide for open meetings of the U.N. organs. But it was not a fatal mistake so long as the opportunities that the U.N. environment offers for negotiations and settlement are fully exploited. It is a positive asset if the public facilities of the United Nations are used to set in motion constructive international actions that will bring the weight of world opinion to bear on parties to negotiate, to agree to cease-fires, or to submit disputes to arbitration or adjudication when that is appropriate; and, finally, to give its approval to agreements that contribute to the achievement of the primary objectives we and most other nations of the world share.

In its nearly universal membership, the United Nations has a potential for the peaceful settlement of disputes that no regional or alliance organization so far has been able to duplicate. The prime value of universalism is that parties to a dispute are committed to seek a peaceful solution, are present, and are necessarily involved. Negotiations rarely succeed without the presence of the parties. NATO tried at various times to deal with the New Guinea problem, and at other times it sought unsuccessfully to contribute to solutions in Cyprus and Algeria. But, given its primary military role, NATO has an image which, like that of abortive Users' Association in the Suez Canal dispute, was not helpful to the conciliation of disputes involving non-NATO and anti-NATO forces. Even in a situation such as the 1965 U.S. intervention in the Dominican Republic, where every conceivable party directly affected had membership in the Organization of American States (OAS), the United States was unable to prevent U.N. involvement – in this case a fact-finding and conciliation team. The reason many favored U.N. involvement was precisely that the OAS, dominated as it is by the disproportionate power of the United States, did not appear to be sufficiently neutral. The United Nations remains the only neutral ground where virtually all parties are present.

One interesting and little-noted characteristic of a third party operating from neutral ground is its ability to supply a financial lubricant or inducement to the settlement process. The International Bank for Reconstruction and Development has effectively acted as the third party in more than one thorny international political situation. The clearance and maintenance of the Suez Canal, in which officials of the I.B.R.D. played a significant role, and the negotiations conducted by Bank officials with India and Pakistan in the long-standing dispute over the waters of the Indus River Basin both represented political disputes with strong economic or financial aspects. This important possibility was underscored in 1966, when the Bank again became involved in Indo-Pakistani relations, this time influencing the policies to be followed toward India and Pakistan following their 1965 hostilities. It is not cynical but realistic to suggest that the largesse with which the Bank can facilitate negotiations may give it some advantage over purely political mediation processes. It provides a third party when one is badly needed, and thus adds to the means for resolving disputes which, however economically involved, are at the same time a source of major political tension and potential danger to the peace.

U.N. PRESENCE

A rule of thumb which was explicitly recognized by Article 33 of the U.N. Charter [3] is that everyone is better off when an international dispute is resolved quietly with a minimum of fuss and without involving the global machinery of the United Nations. There is every reason to encourage the settlement of disputes before they ever come before the United Nations. The United States has played a role of which it can be proud in privately

[3] "1. The parties to any dispute, the continuance of which is likely to endanger the maintenance of international peace and security, shall, first of all, seek a solution by negotiation, enquiry, mediation, conciliation, arbitration, judicial settlement, resort to regional agencies or arrangements, or other peaceful means of their own choice.

"2. The Security Council shall, when it deems necessary, call upon the parties to settle their dispute by such means."

seeking such settlements, and of course if a government is actively using its good offices or otherwise seeking solutions, its independent action is justified. Certain situations cannot be helped by public exposure and debate.

The problem, then, is not the situation that is being constructively dealt with, but the situation that remains unimproved between recurrent crises, and the situation that cannot be handled constructively by "vest-pocket diplomacy." Despite the exigent nature of situations of this order, many nations including our own have been reluctant to use international preventive facilities, choosing instead to rely on bilateral diplomatic activity or, more often, on the wait-and-see principle.

The Suez case is a classic illustration of how we become prisoners of outmoded ways of thinking about the capabilities of the United Nations for preventive peace. Throughout the intense and futile negotiations in the summer of 1956, the United States and its partners rigidly shunned any positive use of U.N. instrumentalities. One American motive was to avoid the possibility of a public discussion of the Panama Canal, by association, as it were. Consequently we relied exclusively on the so-called London group. This forum was unacceptable to Egypt. At the same time we failed to avail ourselves of a wide range of possible actions through the United Nations, including appointment of a U.N. mediator, or of a U.N. agent-general to operate the Canal in the interim without prejudice, or the establishment of a joint regime, or, at a minimum, recognition through a U.N. resolution that the Canal was international in character. Reasonable proposals that enlisted heavy U.N. support could conceivably have altered Egypt's intransigence. We now see that when the British and French finally went to the United Nations in early October it was to clear the way for unilateral action. Only when fighting broke out did we ourselves turn to the United Nations to stop it. This was of course the one thing the United Nations was unable to do, apart from exerting a purely moral force and apart from whatever outside pressure individual members such as the United States and the Soviet Union could apply.

Western statesmen have spoken for years, quite correctly, about the great value of the United Nations in getting the parties to a dispute around the table, substituting talk and mediation and conciliation, however endless and frustrating, for bullets, and offering a variety of institutional means for limiting the conflict and facilitating peaceful change. In the case of Suez we underestimated the preventive capacity of the United Nations before the crisis became acute, overestimated its capabilities when the crisis arrived, and again lost interest when the crisis had passed.

Our attention immediately wandered to another dimension of the problem – the possibility of overt Russian military aggression. The resolutions regarding a peace settlement for Palestine and the refugee problem that the United States introduced in the early hectic nights of the crisis were never again referred to, and instead Washington brought forth the "Eisenhower Doctrine" for the Middle East. This is not to deny the possible value of posting a U.S. keep-out sign in the area, however belatedly and even though the possibility of overt Russian aggression was comparatively slight. The trouble was that this was our only real move to remedy a whole array of critical local problems – problems that did not primarily involve the Communist bloc but instead reflected the basic sources of conflict in the area.

Other factors have inhibited the avowed American determination to wage preventive peace. The number of crises alone has been sufficient to distract attention within the Government from longer-range approaches to the general problem of disputes and the means of dealing with them. In a period when the highest American decision-makers were involved in personal negotiation of one current crisis after another, there was a powerful bureaucratic disincentive to forfend future crises by timely and decisive action with the use of such available tools as U.N. machinery provides.

The plainly discernible result has been the decreasing use that we have made of U.N. facilities in settling potentially dangerous international disputes. The United States in obvious embarrassment discouraged proposals to use the Peace Observation Commission in the 1954 Burma situation involving the alleged activities of Chinese Nationalist elements along Burma's northern frontiers; along with Great Britain it attempted bilateral good offices in the situation between France and Tunisia in 1957, with unimpressive results; and it has minimized the possibility of using the United Nations to forestall new incidents in both the recurrent

Formosa Straits crises and the contingent situation regarding both Berlin and the access routes from West Germany. We brought the Vietnamese crisis to the United Nations only when all the parties to the dispute (less than half of whom were U.N. members) had become frozen in their public postures and when the only conceivable result of Security Council debate could be to assign blame to one side or the other.

The fate of the Peace Observation Commission is a revealing indication of the preference of nations like our own for do-it-yourself diplomacy in the realm of prevention, by contrast with their instinctive flight to the United Nations after a situation gets out of hand. The POC, established under the Uniting for Peace Resolution in 1950, was designed to "observe and report on the situation in any area where there exists international tension the continuance of which is likely to endanger the maintenance of international peace and security." [4] The POC was used exactly once, in Greece.[5] It has been allowed to languish as though there were no problems for it to deal with and no areas sufficiently combustible to warrant a neutral international presence before the flash point is reached. The White House Conference on International Cooperation in 1965 was presented a recommendation for a new Peace Observation Corps that ought to be taken more seriously than was its predecessor.[6]

In the face of the obvious limitations of purely national diplomacy, and despite the fact that the Peace Observation Commission has not developed as intended, one of the insights of the postwar years is that multilateral instruments have developed a role in the settlement of disputes that goes beyond the original concept of a group of governments publicly debating, investigat-

[4] General Assembly Resolution 377 (V) Part B, November 3, 1950.

[5] A POC subcommission, replacing the former U.N. Special Committee on the Balkans, conducted observation of Greece's northern frontiers; at the latter's suggestion, it was discontinued on August 1, 1954. On May 29, 1954, Thailand brought the Indochinese situation to the Security Council as a threat to her own security, requesting that the POC establish a subcommission which would dispatch observers. On June 18, 1954, the Soviet Union vetoed the proposal, and there have been no other serious attempts to utilize the POC machinery.

[6] *Report of the Committee on Arms Control and Disarmament* of the National Citizens' Commission, White House Conference on International Cooperation, Washington, D.C., November 28–December 1, 1965.

ing, and, in effect, judging. One such innovation is what has come to be called a U.N. "presence." Looking back on the procession of crises and outbursts in the postwar years, we see that a U.N. "presence" has often proved itself to be among the most effective instruments available in the realm of preventive peace.

There is a wide and versatile range in which a U.N. presence can manifest itself. It can take the form of a civil field commission with a political function but able also to observe and report, as the U.N. Commission for Korea did to our great advantage on the night of June 24, 1950; or it may be a body of military personnel such as the U.N. Truce Supervisory Organization in Palestine. It may be a subcommittee of the Security Council, bypassing the veto by, at least technically, making no "recommendations," as in Laos in 1959. It may be representatives of the Secretary General in Cyprus starting in 1964, and in the Dominican Republic in 1965–1966. Or it may be a single individual who speaks and acts in the name of the U.N. Secretary General, as Mr. Pier Spinelli did in Amman, Jordan, in the tense summer of 1958.

The Korean precedent is doubly significant. Without the report from the U.N. Commission for Korea at the time of the 1950 attack, there would still be doubts on the part of many nations as to who actually attacked whom. That Commission, in Korea with the responsibility of using its good offices to bring about the unification of Korea, was on the scene at the time of the attack, and the reports submitted in the name of its Indian Chairman gave immediate authenticity to U.S. charges based on our own reporting.

The function of international observation need not be explicit. The vital point is the international presence itself, which by its very nature is capable of the kind of double duty performed by the U.N. Commission for Korea, a function for which no national diplomatic presence can provide a substitute.

The United States should make a far more conscious and determined effort to place international personnel on troubled frontiers to make impartial observations in the case of charges of external aggression or infiltration that ought to be reported back to the entire world community. Greater use of this technique, whether through the machinery of the POC or not, could serve our interests in the majority of disputes that involve charges of threatened aggression or of other forms of externally directed penetration. Propaganda could be revealed for what it is, and U.N. machinery should be elaborated to monitor and report on belligerent radio and other programs beamed to foreign countries. The moral influence of the General Assembly could be better utilized by giving it greater opportunity to act on the reports of its own agents.

A possible function that could have special high value in several of the most explosive situations in the world would be a form of "U.N. Electoral Commission" empowered to assist in ascertaining the will of inhabitants (as was done much less formally by U.N. personnel in the territories of Sabah and Sarawak in 1963), or actually to conduct a plebiscite. Invited in like a firm of auditors, such a team might be of inestimable value in areas such as Vietnam [7] or some day perhaps Taiwan, when the issue turns on the desires of the inhabitants.

The invoking of a U.N. presence is a use of the United Nations that does not depend on a change in the complexion of world politics or of international life in general. The means are already at hand to improve our capacity to deal with international disputes as they arise. Only determined leadership will make this possibility a reality; *i.e.,* insistence, as a matter of fixed policy, that an early rather than a desperate last step be the dispatch of a U.N. presence to the scene for observation, reporting, and whatever other neutral functions seem desirable.

THE U.N. SECRETARIAT AND INTERNATIONAL DISPUTES

In the discussion of the indispensable third-party function in the peaceful settlement of disputes, we have identified two vital ingredients: the availability of neutral ground, supplied by the existence of the universal organization itself; and a U.N. presence in areas of international tension, preferably placed there in advance of hostilities.

A third ingredient is the availability of acceptable personnel

[7] South Vietnam did in fact request U.N. observers for the September 1966 elections. A majority of states, however, apparently feared that this would constitute endorsement of Saigon, and the plan received little support outside of Washington.

to carry out the functions described. Little success has accrued from schemes to make national personnel available on a standing basis, such as the Panel for Inquiry and Conciliation established by the Assembly in April 1949,[8] or the United Nations Panel of Field Observers created later the same year.[9] Perhaps more promise attaches to the recommendation made at the same time that greater use be made of the technique of appointing a *rapporteur* to exercise a conciliatory function with the parties to a dispute, a technique employed with some success by the League of Nations and so far relatively neglected by the United Nations. These suggestions were reiterated in another committee report to the 1965 White House Conference.[10]

But these suggestions for standing groups of national personnel do not seem to get to the heart of the problem. As things now stand, the parties to a dispute come to the United Nations not as to a court where impartial judgments are passed, but as to a place where the processes of diplomacy in various forms can be applied to the amelioration of situations and disputes. In terms of its readiness for compulsory measures for settlement of disputes, the world is somewhere midway between the primitive stage of self-judgment and compulsory submission to legal processes. At the present stage essentially political disputes seem to yield best to a facility that is international and nonpartisan in nature but at the same time utilizes the process of diplomacy rather than of law. While the panels of mediation and similar proposals have gathered dust, the potentialities of the diplomatic role of the Secretary General and his staff offered, for a time, great promise.

In the 1950s, for perhaps the first time in history, parties to a dispute found a truly third party; the Secretary General of the United Nations furnished a third party who was not judicial but political, representing no government but at the same time not bound by rules of law or by preference for the *status quo*. The Secretary General acted in Middle East diplomacy as perhaps the

[8] General Assembly Resolution 268 (III) Part D, April 28, 1949.

[9] General Assembly Resolution 297 (IV) Part B, November 22, 1949.

[10] *Report of the Committee on Peaceful Settlement of Disputes* of the National Citizens Commission. White House Conference on International Cooperation, Washington, D.C., November 28–December 1, 1965.

only world agent able to deal confidentially, authoritatively, and acceptably with the various parties to the several disputes and situations in that region. Examples of his successful efforts ranged from settling the Mt. Scopus dispute in Jerusalem in 1957–1958 to arranging the final compensation for Egypt's nationalization of the Suez Canal.

For a time predictions were being made that the enlarged General Assembly would by its very nature encourage the development of the "executive arm" of the United Nations, and that the members would turn increasingly to the Secretary General in periods of crisis. Dag Hammarskjöld was able to make of his office a truly nonpartisan but powerful factor in world politics. The U.N. Congo action was in fact taken on his initiative, acting under the never-before-used powers contained in Article 99. But his success during the Congo crisis proved so damaging to Soviet purposes in Central Africa that it led eventually to Soviet refusal to pay the assessed share of the costs, and subsequently to the financial-constitutional crisis that nearly incapacitated the organization in 1964–1965. During the renewed Indo-Pakistani fighting in the fall of 1965, the Soviet Union was adamant in denying the Secretary General even modest authority to increase the U.N. observer corps without Security Council direction. The backlash from Moscow, and Paris as well, combined with the tragic loss of Dag Hammarskjöld in 1961, seemed to put an end to the evolution of U.N. peacekeeping and the very notion of U.N. "presences."

The question is how this highly significant and promising development can be revived and hopefully regularized. One possibility would be to seek to exploit a related development – the extension of the Secretary General's third-party role to other officers and agencies of the U.N. Secretariat.

A notable example was the little noticed but historically momentous Beck-Friis Mission to Cambodia and Thailand in 1957–1958, a successful mission of conciliation organized and dispatched by the Secretary General at the request of the parties to a dispute without specific reference to the political organs of the United Nations. Another highly significant example was the dispatch, despite the public displeasure of the Soviet Union, of Mr. Sakari S. Tuomioja, Executive Secretary of the U.N. Economic Commission for Europe, to Laos as the Secretary General's personal representative in mid-November 1959. The purpose was to supply a continued U.N. presence even after the departure of the Security Council subcommittee on Laos. A group of Secretariat officials undertook the sounding of opinion in the British territories of Sabah and Sarawak before they were absorbed in Malaysia in 1964. In the summer of 1966 Secretary General U Thant sent a special representative to check on the Thailand-Cambodia border problem, an initiative for which he was mildly reproved by the Soviets. I have already mentioned the role of U Thant's representatives in Cyprus and Santo Domingo.

These precedents represent a new philosophy of the uses of intergovernmental machinery, preserving impartiality and eschewing publicity but far advanced beyond the self-effacing role of international servant typified by Sir Eric Drummond as Secretary General of the League of Nations. In the Security Council debate on the Lebanese situation in July 1958, Mr. Hammarskjöld, justifying his intention to enlarge, on his own authority, the U.N. Observer Group in Lebanon, said:

> I believe that it is in keeping with the philosophy of the Charter also that the Secretary General should be expected to act without guidance from the Assembly or the Security Council should this appear to him necessary toward helping to fill any vacuums that may appear in the systems which the Charter and traditional diplomacy provide for the safeguarding of peace and security. . . . Were you to disapprove of the way in which these intentions are translated by me into practical steps, I would, of course, accept the consequences of your judgment.[11]

Mr. Hammarskjöld was not unmindful of the jealously guarded prerogatives of governments. In his speech in Copenhagen a year later on the potential uses of the United Nations in the Berlin crisis, he drew the line sharply between what he called "the imposition . . . of executive authority on the United Nations for administrative tasks which require political decisions," which he excluded, and "the right [of the Secretary General] to take a stand in these conflicts to the extent that such stands can be firmly

[11] *New York Times,* July 23, 1958.

based on the Charter and its principles and thus express what may be called the independent judgment of the organization." [12]

But he went on to say:

> Something like an independent position for the Organization as such has found expression both in words and deeds . . . [The Beck-Friis Mission] is an example of what I should like to call active preventive diplomacy, which may be conducted by the United Nations, through the Secretary-General or in other forms, in many situations where no government or group of governments and no regional organization would be able to act in the same way. That such interventions are possible for the United Nations is explained by the fact that in the manner I have indicated, the Organization has begun to gain a certain independent position, and that this tendency has led to the acceptance of an independent political and diplomatic activity on the part of the Secretary-General as the "neutral" representative of the Organization.[13]

But even apart from the predictable communist mistrust of an active Secretariat, there is widespread concern among some other governments that some individuals in international secretariats are not really impartial, and that in fact some are actively working toward the results desired by one or another government. Such suspicions deepened in the face of open collusion between Secretariat officials and the seventy-seven-member "have-not" bloc at the 1965 UNCTAD meeting in Geneva. It is difficult here to distinguish between the legitimate concern over suborned or unduly officious or hostile Secretariat employees and the less justifiable concern over the influence or beliefs of an individual that may run counter to a given nation's wishes. The principal remedies for abuses that do exist lie not only in proper Secretariat supervision, but also in higher-caliber representation from small governments. Mediocre delegations can offer policy vacuums that are often willingly filled by politically ambitious Secretariat personnel.

Such objections, while compelling in the individual instances which have occurred particularly in the economic and social field, are secondary in the light of the larger objective, which clearly points to the need for a vigorous and consistent American

[12] U.N. Press Release SG/812, 1 May 1959.
[13] *Ibid.*

policy of supporting and strengthening the third-party capabilities of the U.N. Secretariat. In the postwar years, despite frequent proposals and a number of modest administrative efforts, there have never been any concerted effort by the U.S. Government to place top-flight Americans in the U.N. Secretariat.

Perhaps one reason for relative American indifference to the staffing of the U.N. Secretariat was that for a long time there was no real element of competition with the Soviet Union. For years the Soviet Union neglected to fill the quota of positions assigned to it and seemed uninterested in the Secretariat (below the top level) except perhaps as a means of espionage. But the Soviet attitude has changed. In recent years Moscow has seemed to make a serious effort to fill vacancies and has complained of discrimination against Soviet candidates. At the same time promised posts were left unfilled, and it remains the case that Soviet nationals are never left in a Secretariat long enough to do a job effectively. (An Assembly vote in 1966 may make *most* U.N. jobs temporary.)

Another reason for American relative inactivity is in part explained (and justified) by the desire not to influence the Secretary General. But unlike many other governments, the United States has never encouraged such service as an honor, or, in the case of government officials, as a basis for continued advancement in the national service. Even though the number of positions open to Americans is limited and becoming more so as the membership increases, service with the United Nations should be made a matter of both professional honor and national interest rather than, as it is now, tacitly if not openly stigmatized. This in turn can be advanced only by a rational acceptance of the interest this country has in the goal, and its diffusion by responsible leaders to the agencies they direct.

But encouraging top-flight Americans to serve is only part of the answer. Americans occupy some key positions, but openings are few. The Secretary General will need top-flight alternates and other staff members to carry out the growing third-party function, and these must necessarily come from countries other than the United States and other great powers. In view of the kinds of cases that can be anticipated, there will be a growing need for trained nationals of Asia and Africa, supplementing such traditional Western sources as mediators as Sweden. Efforts ought to be stepped up to improve the qualifications of personnel from the areas concerned. Various programs have been sponsored by private foundations, by governments, and by the United Nations itself to improve the training of young diplomats and administrators for the newer countries. The U.N. Institute for Training and Research (UNITAR) may go a distance toward filling the gap so far as international service is concerned. Perhaps consideration should be given to the creation of a service academy for the United Nations, in which personnel from all member countries, particularly from those with limited higher-educational facilities, would receive training for service as Secretariat officials similar to the specialized training for a national diplomatic corps. An incidental by-product of a Secretariat training program would be to provide an outlet in underdeveloped countries for surplus trained and educated personnel, who might constitute a focus of discontent and instability in the period before their own national economy can usefully absorb their talents and energies.

THE WILL TO PEACEMAKING

The various devices discussed above can all aid and abet the peacemaking process. But none is of any real value in the absence of a basic will on the part of nations to move toward a world in which pacific procedures will really take the place of force. We have seen that many nations including our own have been selective in their diplomatic efforts, tending to avoid third-party settlement processes in disputes in which national prestige has become involved, as was the case for a lengthy period in Vietnam and remains so in Central Europe. Alongside this fundamental defect in the international system itself is the fact that in our crisis-ridden times the tempo of events has favored the fire-brigade approach, putting out fires after they have started rather than enlisting the efforts of a fire marshal to prevent their outbreak.

Settling disputes is an even more demanding task than pacifying them. One of the prime assumptions about the international-organization movement was that dispute-settling devices would become habit-forming. No other area of multilateral diplomacy has been the object of such intensive and protracted study, from the days of the League of Nation until the 1965 White House Conference on International Cooperation and the similar initiative in the U.N. General Assembly the same year. The concrete proposals to emerge from two generations of research are intelligent, modest, and persuasive. But the sad truth is that virtually none of the recommendations have been put into effect. The sense of progress in peacemaking, in fact, declines with the passage of time. Obviously something is very wrong, and obviously it is not going to be fixed by one or more study of pacific-settlement procedures.

Several explanations account for this monumental shortfall between expectations and reality. Is it possible that the trouble *does* lie somewhere in the institutional structure and procedures of the U.N. and the World Court? This still seems implausible, given the ready availability of the various devices mentioned in Chapter Six, the Security Council, the gradually disappearing Panel of Mediators, and the plethora of recommendations already made. Or perhaps the answer lies in the relative lawlessness of the age, in the preference for unilateral remedy seeking. Since 1945, Russia, China, Britain, France, and the United States have all contributed at one time or another to the idea that for really important issues a state may use force, and *raison d'état* overrides all else. This is a tempting explanation to account for everyone's sins, including one's own. Moreover, the Communists and nationalist revolutionaries aim to change the *status quo* and to overturn one or another part of the established order — precisely that part which law, peacekeeping, and cease-fire diplomacy would tend to protect. And yet, is our age really any more lawless than those preceding? Hardly.

Perhaps the truest explanation lies in the understandable proclivity of overworked statesmen to focus on the present, to approach cases *ad hoc,* to concentrate in the demanding crisis of the moment, to apply preventive diplomacy only when violence actually threatens. Vietnam was the most recent culprit. But earlier it was Article 19, the year before that the test ban, the year before that, Cuba, and the year before that, Berlin. When Quemoy and Matsu were under the gun, the United States considered it unthinkable to negotiate a more durable status, even while hinting that common sense dictated it. When the guns fell silent — or relatively so — attention immediately wandered elsewhere. So with the Suez Canal, the Kashmir plebiscite, half a dozen other "dormant" disputes. There is *never* a good time to plan ahead, always a good time to let sleeping dogs lie. Nothing can be done when the issue is acute; no one wants to do anything when it is quiescent.

Given this human tendency, combined with the pragmatic Anglo-Saxon style that generally discourages purposeful planning, it seems unhelpful to continue to issue injunctions to other quarreling countries to have recourse to law and third-party procedures before they become subjects for peacekeeping. Some institutional reforms addressed to the central issue of peaceful change might be marginally useful — perhaps creating an equity tribunal, as some have suggested, or arranging somehow to breathe real life into Article 14 of the U.N. Charter. At the least it is worth study.

But to get at the core difficulty, the leading Western states with pretensions of being "law-abiding" would probably have to make a far more convincing demonstration than before of their own *bona fides*. Perhaps they could agree to binding arrangements for compulsory arbitration or adjudication of all disputes that arise among themselves without reserving the right either to exempt disputes affecting "national honor" or to decide unilaterally if it is an issue of domestic jurisdiction. Such a protocol among the like-minded could create for the first time a fragment of genuine international order. Without the responsible nations setting an example of purposive action, it will remain futile to hope that others will act as we would have them act.

In this important effort to enhance the peacemaking will and capacity of the United Nations, Western leadership is a precondition to any genuine progress.

CHAPTER TWELVE

Peaceful Change

The cease-fire, the standstill, the buying of time, while preserving the peace, offer no guarantees that a dispute will be settled or its basic causes dealt with. There is a growing awareness that the capacity, however worthwhile, to enforce a cease-fire, to suppress outbreaks of violence, to cram a lid on explosive situations, to buy time, can have a negative effect too. If no progress is made toward settling the dispute, peacekeeping may generate even more unmanageable conflict later. The lack of workable provisions for peaceful change stands indicted as perhaps the prime cause of major and minor wars in this century. The United Nations Charter recognized the problem, but has been far from solving it.

There have of course been some conflict situations for which no settlements are possible for an indefinite period. To keep a lid on the Palestine cauldron and thus to buy time has doubtless been the highest form of statesmanship. But when war broke out again in the fall of 1965 between India and Pakistan over Kashmir, it threw into vivid relief the direct relationship between continued violence and the failure to achieve change through peaceful settlement methods. The whispers of 1948 in Palestine and of 1956 in Suez began to be heard again: Perhaps the latest fighting in the Indian subcontinent had been stopped prematurely. It could be recalled that in the Palestine case, to induce Israel's withdrawal from the Sinai Peninsula in early 1957, promises were made about implementation of the 1951 Security Council resolution regarding free passage through the Canal. American officials can feel duly sheepish that the matter was never pursued with anything that could be called diligence.

U Thant in his 1965 Annual Report worried publicly that "the very fact that [these disputes] have become an accepted and semi-permanent part of the way of life in the areas has tended to . . . reduce the sense of urgency which might stimulate a search by the parties concerned for a basic and peaceful solution." [1] The late Adlai Stevenson was prophetic — but perhaps excessively hopeful — when he dubbed this "the age of cease-fire and peaceful change."

DISPUTED AREAS

The heart of many contemporary disputes is the desire to alter the *status quo* in a way that existing law is traditionally unable to accommodate or resolve. Article 14 of the Charter is based on the premise that peaceful change is desirable, and the United Nations has assisted in fundamental transformation such as the creation of new states in Indonesia, Israel, South Korea, and the former Italian colonies. But the United Nations is incapable of legislating changes in the accepted sense of the word, and in any event it is incapable of enforcing such changes when it does recommend them, as the Palestine and Korean cases also illustrated. In the Palestine dispute Israel did its own implementing; but in Korea no agency existed to execute the "mandate" to unify the country, even though a war was fought in the area by U.N. forces. What the United Nations can do is bring into focus pressures for change that a majority considers to be legitimate, and to apply a whole variety of measures to bring about such a change.

No single rule applies in disputed areas. In some areas such pressure contributes to ultimate transformation, as in Indonesia,

[1] Introduction to the Annual Report of the Secretary General of the Work of the Organization, *U.N. Monthly Chronicle,* October 1965, p. 107.

North Africa, Palestine, the Congo, Cyprus, and various of the trust territories. In others, as with West Berlin, it would be improper to bring about change simply because there was pressure to do so. In a third category (Rhodesia, South-West Africa, and South Africa itself) the explosive ingredient of racial discrimination undergirds U.N. efforts to effect internal changes.

Quemoy and the other offshore Chinese islands are not often discussed any more, but during the Taiwan Straits crises of the middle and late 1950s, statements were made in the highest American quarters concerning the illogic and the potential for future crises inherent in a "Western" position so close to the Chinese mainland. But there has been little evidence of serious activity aimed at working out an acceptable formula for the future. One can conceive of negotiated arrangements in which something the United States wants could be traded for the offshore islands. The proclivity to let sleeping dogs lie means that in a future trip to the brink, it remains possible that in order to sustain an admittedly indefensible position the United States would either have to make war on Communist China or evacuate the Nationalists from the Quemoy position, thus surrendering to enemy pressure. It is consistent with American interest to find a peaceful evolution for the offshore islands that represents neither a surrender to the Communists nor something for which a world war would have to be fought.

There are other present or potential situations affecting the U.S. interest in which both the *status quo* and the change desired by one party are inherently undesirable. In the colonial world West New Guinea – West Irian to the Indonesians – was a case in point, and the United Nations was severely criticized for acting as agent for an Indonesian takeover. Foreseeably, West Berlin may be another situation where the present alternatives become intolerable but where holding on appears to be the only acceptable and honorable course.

It goes without saying that such disputed-area situations are explosive – and that some kind of change is inevitable. Clearly it is incumbent on the United States, in view of its grand strategy of seeking durable and stable situations by a process of peaceful change, to seek new alternatives. How can peaceful change be facilitated in situations such as these? What part can the United

Nations play in inducing or aiding the process of peaceful change in disputed areas?

One means of removing a disputed area or territory from contention is of course to give it to one or the other side, as the United Nations in fact gave West Irian to Indonesia (or for one or the other to take it, as India took Goa). This cannot be counted on to produce peaceful solutions, for a whole variety of reasons ranging from ethnic to economic. The plebiscite solution is a useful one in relatively advanced regions as the Saar, and in fairly advanced colonial areas. The addition of Sabah and Sarawak to the Federation of Malaysia was legitimized by this method. Partition has been increasingly resorted to in recent decades, and may be the eventual solution in Cyprus and South Africa.

A kind of neutral solution never used so far would be to place the area in question under international administration for a specified time, or pending final settlement. The analogy to the trusteeship concept is apparent, but trusteeship involves dependent peoples. The United Nations itself has never been designated the administering authority over a trust territory, but the machinery provided by Article 81 of the Charter, which states that the administering authority of trust territories "may be one or more states or the Organization itself," offers possibilities. In a related way South-West Africa might find its halfway house between white rule and independence.

However, a new concept is needed for situations involving more advanced territories that require international disposition but where the real need is to put them on ice, so to speak, rather than to advance the inhabitants "toward self-government or independence." Given strong motivation to find formulas that conform both to the goal of stability and to common sense as well, means for doing this can be sought within the framework of the United Nations. The availability of neutral nations among the membership of the General Assembly, or of the enlarged Security Council to oversee the integrity of a territory in the name of the United Nations, and of U.N. personnel qualified to administer the operation in the interests of the inhabitants, underscores the value of an organization with neutral members and served by a corps of impartial civil and military servants. A territory with strong traditions and a capacity for self-government might merely require the formal designation of an international status, the symbolism of a U.N. presence, and strong guarantees on the part of at least a significant and effective U.N. majority.

A thoughtful study of the possible uses of the United Nations in the earlier Berlin crisis suggested that ample legal ground exists for creating a new legal status for nondependent "U.N. territories":

> Rather than attempt to squeeze Berlin into the established trusteeship patterns, it might be possible to create for it a special status under the aegis of the U.N. If there is no explicit authorization in the Charter for such a step, neither is there any express prohibition. And the broad powers of both the Security Council and of the General Assembly to deal with matters which affect international peace and security should provide ample authority for a new type of U.N. status for Berlin.[2]

It is possible that under some conditions, as a step to settlement of the larger German issue, we could consider a U.N. protectorate for the whole of Berlin that would fulfill the requirements of international status, symbolic U.N. presence, and guarantees by a U.N. majority that the continued freedom of the inhabitants would not be jeopardized.

Another possibility for a U.N. protectorate would be Taiwan after the demise of Chiang Kai-shek. In this case the territory would, like West Berlin, be capable of self-rule. The operative problem here would be to devise an interim status, internationally underwritten, to carry over through an unstable period until satisfactory permanent arrangements were made. Other candidates for a form of interim U.N. territorial status of a nondependent nature might be Kashmir, the Chinese offshore islands, even Rhodesia.

With the passage of time, political solutions might be found that would permit a territory to be peacefully and logically incorporated in a neighboring state, or partitioned, or absorbed in a larger unit; as a final possibility, the territory conceivably could

[2] Louis Henkin, *The Berlin Crisis and the United Nations* (New York: Carnegie Endowment, 1959), p. 18.

remain under international administration indefinitely on the ground that it could not be fitted into traditional patterns of state sovereignty without endangering the peace. For the chief factor in the pacific settlement of international disputes is not always machinery or techniques or institutions or diplomacy, or even a will to settle, important as these are. It is sometimes the passage of time, until the evolution of new foci of international attention, or until enemies become friends and vice versa, or until the problem simply disappears or alters unrecognizably as conditions change.

It would thus not be necessary to be able to forecast in detail the ultimate disposition of territories under U.N. protection. It is sufficient that a new dimension might be added to the present two-dimensional world of national states, which might have real value in those situations where the international atmosphere is poisoned by tensions generated by unresolved territorial disputes.

Granted, the problems this kind of proposal suggests are almost as numerous as the difficulties that prompt it. For the United Nations in its own name to administer or protect a territory means that troublemakers automatically have a voice in the process. It is also doubtful whether either the Peking or Taipei regimes would at this time gracefully accept U.N. administration of Quemoy or Matsu or, ultimately, Taiwan. India would not be likely to favor international administration of Kashmir, although it might be offered for a limited time — say, five years — as a way of buying additional time until the parties could agree on a final solution. West Berlin and the Federal Republic of Germany could be expected to disfavor any arrangement that removed the symbolic presence of Western troops — although the time may come when mutual withdrawal of Soviet and American forces would leave West Berlin as an exposed enclave of freedom and Western orientation within East German territory. Such a situation would require a new form of international guarantee for continued survival in freedom, a contingency which should be planned for now.

But the test of a scheme for international administration would be whether it promised reduction in tensions and creation of greater international stability, along with justice for the inhabitants of the area and assurances to the disputing parties that neither would gain an unfair advantage. Such conditions are not beyond human ingenuity or inventiveness to supply, and the United States can most constructively work toward eliminating present and future territorial sources of instability and possible belligerence by actively studying the possibilities of such a form of international administration, with the aim of developing a concrete plan for presentation to the United Nations.

INTERNATIONAL WATERWAYS

The principle of international administration should also be seriously contemplated for international waterways vital to international maritime commerce, with the aim of taking preventive steps before another Suez-type crisis is upon us. The reactions to the premature and essentially vindictive Egyptian nationalization of the Suez Canal in July 1956 revealed the intensity with which other nations can be expected to respond to unilateral changes in the status of such internationally vital facilities.

It is too late to begin an internationalization scheme with the Suez Canal, but none too early to take steps that might one day add up to irresistible pressures to broaden its management to satisfy the interests of the users, utilizing the universal agency supplied by the United Nations.

When one considers the Turkish Straits or the Panama Canal, it appears that the chief obstacle to a broadened and more internationally acceptable base of sovereignty is the fear of the dominant power that its own interests will suffer if its control is diluted. Turkey has learned with good reason to fear Russian initiatives to alter the Straits regime. Increasing Panamanian discontent with U.S. control of the Panama Canal Zone has produced important American concessions and the necessity to consider a multibillion-dollar canal in less volatile political surroundings. The very fears that discourage planning on other alternatives, such as internationalization, might under new circumstances encourage the trend to far worse possibilities, as Britain learned to her dismay in 1956 in Suez.

As planning goes forward for a sea-level Atlantic-Pacific canal, it should be possible for the United States to develop a proposal that, while broadening the basis of legal sovereignty and inviting the participation of others, would safeguard fully our special security requirements and financial investment. Suggestions have been made that control of the Panama Canal be vested in the Organization of American States. Given the universality of usership of the Canal, a U.N. agency would seem the more appropriate body to serve the interests of the users while removing the wholly bilateral nature of the issue between Panama and the United States.

International waterways such as the Panama Canal involve powerful traditions and strong, if debatable, strategic interests. Attempts to create an international status for the Straits of Tiran leading into the Gulf of Aqaba, to take another example, would present formidable obstacles involving the entire Palestine complex. But the paramount fact is that the process of change in such areas usually works to maximize the possibility of future disasters. The *status-quo* power tends to hang on until it is directly challenged, as Britain was in Egypt in 1956 and as the United States has been recurrently in the Isthmus of Panama. Then, because under present ground rules violent redress of political wrongs is discouraged by the world community, the action turns out to be irreversible. It is very much to the advantage of the United States and of the world as a whole that the peaceful-change process take place in the general interest, rather than always in the interest of the challenger to the *status quo*.

ANTARCTICA

The problems of disputed areas and international waterways loom large in the foreground of the current international political scene. There are already present the forces and omens that urge the United States as a matter of calculated policy to make every effort to raise these problems to the category of urgent international business. Equally important in its own way in considering the long-range prospects for peaceful change is the remaining unoccupied territory of the earth — Antarctica.

Antarctica is at a suspenseful stage in history. Claims to portions of it have been made by Britain, New Zealand, Australia, France, Norway, Argentina, and Chile. These claims have been rejected by the United States and the Soviet Union, who reserve the right to make their own claims. On December 1, 1959, a highly significant treaty was signed reserving Antarctica for peaceful purposes only and opening it up for unrestricted scientific activity by all the signatories.

The present treaty is essentially only a truce, although the obvious hope is that it will establish a durable pattern that may outmode the territorial claims, all of which remain in force. The Soviet Union claims to have discovered a region in Antarctica rich in valuable minerals including mica, graphite, iron, and apatite. If technological developments materialize that significantly affect military or economic strategy, political considerations may come to be predominant again for Antarctica. The present situation is a frozen *status quo* in a so-far frozen continent. The ultimate issues, however – the future administration of Antarctica and the inevitable question of sovereignty – must still be faced.

The next step to be planned for should involve irrevocable removal of the sovereignty of Antarctica from the reach of any single nation, thus converting the truce into a permanent situation. The need is not so much for a form of organization as for an assertion by the community of nations that Antarctica represents, in the language of international law, *res communis,* rather than a *res nullius* always open to claim and occupation. Such an assertion should be made by resolution or convention under the sponsorship of the United Nations, with the U.N. itself acting as the repository of the territory's sovereignty and the guarantor of its continued international status and of free access of all for peaceful purposes. An incidental benefit would be to place agreement on a broad basis rather than limit it to those who by geographic accident or political design have a connection with the problem today. It would be shortsighted to exclude the possibility that a nation remote from Antarctica – Communist China, for example – could take a profound interest in its strategic possibilities or economic potential. A U.N. assertion would be presumed to affect all rather than only the signatory nations.

CHAPTER THIRTEEN

The Developing Countries

American interest in the overall health and welfare of the rest of the world is neither a purely charitable impulse nor is it limited to diplomatic arrangements for dealing with incipient conflicts. True, we are sensitive as a people to the fact that if there is widespread privation, human suffering, and social unrest in the world, the United States, try as it may, cannot comfortably enjoy its own prosperity. But wholly apart from any humane consideration, there is the pressing realization that the very future of our American society has come to depend increasingly on the health of the other societies that make up the world environment in which we must live.

The chief problem area toward which American economic and social strategies are directed today and in the foreseeable future is the portion of the world commonly called "underdeveloped" (or "less developed," "developing," or "emerging"). As officially defined in the 1963 U.N. financing resolutions, these countries included all but twenty-six or so of the members of the United Nations. Here is the home base of neutralist sentiment in the cold war and of anticolonial agitation in the continuing North-South conflict; and, for obvious reasons, it is the prime target of Communist strategies. As one after another of its component regions and subregions awakens to the possibilities of technological and sociological transformation, it has moved from the bottom of the list to first place among Western concerns. The peoples of the areas, who already far outnumber the rest of the world, will inevitably have a decisive impact on the world environment of the future.

The general American purpose can be simply stated. In broad terms, the American objective of a more stable world environment calls for finding ways of influencing the course of the social revolution sweeping the underdeveloped areas, so that when it has run its course we shall not find ourselves isolated in a hostile world. This is the long-range aim, but the battle is now. The very center of the political warfare of today and tomorrow between the Communists and the West is in the regions of Asia, the Middle East, Africa, and increasingly in the Caribbean area and Latin America. The stakes for both Moscow and Peking are denial of this great gray zone to the West in terms of both military strategy and economic resources, and in the long run its conversion to communism – the particular brand being an additional source of competition. For the West the stakes are, at a minimum, denial of additional areas to Communist rule and, at a maximum, the development of new and more acceptable long-range relationships between the peoples there and the predominantly white Western world.

What is taking place in the underdeveloped countries is the long process of modernization. Where that process is in its early stages, political democracy as we know it seems distant. Even in the more advanced stages of modernization, the economic, social, and educational preconditions for genuine democratic institutions do not always exist in full measure.[1] The task for those who cherish freedom is to develop the capabilities of these societies for democracy, and to see that the possibility of their enjoying economic progress in freedom is left open to them.

Achieving long-range goals may involve short-term means that

[1] In 1966 the following non-Communist countries were living under regimes which in one way or another have been described as "military": Republic of China, Thailand, Pakistan, Iraq, Lebanon, Sudan, Syria, United Arab Republic, Portugal, Spain, El Salvador, Paraguay, Laos, Dahomey, Nigeria, Ghana, South Vietnam, Upper Volta, Congo (Kinshasa), and Central African Republic.

seem contradictory and even repugnant. For example, for the United States to support the emerging countries in some of their unpolished, often brash assertions in the United Nations may seem to be weakening our essential ties with European allies. Distinguished members of Congress insist, incorrectly, that the United States must choose between the two, but we have important interests on both sides and there could be no greater folly than to sacrifice either for an apparent consistency.

Similarly, to aid some societies where pure capitalism seems inapplicable, or where Western-type constitutionalism and the multiparty system are for the moment irrelevant and even destructive, may appear a betrayal of our own values, as may defense of a corrupt or unpopular regime that is threatened by Communist takeover. But there appears to be no other answer to this disturbing dilemma than to stay riveted on the main objective and be prepared to accept the short-term costs involved in helping these countries get through the modernization process. Meanwhile it is clearly in our interest to build up the United Nations in order that it may better facilitate changing relationships between the new states and the old and, as vitally required by political wisdom, give the former a larger stake in the political world that we prefer.

ECONOMIC DEVELOPMENT AND THE UNITED NATIONS

The United Nations from its inception has been heavily engaged in relieving human misery in the aftermath of war, in raising levels of nutrition and literacy, and in protecting human and political rights. More recent challenges have arisen from a widely held conviction that it is possible to do away with misery as the natural condition of man, and from an accelerating revolution in man's knowledge of how to control the material conditions of his life. The growing imperatives of technological advance gave birth to two new U.N. agencies, the World Meteorological Organization and the International Atomic Energy Agency, but the old agencies have felt the effects too. Where once their efforts were directed primarily to research and the setting of standards for the international community, now they are directed to transferring skills and resources to the less-developed nations. United States officials have described as massive and historically unique the sweeping effort of this country to transfer and adapt science and technology from the limited areas in which they have flourished previously to the international community as a whole.[2] Four-fifths of the resources of the United Nations in terms of money and manpower are now devoted to technical and economic goals.

There is no disagreement as to the needs. The U.N. Development Decade – the 1960s – has as its target a 5 percent annual growth rate in the aggregate national income of the developing countries, with self-sustaining growth to be achieved by 1970. With the midpoint well passed, progress toward this goal has been far from spectacular. Even in a favorable international economic climate, the rich have grown noticeably richer, while the poor, though perhaps not actually poorer, are not significantly better off. The general economic expansion of recent years has only highlighted the persistence of certain underlying problems.

One of these problems is the soaring birthrate, which, unless checked, will gobble up every increment of economic growth. Another is the inability of the developing countries, notwithstanding existing bilateral and multilateral programs of financial aid, to finance from their export earnings the imports of capital goods they need for economic development. These countries thus tend to question seriously the prevailing trends of international trade. Some helpful prospects are offered by the reduction of trade barriers under negotiation by the General Agreement on Tariffs and Trade (GATT) in the "Kennedy" and other "Rounds." But whatever the outcome, the developing countries wish to see basic changes made in the patterns of trade that will make the process more predictable – and thus more profitable – from their standpoint. To this end, they sought and finally achieved a U.N. Conference on Trade and Development, which convened in Geneva in 1964. Over the opposition of the United States, they agreed on the establishment of so-called "continuing machinery" in the form of a U.N. Conference on Trade and Development as an organ of the General Assembly, to be convened every three

[2] Ambassador Adlai E. Stevenson applied this to the United Nations in a speech on "The Promise of Science and Technology," Rochester, N.Y., November 12, 1964, *Department of State Bulletin,* December 7, 1964.

years; set up a Trade and Development Board of fifty-five members; and created a permanent staff group within the U.N. Secretariat.

These results were achieved by the extraordinary cohesion of the seventy-seven developing countries that caucused, negotiated through a common spokesman, and voted together despite the very considerable differences that existed among them. At times this unity resulted in majority votes which the developed countries obviously did not find in their own interests and therefore will be likely to disregard. But the opinions of the seventy-seven are, for what they are worth, clearly on the record. In addition, a forum has been provided to examine systematically the problems of the developing countries and to seek remedies for them — two other major goals. Still another institution, the U.N. Organization for Industrial Development (UNIDO) was established subsequently.

One of the lessons learned over the years has been that capital investment is productive only when a certain amount of essential preliminary work has been done. This work involves surveys, feasibility studies, and planning for adequate managerial and technical skills. It is in this so-called pre-investment field that U.N. efforts have been notably successful. The former U.N. Special Fund, merged in 1965 with the Expanded Program of Technical Assistance as the U.N. Development Program, has focused its energies on projects designed to supply developing countries with the knowledge, skills, and institutions needed before substantial investment capital can be attracted and used. Their potential may be estimated from results already in.

As of January 1966, twenty-five of the national-resource surveys carried out at a cost of $33 million had already led to $1,068,000,000 of capital investment. In all, 522 projects were then under way at a cost of $1.5 billion of which only $478 million was provided by the Program, the rest being furnished by the recipient governments. All Development Program funds are pledged voluntarily.

For the United States in particular, a persistent basic issue has been that of bilateral versus multilateral aid. The bilateral approach, which gives the donor country economic and political control over the terms of aid and permits it to reap credit if things go well, has appealed to American policy makers. As a result, and because the American contribution would doubtless be excessive, the United States has consistently and successfully opposed the establishment of a Special U.N. Fund for Economic Development (SUNFED). When it has supplied capital funds, it has preferred to work through such organizations as the World Bank, the International Finance Corporation, and the International Development Authority, in which weighted-voting procedures apply.

But there are important advantages in stressing the multilateral approach, particularly in areas where the U.S. political interest is not too closely tied to a security interest as it is in Vietnam, Korea, and Turkey. Some of the advantages are the improved climate when the recipient of aid is a partner in a multilateral enterprise; the opportunity to coax contributions from countries that could not afford to offer a separate aid program; the benefits of being able to draw from a worldwide talent pool; the opportunities for taking a regional approach – the Mekong River Basin project and Asian Development Bank are obvious examples; the chance to use aid to promote political settlements, as in the dispute over the Indus waters; and the opportunity for numbers of participants to work together and build a community of interests. Perhaps, as purely American foreign aid encounters increasing obstacles at home, political pressures may in fact mount to favor the multilateral approach.[3]

But if multilateralism is to be taken seriously, new techniques will be needed to square the principle of "one nation, one vote," so dear to the hearts of the small and weak, with the fact that the rich and powerful will not support policies and programs they believe violate their interests. In the specialized agencies, as in the United Nations itself, the United States is increasingly in the minority on issues reflecting impatience with Western moderation (as in the World Health Organization's 53–23 vote

[3] See, for example, Senator J. William Fulbright's declaration to the Senate (in connection with the Fiscal Year 1968 foreign-aid legislation) that what had become a "national private charity" must now be "internationalized" (*New York Times,* July 27, 1966). Another influential voice was that of John D. Rockefeller III, who recommended that to correct the "overpowering impact of Americans on Asians," the present U.S. emphasis on bilateral aid be reversed (*New York Times,* May 18, 1966).

in May 1966 to bar Portugal from its regional African activities) or parsimony (as in the same organization's adoption of a record budget for 1967 over not only U.S. but Soviet, British, and French objections). In this connection the procedures that substitute a search for consensus for divisive formal voting in the U.N. Conference on Trade and Development will be interesting to watch as a technique for meeting this problem. The uproar in Congress over a minor Special Fund survey in Cuba indicated quite clearly the political pitfalls for the United States in placing significant funds in the hands of an uncontrollable third party. There are ways of broadening the framework of economic assistance without losing control to either Communists or recipients. An association of the non-Communist industrialized states of the world – the OEEC members, the United States, Canada and Japan – was proposed by the United States in early 1960. The Organization for Economic Cooperative Development (OECD) has contributed substantially to the developing countries, only a fraction of this aid going through U.N. agencies.

Still, the pressure will continue to do at least part of the job cooperatively with the underdeveloped countries. Moreover, the political consequences of not doing so could profoundly affect the success of our purpose in extending aid in the first place.

IDEOLOGY AND ECONOMIC POLICY

In the protracted competition between the ideologies of freedom and authoritarianism, it is useful to have a place where the values of the modern free-enterprise system – what some are coming to call "peoples' capitalism" – can be publicly expounded and demonstrated in action. The United Nations at least in theory offers a forum in which both to demonstrate in detail the virtues of our system and to defend it publicly against attack.

But it has not quite worked that way. While the profit motive may prove far more enduring than Marxist economics, the accompanying spread of planned economies has engendered a fear that the American economic philosophy will be engulfed by alien ideas and practices. Two issues in particular have proved difficult to resolve.

The first has concerned trade policy. Traditionally the developed countries have believed that lowering trade barriers on a reciprocal basis will benefit all trading nations. It has taken years for the United States and others to appreciate that developing countries cannot increase their foreign-exchange earnings to finance capital-equipment and other requirements for development unless they are given some concessions on duties and other penalities on their exports, unless they are permitted some protection for their new industries, and unless commodity markets are stabilized. As has been frequently pointed out, economic aid can be and has been canceled out by a fall in world commodity prices. Roy Blough, looking back at twenty years of U.N. discussion, research, and, more recently, operational programs, has summed it up thus:

> The inherently different positions of the more developed and the less developed countries were evident before the United Nations was established and have affected its activities throughout the two decades of its experience. By 1965 it could be said in general that the view of the less developed countries had finally been publicly accepted in principle by the more developed countries but that the practical application of the principle was as yet only in its early stages.[4]

There is no evidence that these trends pose any serious threat to American prosperity in the short or long term. In fact, the growing consensus on economic development (outside the Communist world) recognizes that eventually most of the development, if there is to be any at all, will have to be done by private business — a fact that can only benefit the United States.

The other issue, which has somewhat less real substance but no less political significance, is essentially ideological — the pressure to include in the concept of self-determination the right to nationalize foreign property. Quite correctly, the United States has insisted that nationalization could be made acceptable only by simultaneous recognition of the right to compensation under international law, and this has become the agreed formula. But actually, if foreign property is nationalized, provisions for fair compensation will be offered according to the political situation between the parties and not because of a resolution on the

[4] "The Furtherance of Economic Development," in *The United Nations in the Balance,* Norman J. Padelford and Leland M. Goodrich (eds.) (New York: Praeger, 1965).

matter by the Economic and Social Council or by the General Assembly. The significance of the U.N. debates and resolutions on this subject has so far been largely symbolic, suggesting that somewhere under the surface is a very real force endowed with deep political passions.

Nasser's nationalization of the Suez Canal, ultimately followed as it was by internationally negotiated compensation, was, according to the U.N. compromise formula, legal. But the Suez military action was fought on completely different strategic and political grounds. The nationalization by the Bolsheviks of American property at the time of the Russian revolution, still uncompensated, was entirely illegal under international law, but there is no sign that this fact by itself significantly affects the course of political and military relationships between the two nations.

In this sense the United Nations is a proving ground for abstractions about economic and political theories but does not particularly affect the course of events. Nevertheless the ideological debates are useful not only to demonstrate to one's own constituency the fidelity with which the home team is being defended, but also to carry on a dialogue between the developed and the less-developed nations.

For example, the less-developed nations, insisting as they do on the right to sovereignty over their natural resources and on freedom to nationalize them, are also beginning to recognize that inducements are needed to attract foreign investment. For its part, the United States has faced a serious problem of balancing its own economic principles against the need for an international stance of maximum attractiveness to the majority of nations. The U.N. dialogue should continue, and having the issues made clear cannot be harmful to the cause of more responsible international behavior.

THE POPULATION PROBLEM

Of many remaining economic and social activities and potentialities of the United Nations that touch on U.S. interests, there is one that cannot be evaded. Overshadowing the entire picture of economic development is the population problem. The dimensions of the problem have been well established. The total number of people who had lived in our world until the present century was under 1.5 billion. Two-thirds of the way through the century the figure has doubled. By the year 2000, given a continuation of present trends, the figure will be more than seven billion.[5] In the United States the annual increase of 1½ percent tends to be concentrated in the least privileged groups, with consequent intensification of problems related to health, family life, housing and opportunities for education, employment and economic betterment. In the less developed countries the average annual increase is about 2½ percent, enough to double the population every twenty-five years. The result is not only threatened starvation in some areas, but an absorption of every increment of economic growth by the necessity to feed a continually larger population. Developed and underdeveloped nations are generally united now in focusing on the quality of life rather than the quantity. Runaway population growth has at last become the recognized threat to the possibilities of improvement. And, crucial to the political consequences, four-fifths of the world's population will by the year 2000 be living in Asia, Africa, and Latin America.

Birth control has religious implications that have made it a sensitive issue politically. The magnitude of the problem is now so well recognized, however, that more tolerant consideration of solutions has become possible. In the area of disseminating information about the facts, and techniques of family planning, the efforts of private organizations have at last been supplemented by public funds in the United States — through the Agency for Economic Development (AID), the U.S. Public Health Service, and the Bureau of the Census. The United Nations has also been active in this area through the World Health Organization (WHO) Population Commission and through U.N. regional economic commissions in Latin America, Africa, and Asia. The United Nations also sponsored World Population Conferences in 1954 and 1965.

When it comes to actually implementing family-planning programs, much less has been done. President Kennedy first publicly encouraged the dissemination of technical information to

[5] The facts and conclusions in this section have been drawn in large part from the *Report of the Committee on Population,* the White House Conference on International Cooperation, November 28–December 1, 1965.

those countries requesting it, but not until 1965 was AID authorized to respond positively to requests for technical, financial, and commodity assistance in support of family-planning programs. In 1965 also, WHO for the first time called on its Director General to provide advisory services in support of family-planning programs. The U.N. Children's Fund (UNICEF) is considering a possible role in this field, and the Economic and Social Council has requested the Secretary General to offer advisory services and training on action programs in population.

Now that a breach has been made in the traditional aversion to governmental action in this vital area, it is in the U.S. interest to press hard on all fronts, keeping in mind that the functional and technical agencies of the United Nations have a special competence and acceptability in this area that give them unique value for U.S. foreign policy.

In the broad context of welfare and evolution as they relate to U.S. interests in the underdeveloped areas, several principles suggest themselves regarding the uses of the United Nations.

First, there probably exist important advantages in utilizing the United Nations more decisively for action programs such as financing of large-scale economic-development projects. In doing so the United States must be prepared to abandon total control over funds, and perhaps a degree of efficiency in the programs, in order better to serve our broader goal of aiding the underdeveloped countries to achieve relatively stable and less vulnerable economic and social orders and, hopefully, democratic forms of political organization.

Second, the United States should approach the trade problems of the developing countries with an open mind and should encourage the success of the new Conference on Trade and Development (UNCTAD), even though this country fought the new institution all the way, much as it had fought the proposed International Trade Organization (ITO) years before. In both instances the U.S. hoped to keep any new trade agency within the purview of the Economic and Social Council, where the developed countries are heavily represented.

There are unquestionably grave disadvantages in the rapid multiplication of semi-autonomous economic agencies within the U.N. system — the consumption of high-level time at meetings alone is prodigious — but the United States in striving to lead the way to coherence and coordination must avoid appearing insensitive to the very real problems of the underdeveloped nations. One way to do this would be to accept the reality of a multitude of poor countries applying pressures on the rich in an organization where the latter are outvoted. The only real alternative to pulling out of the organization is to take initiatives that might attract majority support toward ends which we already accept as serving important American interests.

Third, the population problem should be tackled on every front with particular emphasis on using the broader and more diffuse machinery of the United Nations to assist those countries desiring technical and educational assistance.

CHAPTER FOURTEEN

Colonialism and Human Rights

COLONIALISM AND THE WEST

The most lively process of political change in our age has been the liquidation of Western colonial rule over dependent peoples in Asia, the Southwest Pacific, Africa, the Middle East, and the Caribbean. The process is nearing completion. Of the eleven territories placed under the trusteeship system, only Nauru, New Guinea, and the Trust Territory of the Pacific remain, each a special case. (It is ironic that the Western power most indicted by its allies for pushing them toward decolonization – the United States – is the chief remaining power involved in the trusteeship system. The Trust Territory of the Pacific, consisting of the Marshall, Mariana, and Caroline Islands, and administered as a "strategic trusteeship" under the provisions of Articles 82 and 83 of the U.N. Charter, presents almost insuperable problems in terms of ultimate independence. United States sovereignty also continues to be exercised over Guam, Samoa, and, under the label of "commonwealth," Puerto Rico.)

Elsewhere independence for even the most minute, nonviable pieces of territory has become a commonplace (*e.g.*, the Maldive Islands and Gambia), and the process was delayed in such areas as Guyana and Aden only because of the absence of governments capable of exercising control. The principal exception to the trend is in the southern portion of Africa, where a number of hard-core dependent areas such as Angola, Mozambique, and South-West Africa remain, their status reinforced by powerful European economic interests and, in some cases, by European populations.

Compared with the situation in 1945, when the United Nations established its concern for dependent territories, Western colonialism has just about ended. But the cause of anticolonialism has never been more vehement. (An analogy from astronomy may throw light on the phenomenon: a receding star in the heavens appears to move into the red band of the visible spectrum. This is the so-called "red shift," named after the spectroscopic appearance of the change. I would suggest that the anticolonial revolution against the European West is having its "red shift" just before colonialism ceases to be an issue of contemporary substance.)

There is and will be perhaps for another generation a continuing attitude of resentment, drawing sustenance largely from continued white rule in southern Africa, that can neither be shrugged off nor dealt with wholly by reason. The emotion goes deep, to the level of loyalties, or racial pride, of very different perceptions of history and justice.

One conclusion frequently drawn from this fact is that the United States must make a choice between the neutrals and its NATO allies, who feel themselves to be the chief victims of the former. There would undoubtedly have been some benefits from a public opting for our allies. Some French, and to a lesser extent British and perhaps Belgian interests would perhaps feel closer to American policy if the U.S. had repudiated the anticolonial bias of the United Nations. United States relations with South Africa and Portugal would be eased (including the continuing issue of United States base rights in the Azores), if we had not joined the overwhelming United Nations majority critical of Portuguese rule in Angola and of South African policies of racial repression and refusal to internationalize the former mandate of South-West Africa.

But the choice is a false one, for two reasons. One is that matters have not yet reached the point at which a choice is forced on us, and with a reasonable amount of statesmanship never should. The other reason is that such an option is not really open to United States policy. Policy must be addressed to interests; and the vital truth that is missed by those with the radical solutions is that there *are* divergent interests involved, interests which are served by divergent policies. The divergence is most visible in the United Nations, for obvious reasons, but it was not created there. The NATO countries have a profound common interest in the Atlantic basin, but their worldwide interests are not always common interests and United States policy cannot proceed as if they were.

Nothing could so disserve the United States' national interest as tying the U.S. future in Africa to the policies of Portugal and South Africa, both of which appear to be leading to an inexorable tragedy, however understandable all the reasons. It is unthinkable that we should reverse our present attitudes in order to support and condone the undemocratic character of both rules, and in particular the increasingly repressive quality of the South African white racist regime. To act otherwise would mock our judgment, our instinct, and our system.

It is arguable that the United States has been generally correct in its reading of the colonial problem, and that United Nations pressures in which the United States has joined have had a beneficial effect, even at the cost of lost affection — not a particularly important value compared to interests. American leaders began nagging our British cousins for Indian and Palestinian independence while we were actually their fighting ally in World War II. Similarly, we have used persuasion on both the French and the Dutch, to their profound displeasure but perhaps to their ultimate benefit, in North Africa and the East Indies. The results have been salutary, not because their rule was necessarily worse than what followed (although I happen to believe that a people are fundamentally better off if they rule themselves than if they are governed by a foreign occupier, however enlightened). The result was positive in terms of the Western image, on which we depend so heavily in the spiritual and psychological warfare with communism. Colonial rule, however enlightened, carries with it the attributes of racial superiority, economic exploitation, and social humiliation. That these are pathogenic, so to speak, is amply illustrated by the heritage they leave.

We cannot expect allies such as Portugal to appreciate or even understand what in some cases may seem to them a betrayal of our relationship. But whatever befalls, the United States cannot be party to a deluge which the modern Bourbons, learning nothing from history, are willing to contemplate as the cost of their policies. The anticolonial revolution has its full share of unattractive qualities. Indeed, just because the United States *does* believe that its anticolonial attitude reflects accurately its deeper interests, the Indian invasion of Goa in 1961 strained to the utmost the constancy of our political vision.

Nothing in the erroneous policies of Western colonialism exonerated India from using force in Goa to attain political ends — an act that was at once stupid, illegal, immoral, setting a precedent India herself may well come to rue. Equally damaging to the anticolonial cause was the way in which the Security Council minority averted its eyes and refused to apply the principles of the Charter. This moral abdication profoundly distressed Americans. It was to be expected that the Soviet Union, with its profound political cynicism, would further incite India in a cause certain to be popular with the street mobs. But it was shocking that the United Arab Republic, Ceylon, and Liberia joined the Soviets in blocking action by the Security Council — an action which would not have enabled the United Nations to intervene physically, but simply to register disapprobation at a flagrant departure from one of the few established norms of acceptable international conduct. It will be that much harder for those anticolonial powers to secure protection when they in turn are attacked by someone acting on the same grounds of *raison d'état*.

No nations are so guilty of shortsightedness as those who get away with petty aggressions, or those who (like Guinea before the General Assembly in January 1962) threaten that, unless the organization accedes to the bidding of the impatient radicals, they will resort to violence. Indonesia's threats regarding West New Guinea fell into the same category. There are other manifestations of hypocrisy (or, in any event, inconsistency) in the radical position. The very concept of self-determination, which for so long supplied an ideology for anticolonialism, has suddenly been forgotten by some of the new *status-quo* states. Former President Sylvanus Olympio of Togo, whose international career was launched as spokesman in the United Nations for an Ewe national state, suddenly began to deprecate the notion of self-determination as obviously inconsistent with his new nation's nonethnic boundaries. Similarly, President Sukarno of Indonesia rejected self-determination for the Papuans of West Irian until they were firmly in Indonesian hands and after.

For a time many seemed to share the myth that the great powers are guided only by expediency, while the neutralists in some magical way constitute the sole repository of moral wisdom. In the clamor over Goa and West Irian, it was forgotten that in the 1940s India had forcibly suppressed a self-determined independence movement in the province of Hyderabad, and Indonesia, one in the South Moluccas. The gravest threat to the integrity of the Congo after U.N. forces left in 1964 was a rebellion in the eastern provinces directly supported by some of the radical African states who were determined to overturn the government of Premier Moise Tshombe, still unforgiven for his secessionist movement in Katanga and his involvement in the murder of their hero Patrice Lumumba. Their efforts to subvert a fellow African state made somehow hollow their subsequent outrage and vituperation at the Belgian-American rescue mission of embattled whites in Stanleyville in the fall of 1964. Perhaps it is as well that the air has been cleared and a start made toward doing away with an irrational moral division of the world.

COLONIALISM AND U.S. POLICY

There is much in the present situation to support Canning's maxim that interests should be the "shibboleth of policy." Our despair at the intransigence of Portugal might estrange us from a NATO ally; our distaste with what seemed for a time to be the shortsightedness of India or Indonesia or Ghana might have stopped us from caring about the modernization process in these nations. A combination of despair and distaste might (and does) fan the embers of isolationism. But the only proper answer is to pursue our interests after calculating those interests on a rational basis. In my opinion, the results of such a calculation would not differ markedly from the present course of action, *i.e.,* the role of middleman, urging greater speed and progress on the European powers and at the same time counseling patience and adequate preparation on the dependencies. This has not been a comfortable role, but it has been an honest one. The United States cannot afford to advocate independence before a territory is ready to administer its own affairs — a point that usually comes earlier than the administering powers acknowledge but later than the independence-movement leaders insist upon. American objectives involving greater stabilization in international politics will be served by continuing to assist with the process of liquidation, to ensure that it is as orderly as possible and that the claims of neither side are permitted to rend irreparably the fabric of world peace and order.

If it is true that United States interests are not always identical with the interests of our Western European allies except in the North Atlantic area itself, the role of the United Nations in United States policy becomes clearer. The United States enjoys, in effect, a three-way relationship with the allies and with the neutrals. For us, the United Nations is a place where this relationship can be, so to say, triangulated. It is most significantly a means by which the United States can relate itself to its nonallies, and perhaps it is the only existing means for doing so. Nothing about NATO obviates that need. The argument that "when the chips are down" the United States can count only on its allies is doubtless true, but it overlooks the world we must live in when the chips are not down, or when those chips are only a part of the stakes in the game.

We need an organization in which we can discuss international problems on a regular basis with all the other countries in the world. This may seem self-evident, but it tends to be overlooked. We cannot do the job only in meetings of allies, because there are problems we have to discuss with other than our allies. It is not convenient to call an *ad hoc* diplomatic conference every time a number of countries want to talk things over with one another. As a continuing diplomatic conference, therefore, the United Nations is a great convenience — never mind the aspirations, the intimations of world order, or the police functions. The United Nations is, at the world level, what man has always needed, wanted, and has therefore had at every other level of political interaction, whether in the form of bazaar, agora, forum, convention, town hall, exchange, parliament, legislature, or congress.

In considering how the United Nations can best serve American strategic interests we ought to distinguish between the symbolic and the more tangible types of U.N. involvement. The racial issue, where little action is foreseen but profound and subtle psychological reactions are nonetheless involved, is perhaps the prime example of U.N. symbolism. In the colonial issue the effect of the United Nations has been most concrete with respect to the trust territories. It has been most symbolic with respect to the other non-self-governing territories, over which it has little direct authority but which have occupied more time in debate and more committees, particularly after the 1960 Declaration on Colonialism, and have generated more heat than any other issue before the United Nations. Crucial impressions about American foreign policy have been formed and acted upon as a result of purely verbal diplomatic performances by our government. The debates, however ineffective on the policy of the metropolitan government concerned, evoke the values of highest significance to the anticolonial forces — values of independence, self-respect, self-rule, cultural autonomy, and the whole complex of meanings bound up in the concept of self-determination.

While the United States has finally felt emboldened to assert its belief in the inevitability of the process that is taking place in the colonial world, this has not proved the end of the matter. Finding the bright morn of independence dimmed by serious economic, social, and political problems, many leaders of the new states have found the villain to be "neocolonialism." As the prime influence in one way or another over more than half the world's economic resources, the United States, finds itself the prime target, accused of behind-the-scenes manipulative power which is impossible to either prove or disprove. In general, this is a storm that the United States ought to plan to ride out with a firm grip on its principles, principles which have in other times supplied the very basis for the ideology of the new countries most critical of us today.

In addition to the largely symbolic side of debates and resolutions, however, there is an area of U.N. action which can be geared to our strategy.

In the economic and social fields, the general principle that should govern U.N. programs is almost identical with our own broad objectives. The United Nations is in a unique position to help develop and foster institutions within the developing countries which in the end will be democratic. Programs designed to train civil servants, to create administrative services, and to improve the internal foundations for social health and political freedom, all contribute to this objective. The U.N. Economic Commissions for Asia and the Far East, for Africa, and for Latin America, as well as the several technical-assistance programs of U.N. agencies, should be regarded as serious means toward the goal, with the special virtue that planning and action are done collaboratively with the potential leaders and with the people of the areas in question. With its multiple avenues of contact with the dependent areas, the United Nations can be reliably counted on to identify and bring to general attention problems in these areas – problems that profoundly affect the political possibilities, or that supply significant preconditions for an orderly political transition, which might not otherwise come to the attention of other nations until dangerously late.

HUMAN RIGHTS

Without doubt a great deal more will be heard of human rights in the United Nations. The Universal Declaration of Human Rights, adopted without dissent in 1948 (with the Soviet bloc, Yugoslavia, South Africa, and Saudi Arabia abstaining, and Honduras – which approved later – and Yemen being absent), has reportedly been the partial stimulus for two regional conventions. Its influence has also been felt in the constitutions of seven states, in the peace treaty with Japan, in the Austrian State Treaty, and in legislation in numerous other countries.

For ten years draft convenants on civil and political rights and on economic, social, and cultural rights awaited Assembly action. With the passage in 1963 of the Declaration on the Elimination of All Forms of Racial Discrimination, the question took fire once again.

There is no conflict, but rather a positive harmony, between United States interests and the ends of 1968's International Year for Human Rights. The United States has some unfinished business to complete in this realm. The late Secretary of State John Foster Dulles, in an effort to appease opposition, acted to discourage the drafting of formal human-rights covenants; he would not submit them to Congress for ratification. U.S. policy subsequently changed, and in 1963 President Kennedy submitted to the Senate, the U.N. and ILO (International Labor Organization) conventions on slavery, forced labor, and political rights of women.

The United States' record on racial matters is one of which it need no longer feel ashamed. It has confronted its own racial problems with far greater authority and success than, for example, has India in dealing with its even more brutal and degrading caste system (or, needless to say, than South Africa, whose official policy is one of segregation). Moreover, this has not always gone unnoticed. In the discussion of the *apartheid* issue at the 1964 Assembly, many of the speeches by African delegates, while condemning South Africa, gave credit to the United States for its opposition to South Africa's racist policies.

A healthy reversal of a long-standing policy of noninvolvement in treaty-drafting in this field took place in 1963, when the Administration sent the three human-rights conventions to the Senate. This is a start that ought to be followed up. It is important that the United States take action on these conventions, and also on the long-pigeonholed Genocide Convention, in order that we be in a position to bring moral pressure to bear on others, to influence the drafting of future covenants, and generally to appear — as we have every right to appear — as one of the leading forces supporting the still revolutionary notions of political freedom, racial equality, and equal opportunity for all men.

It is equally important that the United States confront the implications of leadership in forums in which a majority of members are no longer satisfied with purely national action in the protection of individuals. In voting for mandatory sanctions against the Rhodesian government in 1966, the Security Council took a major step in what is at root a question of human rights. There will be increasing pressures to move even more effectively against Portugal, and South African *apartheid*. Perhaps most potentially significant of all was the determination expressed by 114 nations at the 1966 General Assembly to divest South Africa of its League of Nations mandate over South-West Africa.

The proposal has been made by the United States for a U.N. High Commissioner on Human Rights, whose role would include collecting all the information about human-rights violations which now goes to any number of other bodies, such as the Special Committee on Colonialism, the Special Committee on Apartheid, and the Commission on Human Rights. The High Commission would use fact-finding machinery and the influence of the office in the search for solutions. This appears to be a promising development that would serve both to advance the cause of complainants and to protect governments that are targets of malicious or unjustified attack.

PART V The Goal of World Order

CHAPTER FIFTEEN

The Creation of Community

CHAPTER SIXTEEN

Toward a Rule of Law

CHAPTER FIFTEEN

The Creation of Community

We finally turn to the third and last category of time in which to explore the possible uses of the United Nations: the long range. We have said that the overall long-range U.S. objective is

> to build a more reliable, predictable, and tolerable world order, based on values reflecting freedom and voluntarism rather than totalitarianism and coercion.

We have suggested that this objective calls for strategy designed

> to substitute processes of cooperation, order, and eventually world law for the anarchy and narrow nationalism that continue to endanger world peace and stability.

THE IDEA OF WORLD GOVERNMENT

The most explicit suggestions for actions toward the realization of this ultimate goal have come from the small minority advocating world government or from those who advocate political union among nations of the Atlantic Community. Such proposals have called for steps going far beyond present levels of constitutionalism and intergovernmental cooperation. As a consequence, although in the abstract these suggestions might have appeared logical and entirely rational, they have seemed anything but rational to professionals who were struggling, with only limited success, to bring to life even the multilateral machinery already in existence.

Advocates of world federation like to cite the experience of the American colonies as relevant and even analogous, particularly the transition from the Articles of Confederation to the Constitution. But they often miss the point that

> Those who seek to bring about America's participation in projects for international control and even world government would be well-advised to settle for a vague commitment at the outset and to trust history to define the reality. It seems very unlikely that the American Constitution would have been ratified if it had been clear that the national government enjoyed the powers claimed for it by [Chief Justice] Marshall in *McCulloch v. Maryland.*[1]

Proposals have occasionally been made to give the United Nations legislative powers, or to eliminate the veto. Such proposals clearly require acceptance of some basic concepts of sovereignty which have hitherto not been accepted. One of the most encouraging contemporary developments is the evidence of some gradual steps to crystallize a community of interests among certain nations on the basis of a consensus on specified values or objectives; but it is a far cry from such beginnings to the allocation of genuine legislative power to the General Assembly of the United Nations. That lies on the other side of the Rubicon, and it involves acceptance of a form of international constitutional government which the majority of nations have shown themselves unready to accept.

The argument about world government has all too frequently centered around questions of feasibility rather than on questions of values. Much thought has gone into blueprints for ideal global governmental arrangements, but little analysis has been made of the values of personal liberty in relation to world government. A world government, while satisfying certain administrative and security needs, conceivably might, by applying a lower common

[1] Robert G. McCloskey, "American Political Thought and the Study of Politics," LI *American Political Science Review* (1957), p. 129.

denominator than that which we are used to, jeopardize the high standard of individual liberties painfully acquired by certain Western peoples; and it might reduce the initiative of local governments upon which the bulk of social and economic progress depends.

Another problem, which is not often cited but which must be anticipated because of the very nature of the political process, is that of providing satisfactorily for the process of change. The nations comprising present world society are characterized by highly unequal stages of economic, political, and cultural development. As in similarly unbalanced civil societies, insurrections would predictably take place against the newly established world government; and local insurrections could well grow into civil war on a global scale.

Apart from the theoretical considerations, the chief disability of world-government proposals is that they must assume the disappearance, or at least the drastic transformation, of the Soviet Union and Communist China. Today both countries are, in different degrees, revolutionary and imperialistic powers determined to organize the world in their own image. To validate the proposals for world government, they must be postulated into sharers of Western liberal values and advocates of permanent stability.

In short, the debate on strategy to achieve a new world order has almost completely ignored a first truth: that, since the goal of world order depends upon a minimum consensus of political and societal values (unless by world order we mean world tyranny) the focus of logic must be not on the form of structure of a possible world order, but on the inescapable prerequisites of consensus and shared values.

American planners have sensed this fundamental fact, but American policy has reflected not so much a conscious consideration of the problems it implies as an acceptance of those problems as an excuse for inaction. American policy, although correct in assuming that a gradual rather than a drastic approach to world order will command the best chance of success, has in using this reasoning given "gradual" the comfortable quality of meaning anytime, or perhaps never. Thus the task remains of formulating a coherent American strategic doctrine in the political realm that orchestrates the short-range, the middle-range, and the long-range approaches to the kind of world order the United States seeks.

The issue of supranational institutions has arisen most directly in American foreign policy in the 1960s in connection with proposals for General and Complete Disarmament. The United States draft treaty [2] contains provisions for international military forces potent enough to enforce the disarmament regime when it comes about. It is apparent that to do this it would be necessary to create appropriate political decision-making institutions that inescapably add up to world government.[3] The logic of this connection is impressive, and perhaps if there were a disposition for drastic disarmament, the political arrangements to accompany it would also be feasible. Today both appear equally remote.

With or without disarmament, the United States holds important goals bearing on world order. In planning toward the achievement of those goals, it is essential to maintain an atmosphere of reality and concreteness. If steps are to be taken now to begin to implement our goals, the realistic approach is particularly desirable when it comes to contemplating the uses and development of international political institutions. But this is only half the need. The other half is a fresh willingness to regard our long-term goals as capable of implementation instead of regrettably but safely meaningless. It is not easy to surrender the comfort of dreams in favor of the realities of a program of limited action; but limited action is at least a start toward distant goals, and some start must be made if any meaning is to be given our concept of world order based on democratic and libertarian principles. Even if the world is not yet ready for a universal version of such a program, we are not entitled to sit still. Burckhardt said it well:

[2] "Outline of Basic Provisions of a Treaty on General and Complete Disarmament in a Peaceful World," submitted to Eighteen-Nation Disarmament Committee in Geneva on April 18, 1962. U.S. Arms Control and Disarmament Agency Publication 4, General Series 3, May 1962.

[3] See the author's "Arms Control and World Government," *World Politics*, July 1962; also Lincoln P. Bloomfield *et al.*, *International Military Forces — The Problem of Peacekeeping in an Armed and Disarming World* (Boston: Little, Brown, 1964), especially Chapter Two, "World Force and World Order."

> From time to time a great event, ardently desired, does not take place because some future time will fulfil it in greater perfection.[4]

The starting point must of necessity be a modest one, and progress predictably slow.

We are powerless to make even limited progress unless we believe that time is on our side in the struggle with communism. If we believe that Western civilization is the Roman Empire of this century, and that it is fated forever to remain on the defensive, the outlook is hopeless. The truth is that in the process of defending against assault, the West has shown itself capable of creating new strengths and setting in motion new energies of its own. Although the West is fundamentally and almost by definition in a defensive position and cannot act the revolutionary (no matter what verbal gymnastics may be recommended by salesmen for America overseas), the course of revolution invariably produces a new dialectic. The Soviet Union as a new imperial power represents an established order, behind whose façade the forces of change are working just as surely as they worked on Rome. If the West can seek out the dynamic principle of those forces, so to speak, it can consciously accelerate the effect of contradictions within the Soviet empire. Above all, with a positive organizing principle of its own, the West can act purposefully to foster its own version of history. This is the appropriate strategy even while containing a new and potentially imperialist force such as China.

During a period when both superpowers are generally balanced by a rough equilibrium in technology and, given the various trade-offs, in the deliverable megatonnage of nuclear destruction, the primary determinative forces are not military but political and ideological. The kind of political strategy needed by the West is one that can unbalance the *nonmilitary* equilibrium in our favor. As the anthropologist Clyde Kluckhohn has written:

> There are moments in the careers of nations, as well as in the careers of individuals, when opposing external forces are about equally balanced, and it is then that intangibles like "will" and "belief" throw the scales.[5]

[4] Jacob Burckhardt, *Force and Freedom* (New York: Meridian, 1955), p. 325.
[5] Clyde Kluckhohn, *Mirror for Man* (New York: Whittlesey House, 1949), p. 198.

CONSENSUS AND COMMUNITY

The unpredictable rhythms of history, of which our century displays only the most recent examples, offer little prospect for an end to the dynamic interplay between the established order and the invariable rise of forces dissatisfied with the conditions of their membership in it. That dynamic process and its effect on the prospects for world order are the raw materials with which planners must work if they are not to fall into one of the three pits described some years ago by Walter Lippmann when he wrote:

> The American refusal to recognize the struggle for existence has in this century crystallized in three recognizable patterns of conduct: in a neutrality which assumes that the struggle can be ignored and avoided; in crusades that assume that by defeating the chief troublemaker the struggle for existence will end; in the sponsorship of a universal society which assumes that the struggle can be abolished.[6]

The basis for true community, political experience tells us, is a genuine consensus about the values which the community cherishes. Law, in turn, can become acceptable and effective only if it reflects that consensus. Political community in its ideal form rests on commonly shared values on the proper role of man in society. Translated in terms of today's world, world government would be a possibility if all the politically determinative sectors of world society shared the same concepts of human rights, political freedom, and perhaps economic organization. We know in our very bones that this is not a feasible possibility at the present stage of history.

But we also know that there is a highly developed consensus on some limited values – allocation of radio frequencies, epidemic control, weather-reporting, mail service – as well as on the importance attached to the process of industrialization and societal modernization, and (one can guess even including China) on the mutual interest in minimizing the possibilities of global war. Furthermore, there are some nations that share primary political and social values, achieving a *de facto* community of interests

[6] Walter Lippmann, "The Rivalry of Nations," *Atlantic Monthly*, February 1948, p. 19.

from which have already come limited experiments in economic integration and in intellectual and cultural harmony.

Finally, we know that among the citizenry of virtually all nations, if not necessarily among the ruling elites, there is a shared longing for conditions of greater international tranquillity, material betterment, and individual fulfillment. This longing assumes political shape in the logic Walter Lippmann articulated when he wrote:

> A universal society is inevitable. . . . The feeling that it is possible proceeds from the fact that modern war has become a universal calamity, that therefore a universal society is necessary, and that necessity is the mother of invention.[7]

There are, then, operational bases for action. They are at present limited, fragmentary, and nonuniversal; but their very existence gives promise for an improved world order. But prospects for world community cannot rest on the expectation of an abstract commitment by members of an essentially nonexistent community; they must be advanced by degrees by focusing attention on those specific interests, small or large, that are shared by groups of nations, whether they represent the entire world or not. One of the wisest contemporary thinkers has developed this theme in these words:

> Our actions and attitudes on detailed questions of daily policy, on questions of tariffs and immigration quotas, on technical assistance programs and investment in underdeveloped areas will contribute more to the international community, which all far-seeing Americans see in the making, than any abstract commitments to ideal and impossible world constitutions which some idealistic Americans regard as important. World community must gradually grow through acts of mutual loyalty. Mutual loyalty in situations of great disproportions of power and fortune is difficult but not impossible. . . . Our problem is that technics have established a rudimentary world community but have not integrated it organically, morally, or politically. They have created a community of mutual dependence, but not one of mutual trust and respect.[8]

[7] Walter Lippmann, "The Great Revolution," *U.N. Monthly Chronicle*, April 1965, p. 67.

[8] Reinhold Niebuhr, *The World Crisis and American Responsibility* (New York: Association Press, 1958), pp. 80, 85–86.

What, then, is the governing principle around which long-range Western strategy should center? The creation of segments, however imperfect, of true community.

What basic strategy does it call for? To support integration in economic and political fields which minimizes separatist nationalisms and ideologies and maximizes principles of cooperation and common purpose.

What can be done now? The United States can seek out new areas of consensus and common interest and creatively support their transition to prototypes of the world order to which we aspire.

THE CREATION OF LIMITED COMMUNITIES

The first category of potential communities that the United States should strive to bring into being embraces the international community of science and technology. We have already commented on the degree to which common interest in science transcends ideological differences, with the caveat that political considerations continue to define the broad limits of intergovernmental collaboration. One prediction that can be confidently made is that further radical and transforming changes are to be anticipated in the realm of science and technology, and that there is no theoretical limit to the need for institutional means to deal with these changes constructively. I have already noted that the challenge of outer space, beyond its purely military and scientific objectives, offers both need and opportunity for the development of institutional forms of international cooperation on a problem of irrefutably common human concern.

Soviet motives in cooperating in limited ways can be deduced from Soviet doctrine. In general such collaboration as takes place is doubtless believed to advance Soviet ideological aims and Russian national interests. American motives, however, are not so focused and remain confused, with scientific and military claims alternating on the center of the stage. So long as the United States does not more sharply define in concrete organizational and institutional terms the image it wishes to imprint on the Space Age, the direction which collaboration takes is going to be fixed at every point by Soviet rather than American planners.

Alternatively, political arrangements will continue to be prisoner of what I earlier described as "politically mindless technology."

There are other scientific and technological areas in which common interests exist, whether yet identified as such or not, and where the United States can move toward its larger political objective by innovations and experiments in institutionalizing those interests. The International Geophysical Year furnished a world pattern that can and should be exploited. Scientists have repeatedly argued that the long-range hope for peace lies in the establishment of "transnational communities" in which scholars, scientists, and others with common interest work together for a new world order.[9] As an official of the National Academy of Sciences wrote about the International Council of Scientific Unions (I.C.S.U.):

> I.C.S.U. and its affiliated bodies welcome participation in their activities of scientists from any country or territory and . . . such participation [does] not carry any implication whatsoever with respect to recognition of the government or territory concerned. This principle made possible the virtually universal enrollment of national scientific communities in the I.G.Y.[10]

Certainly the success of the International Geophysical Year, with its widely publicized emphasis on the international interests of the scientific community, was a landmark in international relations. Indeed, some have seen it as a progenitor of completely new patterns of international political relations:

> The I.G.Y. may turn out to be a brilliant new approach toward world organization. The geophysicist is inevitably a truly international scientist. During current Antarctic operations all considerations other than scientific have been set aside. Cooperation among all participating nations is real.[11]

It may well be that the most fruitful areas of cooperation today lie in realms that depend sufficiently on the scientists, with their

[9] J. Robert Oppenheimer, *New York Times,* April 16, 1958.

[10] Wallace W. Attwood, Jr., "The International Geophysical Year in Retrospect," *Department of State Bulletin,* May 11, 1959, p. 684.

[11] Laurence M. Gould, "Antarctica in World Affairs," *Headline Series,* No. 128, Foreign Policy Association, New York, 1958.

usually detached political outlook, to minimize political differences.

But, although scientific contact should be outside the political forum, the importance of the issues of scientific cooperation can be underscored only by giving them the floor, so to speak, in political forums such as the United Nations. If it appears that there may be danger that such interconnections make scientific subjects political, the answer is to concentrate on nonpolitical bodies, such as private scientific or the U.N. specialized agencies, for the actual scientific collaboration and contact. But the United Nations should be used for the purpose of institutionalizing such cooperation and for the dissemination of results through the widest media.

From the International Health Year in 1961 through International Cooperation Year in 1965 (which spawned a multitude of new ideas and approaches), to the International Year for Human Rights in 1968, from the World Food Program to the World Weather Watch, the United Nations has in fact increasingly become the umbrella for attacks on human and technical problems of international concern.

American strategy should continue to encourage proposals through the United Nations for intensive collaborative investigations and endeavors in various scientific fields that bear on the solution of the common global problems now or eventually affecting every human being. We have noted the problem of overpopulation. Others include the dwindling water supply and the search for new sources of energy. The U.N. Conference on the Application of Science and Technology for the Benefit of Less Developed Areas (UNCSAT), which met in 1963, brought together for the first time scientists, economists, diplomats, and administrators from eighty-seven countries. The resulting eighteen-nation Advisory Committee is seeking to improve the United Nations' contribution to these areas. The social and political impact of this search for solutions could be widespread.

One way of moving such vital issues from the technical level to that of maximum public and political impact, yet without overburdening the political agenda, would be for the General Assembly to adopt the British Royal Commission method. Blue-ribbon special bodies of both experts and diplomats would be created *ad hoc* by the Assembly to examine the latest developments in a particular field, reporting back with recommendations for action in political, financial, and organizational terms. (A first step in this direction was taken in 1965 when the Assembly established a fourteen-nation committee to analyze and make recommendations on U.N. finances and financing.) Such reports could package whole areas which political leadership might otherwise neglect. Clear explanations of the social and economic significance of such issues before an international political body could have a salutary effect, both in focusing international diplomacy on essentially constructive nondivisive issues and in elevating to their proper place some problems that deserve urgent attention and the allocation of significant international resources.

To turn to another base for action, there has been in recent years an accelerating trend toward the integration of the economies and, in some cases, the politics of states in limited association with each other. It has paralleled the sharp upsurge of nationalism during the same time and has been obscured by that more dramatic and vivid development. France, for example, has behaved under General de Gaulle as a state torn between the pressures of the two opposing trends. The balance was for a time tipped so that steps favoring further integration within the Western European community were almost completely stalled. This has been accompanied by the withdrawal of established cooperative arrangements under NATO.

Clearly the trend toward greater integration must contend every step of the way with the forces of nationalism; there is no evidence that purely "functional" interrelationships will lead by any natural or automatic process to political integration, or even that integration as such will eventually be the dominant trend. The evidence is still ambiguous. I have mentioned the halting, although promising, Western European experience. In 1959 the so-called Outer Seven, led by England, formed the European Free Trade Association (EFTA). Genuine European integration will probably be a meaningful reality only when EFTA is merged with the Common Market, and perhaps later, pursuant to one of De Gaulle's deeper insights, when the European community comes to include some of the estranged European countries of the erstwhile Soviet bloc, whose integration in the economic side of the Warsaw Pact (COMECON) is increasingly tenuous.

Africa is an example of multiple steps toward and away from integration over a very few years. Many efforts to unite African states have foundered or fallen far short of their original purposes — for example, the abortive Federation of Rhodesia and Nyasaland, the unions of Egypt and Syria, and Egypt and Yemen, the Union of Central African Republics, the Union of Ghana, Guinea, and Mali, the East African Common Services Organizations, and such coalitions as the Monrovian and Casablanca groups. But meanwhile an overall continental grouping has taken shape, and ever since its inception in 1962 the Organization for African Unity (OAU) has shown promise, particularly in the peaceful-settlement area. The U.N. Economic Commission for Africa, created in 1960, has taken important strides toward the goal of continent-wide economic cooperation. An African Development Bank has been founded. And even on the subregional level, there has been steady institutional cooperation among the French-speaking states, leading eventually to the formation of the Afro-Malagasy Commission Organization (OCAM) in 1965, within the several frameworks of the OAU. The Maghreb grouping of North African States was organized in 1962. And the combined nation of Tanzania was formed at Tanganyika and Zanzibar.

In Asia there have been several indigenous integrative attempts whose prospects remain unclear. In 1966 the ending of the "confrontation" between Indonesia and Malaysia led to revival of the Association of Southeast Asia, consisting of Thailand, the Philippines, and Malaysia, with promise of also including Indonesia. It already is working toward a joint shipping line and the coordination of commodity prices. Malaysia itself constituted a genuine integration of Malaya with the former British territories of Singapore, Sabah, Sarawak, and Brunei, although Singapore broke away in 1965. The forced intimacy of Tibet with Communist China illustrates vividly the evils of involuntary integration.

Scandinavian regional cooperation, though not integration, takes place primarily within the Nordic Council, formed in 1961.

And in Latin America the seven-nation Central American free trade zone, formed in 1960, while slow in developing is finally moving toward a genuine common market. Possibly even more significant, the presidents of Chile, Colombia, and Venezuela decided in August 1966 to support economic integration for all of Latin America, a move applauded by the United States.[12]

The United States, as I have said, must regard the prospect of world government as a mixed blessing. If the national interest had to be summed up, one might say that we favor the growth of larger-than-national communities of common interest and peaceful purpose that at the same time preserve the high values of pluralism and diversity — a combination often summed up by the word "interdependence." Within this larger strategic context the United States ought to favor the expansion of loyalties and a sense of interests on a widening basis.

The United Nations has only a limited role to play in facilitating or even affecting this mixed set of trends. It has already taken some constructive steps which should be encouraged and built upon. Perhaps the earliest was the decision of the General Assembly in 1949 to incorporate Cyrenaica, the Fezzan, and Tripolitania into the new state of Libya, and the related decision in 1950 to federate Eritrea with Ethiopia. Most instances of regional and functional integration normally take place without reference to the United Nations itself. But regional cooperation should not be regarded as competitive to the principle of universality. Confederations of the sort described above, far from being rivals or threats to the United Nations, are building blocks of consensus and community and political stepping-stones toward the universal society of which the United Nations may be the forerunner.

In speaking of John F. Kennedy's unfulfilled goals, Theodore Sorenson wrote that among "his long-range goals in foreign affairs [was] a United Nations made stronger as national sovereignty became weaker." [13] Where the United Nations can offer ways and means toward this end, United States interests can only be served by a leadership role in such actions.

[12] Speech by President Johnson, August 17, 1966, *New York Times,* August 18, 1966.

[13] Theodore C. Sorenson, *Kennedy* (New York: Harper, 1965), p. 754.

CHAPTER SIXTEEN

Toward a Rule of Law

If we seek to make progress toward a world community, we must explore not only the areas of common regional interests but also the common interests among nations in all continents and regions that are not being reflected adequately in the world's institutions. For the fact that such widely shared interests already exist suggests a fundamental approach to world order – specifically, that action can be taken now to foster the rule of law in the world without waiting for the formation of a universal political consensus on which to base it.

It is true that such a consensus on certain fundamental political values is a prerequisite to the universal rule of law, and that a universal community of political interest must be created before such a law can be superimposed.[1] Nevertheless, even in the realm of international law, the United States might sponsor limited action now, based on existing common interests, that would be realistic, positive, and constructive in advancing its grand strategy.

In the course of such possible U.S. action toward the sort of world order we aspire to, we are confronted by two issues of

[1] For a more thorough exposition of this point of view, see the author's *Law, Politics, and International Disputes*, in *International Conciliation*, No. 516, January 1958.

unusual moment: the problem of making greater use of legal methods in the settlement of international disputes, and the problem of building a legal order in the absence of a true universal community or of the shared political and social values upon which genuine community must rest.

LEGAL AND POLITICAL DISPUTES

The first problem – legal solutions for international disputes – raises once again some long-debated issues about the role of the law in fostering or inhibiting the processes of political and social change. This relationship has some fixed qualities which cannot be disregarded, however powerful our impulses toward reform.

There has long been agreement that in its essence the law represents stability, as distinct from the political process, which is dynamic in nature. The law, in this oversimplified but nonetheless historically striking equation, reflects the *status quo*. Significant and needful changes in the established political, economic, and social order cannot be brought about by appealing to the courts, since it is the function of the courts to uphold the existing order. Although adjustments between those sharing the same ground rules can be accommodated by the law, changes in the ground rules themselves – in the basic distribution of power or status – can, so the argument runs, be brought about only by altering the law.

Even in the most harmonious domestic setting, parliaments rather than courts generally alter the law in the sense of resolving the great conflicts of interest between component parts of society as to the allocation of political power and social strength. These conflicts and their accommodation are the very stuff and substance of the political process. Of course the law has a role even here, in ensuring that conflicts stop short of violence, in guarding the larger public interest against the contenders, or, in a different sense, in rendering decisions that show that it too understands the dynamics of the society it serves. But when all is said and done, in a well-integrated society the means by which the basic constellation of internal forces is rearranged without violence are legislative and not judicial. In an unintegrated society, revolution (or, on an international scale, war) is the traditional vehicle for such changes. It is quite evident that we have some distance to go before we can achieve the preconditions for genuine international legislation with all that it implies. And such a task is Herculean in an age in which the engines of history are political forces with warring ideas about how to organize society. The international dispute-solving process thus functions under extraordinary handicaps and still encourages a sterile black-and-white dialogue between those who insist that if only men would be rational all disputes could be adjudicated, and those who dismiss legal methods as permanently irrelevant to world politics.

The matter is, of course, anything but black and white. Even when political disputes have been most intractable, it has been true that courts have sometimes changed the law, often after, as it were, reading the election returns. The doctrine of changed circumstances (*rebus sic stantibus*) at least theoretically permits obsolete treaties to be legally invalidated. The United Nations, like the League of Nations before it, has machinery available for peaceful change. In the case of the United Nations a genuinely new bias has existed toward change and away from the *status quo* – for example, in the realm of colonialism.

But perhaps the greatest challenge to traditional thinking about law and politics is that the legal order is no longer always synonymous with the political *status quo*. The international *status quo* today is a multiple array of established orders against each of which large-scale forces are in revolt. It bears little resemblance to the two-dimensional confrontations of the nineteenth century that still color much of our political imagery.

The shifts in political equations are in turn reflected in the mirror that law holds up to society. The principle of domestic jurisdiction – the very keystone of modern international constitutional order – yielded with high drama in March of 1960 to the conviction of a growing number of states that South Africa's internal racial policies not only were reprehensible but also constituted a potential threat to international peace and security. The latter concept too had changed when such a threat could engage the Security Council even though no armies were mobilized, no borders violated, no ultimatum issued. Cuba's invocation of the Security Council in its dispute with the United States in the summer of 1960 further illustrated the trend to broaden the meaning of "international." Rhodesia's unilateral declaration of independence in 1965 would a century earlier have been of concern only to Britain; today only the most aloof U.N. members, such as France, have questioned the responsibility of the Security Council to press for a reversal of Rhodesia's action.

The new plasticity in legal concepts is not limited to the colonial area. The very notion of territorial inviolability and privacy has already been shattered by orbiting satellites, and more sophisticated successors can be counted on to appear. Only when such intrusion becomes institutionalized by the organs of international society will the law catch up with the reality.

These are all among the reasons why the present, although a time of change, could also be a time of opportunity. A serious détente between the East and West, if it ever comes about, could permit the processes of evolution to erect new conceptual bridges between the Communist states and the West, draining some presently intractable disputes of their revolutionary quality, and turning the mutual focus away from issues involving the legitimacy of the present distribution of power and wealth. Such an evolution in the East-West contest may be in the far distance, particularly considering the international dynamics of Chinese communism. But as newly independent countries come to reaffirm what President Lleras of Colombia once called their decisive stake in Western civilization, as they come to regard the legal order — such as it is — as the guardian rather than the thief of their patrimony, the international consensus can grow, and with it the possibilities for international law and — by the most natural process of all — international authority.

The issues which may not be "justiciable" at one time could well be at another time, because their adjudication would not be seen as placing in jeopardy the existence or relative power of a nation. And surely there are many matters which are now nonjusticiable only because there is no custom or habit or expectation or pressure for adjudication.

A discriminating brand of statesmanship can isolate legal aspects of political cases and, with strong leadership and proper timing, make better use of the potential of the law. As a minor participant in the American side of the Suez crisis of 1956, I believe that situation may well have offered opportunities at one stage to seek a World Court ruling, by mutual agreement, on Egypt's obligations regarding free passage under the Constantinople Treaty of 1888. But at no time after July 26, 1956, was it realistic to expect Egypt to consult the Court on the proper ownership of the Canal itself. The question of sovereignty had become a closed question, but the more procedural issues might not have been. The 1966 decision of the Court on South-West Africa may have foreclosed for many years this kind of constructive exploration of legal potential. By making a decision on narrow technical grounds after years of hearings on the merits, the Court may well be repudiated by many of the newer states as irrelevant to the political process.

Looking beyond the immediate period of disillusionment and rejection, however, the fundamentals remain. There are two basic preconditions for improved use of the law in the settlement of international disputes. Both reflect hazards to which Americans are peculiarly prone.

One hazard already touched upon is the persistent delusion, popular among a few professionals and many laymen, that one of the things man strives for is to substitute law for politics. At its most extravagant, this fantasy sees as the objective of foreign policy the creation of a world in which there is no conflict or tension – in other words, an end to the dynamic processes by which history spins itself out of the thrusts and responses of man and nature. I have tried to show that under the most favorable conditions the legal and political realms have their natural and legitimate roles to play in ordering social life. In taking a forward step toward greater use of international arbitral and judicial machinery, nothing could be more damaging than to underrate the distinction between the legal and political realms into which constitutional society, if it is to survive and flourish, characteristically and naturally divides itself.

The other hazard is the tendency, upon any temporary easement in world conditions, to slacken off drastically on major international tasks considered imperative when pressure was on. A rather new order of maturity will be required of us if the incentives to community-building are not to atrophy recurrently whenever pressures are lifted in a more relaxed environment.

By the same token, unless there is the same degree of purposeful action and example by leading countries such as the United States, continued tensions will supply a permanent excuse for inaction.

A MORE LAWFUL WORLD ORDER

It is with respect to the distant vision of a more lawful world that frequently enunciated long-term goals seem most abstract and unreal. So long as those goals depend on a universal consensus, the prospects for advancing toward a more satisfactory international society are dim indeed. The realistic view was probably stated most succinctly by former Secretary of State Dean Acheson when he called the pursuit for peace through law "illusory," going on to say that, "in the search for ways to maintain our values and pursue them in an orderly way, we must look beyond the resources of law." [2] But are there no steps we could take before a distant millennium, no promising raw materials out of which to construct meaningful segments of community?

I believe there are, but they require us to modify some assumptions about the nature of a world legal regime. One assumption is that a community upon which to base such a regime already exists — which is patently untrue. Another is that in order to subject nations to a compulsory rule of law, such a total community would first have to come into being — which relegates the possibilities to an indefinite future. To make any progress at all toward the larger goal, for the foreseeable future we must, in the words of Andrew Jackson, "elevate them guns a little lower." We must revise the all-or-nothing premise that underlies much contemporary thinking about the rule of law in the world. For if progress toward a rule of law depends upon a genuine sharing of fundamental political values by the West and the Communist states, we are lost before we begin.

Certainly some of the dominant attitudes in the Soviet outlook have changed, and we should continue to encourage this change in every way possible. But on the evidence so far, Communist leaders reject the notion of judges that can be impartial between systems; according to their doctrine one is either for them or

[2] At the University of Virginia, May 7, 1966. *New York Times,* May 19, 1966.

against them. Particularly is this true of the Chinese. We seem to envisage so-called peaceful competition as a way in which we can "win" in accordance with civilized ground rules; it is not at all clear that the Communists can contemplate losing gracefully or in any other way. I can only conclude that the most promising prospect for enlarging the rule of law today takes the form of agreements between the *most* like-minded rather than the least like-minded states. I suggested in Chapter Eleven that like-minded states should band together in a treaty that makes binding between them the pacific-settlement procedures they urge upon others without however always being willing to abide by themselves. Let us go a step further here.

A considerable number of nations already share certain values in common that would be relevant to the formation of a legal community. One shared value among many Western nations is their relative satisfaction with the established order in broad terms, implying their general willingness to live within it. This in turn suggests that a willingness probably exists to let their legal disputes be arbitrated or adjudicated by an impartial body if they are guaranteed mutual reciprocity from other nations similarly bound, and if they feel they can count on recognizable justice from the mediating third party.

There is a deep tradition of jurisprudence in North America, Western Europe, and Australasia that can be built upon; the legal habits developed by Latin American states on international questions are already strongly embedded. In other areas, as one after another newly independent state comes to reconstruct satisfactory and trustful relationships with the older parts of international society, a similar tradition could slowly develop.

The nature of a potential legal community is to some extent identified by the character of the forty-odd states whose declarations regarding compulsory jurisdiction of the International Court of Justice are still on the books — thirteen are European, nine Latin American, and twelve Afro-Asian, in addition to the United States, Israel, and the four older British dominions. It will be noted at once that such a community would not be limited to any one region or continent, nor would it make a politically myopic distinction between "have" and "have-not" nations.

Actually, the nations outside traditional Western systems have had little or no opportunity to demonstrate their willingness to submit even their legal disputes to the legal process. Moreover they have not been influenced to do so. The United Arab Republic was never seriously challenged by the principal powers to submit the legal aspects of the Suez Canal dispute to adjudication; India and Pakistan have never been pushed to arbitrate their differences over Kashmir, nor were the Netherlands and Indonesia to adjudicate the West New Guinea dispute. In some cases one or the other party knows only too well what the law's reply will be and does not wish to hear it. But in an improved environment, with great powers such as the United States setting the example, the pressures to make such modest progress would doubtless intensify — always, however, with the clear understanding that the legal process can be expected to encompass only the *legal* questions that arise between nations, not those that are basically political.

The Latin American states seemed prepared, in the Bogotá Conference on Pacific Settlement of Disputes in 1948, to agree that *all* disputes, whether justiciable or not, be submitted to a process of adjudication. This goes too far; it feeds the fear that any step at all would involve an unacceptable cost. But political disputes frequently have aspects that can be formulated in legal terms and upon which a legally based judgment would be acceptable. This suggests that a not inconsiderable body of issues could be so handled, and it is a counsel of despair to hold that even the most advanced nations would consider *any* serious dispute political and would refuse to be bound by a third-party legal judgment.

I do not believe that the germ of truth this assertion contains is sufficient to deter the United States from making a fresh start on the assumption that, under appropriate political and constitutional conditions, greater willingness to use legal process for legal questions would be forthcoming. The place to make a fresh start is among those nations throughout the world presently sharing at least a modest consensus of values and political beliefs, constituting them a core legal community open to all who will join it, without awaiting the conversion of the Communist nations to the Western versions of jurisprudence and political philosophy.

The first step, of course is for the United States Senate to repeal the damaging reservation it attached to American adherence in 1945 to the Statute of the International Court of Justice, specifically the article reserving to the United States the determination of whether or not a dispute is within its domestic jurisdiction, a decision that the Court would otherwise make. As a consequence of the American example, eight countries – Mexico, France, Liberia, South Africa, India, Pakistan, Britain, and the Sudan – followed suit. The number of acceptances of the Court's compulsory jurisdiction declined to forty out of eighty-four nominal parties to its statute, and the result has been that the present Court enjoys less stature in the world than even its predecessor before the war.

India, Britain, and France have reconsidered and dropped their self-judging reservations. The abrogation by the United States of its reservation is an indispensable step toward pointing the way to more orderly methods of settling international differences. This act would furnish a new basis for action, which should be followed without losing the momentum of the act itself.

The United States should undertake the formation now of a legal community consisting of those nations willing to live under its rules. Such a community would not be limited to any one region or continent, and it would be open to all nations willing to accede. Within this legal community all legal disputes of the nature contemplated by Article 36 [3] of the Statute of the International Court of Justice would be recognized, without reservations, as coming within the jurisdiction of international jurisprudence. This is the obligation nations assume when they accede to the optional clause of the Statute of the Court, but in the light of the progressive deterioration of this obligation in the recent past, a fresh beginning is needed.

The U.N. Legal Commission, on call of the General Assembly, should be asked to prepare a new protocol that would make the Court's jurisdiction mutually binding on the signatories thereto.

[3] Interpretation of treaties; questions of international law; the existence of a fact which, if established, would constitute a breach of an international agreement; and the nature and extent of reparations to be made for the breach of an international obligation.

The protocol would address itself both to primary legal disputes and to those aspects of political disputes that are realistically justiciable. In addition, the protocol would bind states to establish bilateral or other arbitration tribunals and to arbitrate claims and disputes that might arise out of treaties drafted in the future. It would also include a fresh appraisal of the need for regional or other sub-bodies of the International Court, which were not needed up to now because of the paucity of Court business but conceivably might be needed in the future if enough nations followed this new lead. The United States should indicate its willingness to be the first signatory of the protocol.

If other nations initially were cautious about a new commitment of this sort, it would not be a reason for abandoning the effort. The forty or so nations whose declarations regarding compulsory jurisdiction are operative — with or without reservations — constitute the basic membership of a legal community. A limited legal order encompassing those countries can be established now. Other nations ready for more enlightened patterns of relationships — and there are obviously some — would be offered a concrete means of taking action instead of continuing to be dragged down to the level of the most narrowly nationalistic or isolationist.

In order that countries not members of the United Nations — Switzerland and the small principalities of Europe, as well as semiautonomous territories — might also accede anew, the protocol would be negotiated and drafted at a plenipotentiary conference called by the United Nations but of an *ad hoc* nature. The protocol would come into force with respect to any pair of states as soon as those states had ratified the protocol by their own constitutional means.

If the Russians — and Chinese — did not come into such a limited community for another fifty years, we would still have provided a new beginning for a more lawful world with respect to legal disputes, the adjudication of which would be in no way dependent on agreement with the Communist states. Under this proposal the continued antisocial international behavior of the Communist nations would no longer serve as an excuse for the almost-automatic rejection of legal methods among non-Communist nations. Indeed, the position of the Soviet Union would be quite irrelevant. In no way threatened by our proposal, it would be hard put to attack it on plausible grounds (although, once aware that the United States was actually taking a concrete step toward its own variety of world order, the Soviet Union would doubtless appreciate the scope of the challenge).

Such a proposal should commend itself to the American public and to the Senate, which, apart from abrogating the American reservation, must ratify the proposed commitment. The crucial point is that such a step binds the United States only with respect to states that equally bind themselves. So long as the rule of law is limited to those states that agree in advance to live within it, and so long as it actually only affects a limited sector of their international relationships, the safety and security of participating nations remain free of any jeopardy.

The positive argument is even more compelling. In designing new patterns of international behavior that nations will be prepared not just to applaud but to act upon, nothing will take the place of example and leadership. The Western-oriented nations, by acting decisively and courageously, can give content and reality, however modest, to their version of the proper course of history and the shape of the political future. The United States, once freed of the self-imposed incubus of the Senate reservation, can apply its influence to encouraging other nations to follow suit, not least of all the Communist nations at such time as they cease to repudiate the existing rules of the game and finally decide that they can live and prosper within the kind of mutually tolerant legal and political framework toward which we should now be bending our efforts.

A Perspective

Probably nothing is more important in determining the role of the United Nations on the world political stage than the nature of the U.N. image that leading statesmen hold in their minds. Whether or not those images are accurate or even rational, they define in broad terms national attitudes toward the United Nations. Moreover the process is a reciprocal one, with national attitudes in their turn affecting the prospects of the world organization. Of all its members, the United States has for obvious reasons had the greatest influence in shaping the organization as it is today; for less obvious reasons the United States has had perhaps the greatest difficulty among the principal members in defining its national attitude toward the United Nations in terms of a coherent and integrated strategy.

For many Americans the story of the United Nations has had three parts: early hopes and dreams, rapid disillusionment, and eventual relegation to that cherished but quiescent role assigned to unattainable moral purposes. With the special poignancy with which men react to illusions that never quite materialize, the hopes nurtured in 1945 for One World and for wholehearted international cooperation have been repudiated by those who woke from the dream, and clung to by those who believed that the reality rather than the dream was at fault. The issue between the two attitudes has continued to be success or failure measured in terms of the original vision; meanwhile a number of important things have happened to change the very nature of the problem.

The meaning of the strategic issues confronting the United States and the West have become far more explicit than they were in 1945. The alternatives realistically available to deal with these issues have, in turn, become increasingly well defined. Simultaneously, the United Nations, profoundly influenced by external forces, has itself undergone organic growth, acquiring qualities of uniqueness and individuality according to its own laws of internal development.

It now becomes not only possible but essential to redefine the touchstone in terms of which an American strategic doctrine for the role of the United Nations is formulated. The vision with which we created the United Nations perhaps asked too much of both men and their institutions; it needs to be brought into new focus and related to what we are, what we have, and what we must do from here on. There can surely be no argument with the proposition that the U.N. Charter stands, as Dean Rusk has often said, as an eloquent statement of the kind of world this country is essentially striving for. American long-term goals coincide exactly with the intention stated in the Preamble:

> to establish conditions under which justice and respect for the obligations arising from treaties and other sources of international law can be maintained.

But any estimate of the potential role of the United Nations in the years ahead necessarily takes its cue not only from the original premises of the institution itself, but also and above all from a realistic concept of the United Nations as it is today. It is this concept that must be related to the dictates of the national strategic problem.

The great tasks of national strategy — deterrence of general war, a *modus vivendi* with the Soviet Union, the education of China, and safeguarded arms-control agreements — represent a proper first claim upon national resources. To succeed in them, the United States is utilizing the entire range of instrumentalities

— diplomatic, military, economic, and psychological — that are available to it. These tasks, seen in the large, have been essentially beyond the reach of the United Nations except in marginal terms.

But in reality, as our classification of national goals indicates, these massive problem areas are not the vast and undifferentiated wholes that rhetoric makes them seem. Each is composed of many smaller parts, some entirely national or bilateral in significance, but others revealing important opportunities for international institutions such as the United Nations to contribute to their solution.

Perhaps what emerge most clearly from our analysis are the possibilities of action through the United Nations for attacking significant segments of the short-term problems. It is not difficult to demonstrate that U.N. neutral forces and third-party presences can fill a serious gap in purely American or Western capabilities, minimizing the dangers in the use of force while discouraging military or subversive takeovers and preventing the deterrent situation from being undercut by irresponsible men. With a more consistent role, the United Nations can take purposeful preventive actions, help to damp down local conflicts, and dispense a crude form of international justice sufficient to enable peaceful change to take place. This fact alone lends urgency to the task of finding new modalities for deciding upon and financing peacekeeping actions.

In the light of the overall strategic problem, the United Nations is secondary to other instrumentalities, both national and collective, in meeting the basic short-run issues of survival and security. But even here, when measured against the specific goals of American foreign policy, the U.N. reveals modest possibilities for maximizing the qualities about it that are unique — its inclusion of neutral nations, its capacity to act as the indispensable third party, and the larger symbolism communicated by the presence of its physical agencies.

When we lift our eyes from the short term, the most striking fact about contemporary history is the acceleration of the processes of change. Once we grasp the scope and drama of those processes, a different perspective begins to emerge regarding the connection between the short run and the middle and more distant future — and, by the same token, regarding the potential uses of the United Nations. Because the process is dynamic and not static, we may accept the present limiting realities of the role of the United Nations without letting these continue to determine the ultimate limits of policy actions open to the United States.

The processes of change with the greatest capacity to affect the contours of world politics are those taking place in the underdeveloped countries and in Soviet society. These have important implications for the United Nations as an institution linking East with West and North with South. In Western-Soviet relations, assuming as we must that the process of deterrence continues to discourage great risk-taking, there will open up possibilities of limiting and regulating armaments as both sides come to perceive common interests that are still not mutually explicit; from this tangible expression of common interest, as well as from the common interests arising out of scientific and technological transformations, can flow unforeseeable tasks for the United Nations. In the area of revolutionary nationalism, the process of modernization and development in the underdeveloped countries is by definition a process of nation-building and institution-building in which the United Nations can play a crucial role.

The dynamics of change thus governs strategy itself; a strategic doctrine for the United Nations, if it is to serve us adequately, must be dynamic and not static. Forces of change are at work that organically connect the short range with the long range; national strategy that persists in keeping them in separate compartments — the one representing today's ineluctable reality, the other merely tomorrow's idle dream — has an unpromising future.

What happens during these historical transformations can profoundly reshape history. A false step in the process of seeking Soviet-American *rapprochement* might jeopardize the chances for peace; the way in which the modernization process is or is not steered into wholesome and constructive channels can reorder the strategic map; and what happens now to enhance the power and clarity of the ideological forces at issue in the world can give a decisive advantage to the value system preferred and propagated by one or the other of them.

If the political configurations that emerge from the present conflict are to reflect the value system preferred and practiced by the ideological force representing freedom rather than coercion, national strategy must encompass a far larger enterprise than the tactics of maneuvering safely through short-term crises. Granting every major obstacle to Western diplomacy in this era, in and out of the United Nations, the most important thing of all is not to take them as permanent, as insurmountable, or as excuses for a policy of retreat, withdrawal, or despair.

Conceived in this broader perspective, the United Nations can even now open certain opportunities to the United States and the West to influence a larger area of international affairs, and to help accelerate the growth of a broader consensus and consequently a broader world community.

But for every opportunity there is a danger. A valid assessment can be made only by balancing the national interest against the aggregate of assets and liabilities, and separating the possible from the impossible.

Today it is not possible to assume a situation of harmonious and trustful collaboration between the Soviet Union and the United States, let alone between the United States and China. But it is possible to focus intensely on the common interests that exist or might be brought into being, and to study attentively the possibilities offered by the only political institution joining the two for making those interests concrete and giving them form and operative meaning.

It is not possible to rely on the automatic or inevitable dedication of the developing countries to the values of political democracy and economic liberalism, or for the United States to avoid some of the political consequences of being greatly outnumbered in the United Nations by a solid bloc of newly independent states. But it is possible to utilize the opportunities offered by their presence in the United Nations, and by their political attachment to it, as a means of identifying our interests with theirs. It is possible to apply the institutional resources of the United Nations for constructively influencing their internal development and international maturity, without too much concern about who is winning the popularity contests at any given moment.

It has not been possible thus far to execute a policy that recognizes the reality of the United Nations — that it is not at all the privileged club of like-minded states we have insisted it to be, but a world forum in which virtually all nations are represented or soon will be. On any rational grounds we ought to insist that U.N. membership be regarded as a mandatory obligation of all states, with no one permitted to remain unaccountable and free of the obligations other governments have assumed. The seating of Communist China can be seen as an adjustment to reality—and to an even more turbulent United Nations. But China has not been the only case that reduces the U.N. claim to be universally representative; the divided states of Germany, Korea, and Vietnam are also on the outside.

Planning could now begin to consider whether, for example, a United Nations including both Germanies could not make a contribution toward moving us ahead toward an ultimate German settlement (bearing in mind the possible virtue in having put the Vietnam matter before the United Nations a decade earlier, and the likelihood that from the American standpoint the results could not have been much worse).

Finally, it is not possible to wish into existence a world in which the forces of extreme nationalism yield constantly to the larger interests of mankind. But it is possible to view extreme nationalism as a malignant disorder of a heroic epoch, and nationalism in its benign form as the zealous guardian of individual liberties and the uniqueness of diverse cultures. National sentiment is proving to be the undoing of the erstwhile Communist empire, and the United States must perceive the value of continued separate membership in international organizations and other means of sustaining the identity of states held in thrall.

It is possible to sharpen the utility of the United Nations as an agency for lessening—and, in this sense, civilizing—the virulence of self-centered nationalism by using it to give greater encouragement to the parallel trend toward consolidation and integration, and by international activities, programs, and institutions that transcend the concerns of individual nations and reflect a common interest, however limited to start with. When we falsely postulate a consensus where none exists, we risk perpetual failure and disillusionment; but where there is a legitimate prospect of a genuine community of interests around a specific — rather than an abstract — need, we have every cause to move, and move vigorously. If the communities of interest are less than universal in scope and size, they need not fragment the larger edifice so long as they are fostered within the framework of the United Nations.

In sum, even measured against its realistic limits, the United Nations still represents an opportunity for the United States and the West. It could become a potential danger to American interests if national strategy is passive in the face of the strong incoming tides of political movement and change. It could become a danger if the Western powers misinterpret their larger destiny and shrink to the stature of a bitterly embattled minority, hopelessly out of tune with history. It could become a danger if communism and state socialism appear to offer the only available organizing principle for new societies. But it also furnishes an equivalent opportunity for supporting and reinforcing a dynamic Western view of the future trends of political life. For all that it is a noisy and often ineffective bazaar for everyday international relationships, the United Nations is a symbol of the kind of world society in which American values and concepts of political relations would best flourish — including the values of pluralism, of individuality, and of home rule.

With all its imperfections, the United Nations typifies in embryo that order which we want to see emerge beyond the cold war between East and West, and the civil wars between North and South. It symbolizes the sweep of our own vision of a more perfect union, and it challenges anew our capacity to make plans befitting that vision and our will to transform those plans into reality.

APPENDIX

The Mechanics of U.S. Participation in the United Nations (Revised)

American sponsorship of and active participation in the United Nations during and after World War II represented a radical departure from the past. Isolationism, if not dead, was dying fast. The United States had to create a revised set of attitudes toward the rest of the world; and it had to improvise an understanding of its important role in the new organization. This book has attempted to suggest ways of refreshing and renewing that understanding in the light of more than two decades of experience and of changed conditions and needs.

The historic break with the American past symbolized by membership in the United Nations was inevitably reflected in the machinery employed to conduct the nation's foreign relations. Here, too, some radical departures from the past were needed. What follows is a thumbnail sketch of how the machinery for this unprecedented American diplomatic responsibility was created, used, sometimes abused, and ultimately assimilated into the larger bureaucratic structure of American government.

The first postwar unit of the State Department devoted to the preparation and execution of U.S. policy in the United Nations was the Office of Special Political Affairs (S.P.A.), established January 15, 1944. Parallel to, and technically equal with, the geographic offices, it continued for a time to report to a Special Assistant to the Secretary of State, Leo Pasvolsky. With Mr. Pasvolsky's departure in March 1946, the Office of Special Political Affairs remained, still technically speaking, on a par with the four geographic offices but without representation at the assistant secretary level.

When the geographic offices became "bureaus" on October 3, 1949, so did the former S.P.A. (which on January 21, 1948, had been rechristened the Office of United Nations Affairs). The Hoover Commission report of February 1949 recommended endowing all *five* [1] bureaus with assistant secretaries – the five assistant secretaries "at the action level." References at that time were to "five operating vice-presidents." The only distinction was reflected in the injunction that the Bureau of U.N. Affairs should normally secure substantive area policy guidance from the appropriate regional bureau – which it does.

Functions were added to the Bureau from elsewhere in the Department; for example, in 1948 and 1949, the narcotics control, international health, and social welfare interests from the now disbanded Division of International Labor, Health, and Social Affairs. The Division of International Conferences was acquired on April 1, 1949 from the administrative area of the Department.

On August 25, 1954 the name of the Bureau was changed from U.N. Affairs to International Organization Affairs (I.O.). There were sound reasons for the change, chiefly the Bureau's responsibility for many aspects of U.S. participation not only in the United Nations but in other international organizations as well. I.O. carries the primary "backstopping" responsibility for U.S. participation in the United Nations. It also carries limited (administrative and budget) responsibilities for this country's participation in the U.N. family of Specialized Agencies, in the General Agreement on Tariff and Trade (G.A.T.T.), the Organization of Economic Cooperation and Development (O.E.C.D.), Organization of American States (O.A.S.), International Atomic Energy Agency (I.A.E.A.), intergovernmental refugee agencies, South Pacific Commission, and others. (It does not however

[1] Now seven: the five regional bureaus, the Bureau of International Organization Affairs (formerly U.N. Affairs), and the Bureau of Economic Affairs.

handle any matters before some other international organizations in which the United States does not participate directly, such as the European Community bodies, Latin American and European Free Trade Associations, Central American Common Market, and so on.) The change of name was also made with the tacit acknowledgment that the new label would not inflame quite so many members of Congress who were at that time disenchanted with the United Nations.

Many of the Bureau's officers were recruited during the war to assist in the preparations for postwar organization, preparations that were largely of a research nature. The roster of officers on this staff prior to 1946 reveals some names now familiar outside the Department as professors, college presidents, and research directors. Others stayed on after coming in from the academic world, or at any rate from other than the regular service, and for some years were keenly aware that as a group they were often regarded, particularly by the more traditionally-minded in the geographic bureaus, as "dilettantes" of diplomacy, "intellectuals," even "visionaries" – at any rate, not quite members of the "in-group." This reputation has stuck even though the Bureau is now essentially staffed in the same pattern as the other Bureaus.

Such distinctions were magnified because the vast majority of officers in U.N. Affairs were for almost a decade members of the Department's civil service, while most of the key officers of the geographic bureaus were Foreign Service officers. New integration legislation, signed by the President in August 1954, changed all that. A steady flow of replacements began to stream into the Bureau from field duty. The long-term effect of this change has been salutary both in terms of the diversity of experience it offers former civil service personnel and career Foreign Service officers, and in terms of the needful institutional amalgamation and acceptance of the U.N. segment of our foreign affairs machinery and policies.

In the years since 1944 the United States has built up what is unquestionably the most elaborate policy-making and policy-executing structure of any of the members of the United Nations. At the top of the chain of command of that structure is, of course, the President. The President is responsible for the formulation, execution, and coordination of foreign policies. As chief executive, as commander in chief, and as chairman of the National Security Council, he presides over the process of defining U.S. objectives in the world and coordinating activities to achieve those objects.

In directing U.S. participation in international organizations the President under his constitutional authority determines policy and designates representatives and agencies for its execution.

The Secretary of State is principal adviser to the President in the determination and execution of U.S. foreign policy and is charged with the responsibility for all the activities of the State Department. In directing U.S. relations with international organizations, he performs his functions in the same fashion as he does in all fields of international relations.

The National Security Council also helps the President as prescribed by statute and acts on major policy problems arising in the United Nations in the same way as on other foreign policy issues.

The way in which the N.S.C. is used has varied with Presidential styles. President Eisenhower relied heavily on the staff machinery it represented. President Kennedy used it little, preferring personal direction and ad hoc task forces (such as the so-called "Executive Committee" that functioned during the Cuban missile crisis in 1962). President Johnson uses the Council as a high-level discussion group to bring forward opinions, but not as a decision-making body.

The Assistant Secretary of State for International Organization Affairs is one of the seven assistant secretaries with action responsibilities who, in the words of the Hoover Commission, have "responsibility for decisions within clearly defined limits" and "serve as focal points of contact between the Department and the overseas and international organization missions in both substantive and administrative matters." The Hoover Commission described the Assistant Secretary for International Organization Affairs as "in charge of relationships with international organizations, including the United Nations and its affiliated organizations" and as "the channel for instructions to and from United States representatives and delegations at the United Nations" as well as to certain other international organizations and conferences.

The Assistant Secretary for International Organization Affairs acts as the "desk," or departmental headquarters office, for the U.S. Representative to the United Nations and U.S. delegates to other U.N. agencies (and to some non-U.N. bodies). He ensures that these representatives of the United States follow national policy.

The U.S. Representative to the United Nations is, as prescribed by Executive Order 10108,[2] the chief of the United States mission to the United Nations (U.S.U.N.) and a Member of the President's Cabinet. The mission includes other U.S. representatives and deputy representatives (i.e., those serving in the U.N. Economic and Social Council and its commissions, the Trusteeship Council, Disarmament Commission, Military Staff Committee, etc.) and the deputy representative on the Security Council. There is also a second deputy for the Security Council.

The U.S. Representative coordinates "the activities of the Mission in carrying out the instructions of the President transmitted either by the Secretary of State or by other means of transmission as directed by the President." Thus he is responsible for directing U.S. activities at U.N. headquarters, administers the U.S. mission, is the chief U.S. representative in the U.N. Security Council, chairman of the U.S. delegation to the General Assembly (except when the Secretary of State is present), representative *ex officio* and principal U.S. spokesman in any U.S. body at the U.N. headquarters, and principal U.S. negotiator with the U.N. Secretariat and representatives in New York of other member governments.

The U.S. mission to the United Nations, although unique in many ways, is comparable to a major U.S. embassy abroad in terms of its normal working relation with the State Department. Just as the Bureau of European Affairs is the home desk for our London Embassy, so the Bureau of International Organization Affairs is the home desk for the U.S. mission to the United Nations. U.S. ambassadors in both cases are appointed by and responsible to the President. The appropriate assistant secretary of state, acting for the Secretary, is in both cases responsible for ensuring that they are instructed and advised, that such instructions and advice represent the coordinated views of the government (including where necessary the decisions of the Secretary

[2] 15 Fed. Reg. 757.

and the President), and for receiving the information they report and seeing that it is used in Washington. Under special circumstances, the head of the U.S. mission, like other ambassadors, occasionally receives his instructions directly from the Secretary of State or the President. The head of the U.S. mission takes an active part in the formulation of U.S. policy and tactics both prior to and during U.N. meetings and recommends changes in policies if, in his opinion, conditions require them.

The basic functions of the U.S. representative to the United Nations were stated by the so-called U.N. Participation Act of 1945, as amended in 1949,[3] and by President Truman's Executive Orders of 1947 and 1950.[4] Warren R. Austin was the U.S. Representative at the time. Henry Cabot Lodge succeeded him in 1953. Both men had been influential Republican senators. But there was one important difference: Lodge was also made a member of the President's Cabinet.

President Kennedy followed this pattern by naming a defeated Presidential candidate with world-wide stature – Adlai E. Stevenson. On the latter's death President Johnson asked Supreme Court Justice Arthur J. Goldberg to step down and take the post. Like Lodge, they were members of the Cabinet.

Given personalities of this stature, even though the formal responsibilities of the representative did not change, his domestic political role was sharply upgraded, particularly by contrast with his nominal "home desk" in the person of the Assistant Secretary for International Organization Affairs.

There was one immediate effect in the General Assembly delegation. The Department's practice during the years 1946–1953 had been to furnish the U.S. Representative each fall with what was in effect a ready-made Assembly delegation, cooperatively planned, to be sure, but characteristically "chief-of-staffed" by senior officers of the Bureau. This changed in 1953, and the directing staff positions in the Assembly delegation became fixed to the permanent mission. This practice remains, but since the directing staff members are Foreign Service officers now, often

[3] Respectively, Public Laws 264, 79th Congress, and 341, 81st Congress.
[4] Executive Order 9844 of April 28, 1947, amended by Executive Order 10108 of February 19, 1950.

from the Bureau, the procedure of selecting and briefing delegations in fact remains cooperative.

Important policy initiatives are sometimes pressed on Washington by the U.S. mission, and these are taken seriously. But, the shifts of prestige to New York have not affected national policy in basic ways. The U.S. delegation to the United Nations is an instructed delegation not only in the technical sense but in a real sense as well. Perhaps the sharpest reminder of where the levers of power are in the U.S. government was furnished during the succession of postwar crises such as Korea, Suez, Congo, and Dominican Republic. During these crises the permanent staff of the U.S. mission in New York functioned tirelessly and skillfully as servants and executors of policy made by the hour in Washington. Instantaneous contacts by phone, cable, radio and more recent electronic devices allow for closer contacts between Washington and N.Y.

In the policy-making echelons of the U.S. government, the key figure regarding U.N. participation is the Assistant Secretary of State for International Organization Affairs. This presidential appointee must be able to maintain a relation of mutual confidence and respect with two personages central in our government who both outrank him: the Secretary of State and the U.S. Representative to the United Nations. If these relations break down, the Assistant Secretary's usefulness is, of course, critically impaired.

Protocol places a handicap on the Assistant Secretary of State in carrying out his duties. The U.S. Representative, particularly when he sits as a member of the President's Cabinet, outranks the Assistant Secretary through whom he normally receives his instructions. (A problem which some anticipated but that does not seem to have arisen concerns the ambiguity of the U.S. Representative's role vis-à-vis his superior, the Secretary of State – both Cabinet-level officials.) All U.S. ambassadors, of course, enjoy nominal relations with the President that transcend, again nominally, their obligations to the Secretary of State's deputies. These deputies, however, are clearly in a command position, both over the cables and in their functions as regional chiefs of mission meetings, over which a regional assistant secretary generally presides.

One consequence of the Secretary of State's confidence in the assistant secretary charged with U.N. affairs has been the preoccupation of the latter with political, as opposed to economic, social, trusteeship, technical, and other facets of his responsibilities. The reasons for this preoccupation are several. The most obvious is that great political crises have dominated the foreign policy scene over the last decade. Another basic institutional factor has resulted from the dominantly political interests and proclivities of the Secretaries of State.

Nonetheless, the other problems claim the assistant secretaries' attention and have to be dealt with. The utilization of deputy assistant secretaries has from time to time resulted in a fairly sharp division of responsibility below the assistant secretary level. This also conforms to the administrative structure of the Bureau, which is divided in administration, political affairs, economic and social affairs, international conferences, and international administration. In recent times one deputy served across the board, a second followed the economic and social work of the Bureau, and the third oversaw the administrative decisions and often certain specialized interests, such as inter-American organization matters and, at times, refugee problems. Special assistants are also used to follow certain highly technical subjects for the Assistant Secretary.

Since the objective of U.S. participation in the United Nations is to realize this nation's role and forward its interests in multilateral diplomatic bodies, there are two objects in organizing and disciplining the government machinery for participating in this process: (1) to ensure that the United States speaks with one voice on issues arising in the international forums, and (2) to ensure that this voice represents the best judgment and skill that can be brought to bear on problems of foreign policy.

U.S. participation in international organizations works like a funnel. At one end, experts in government agencies recommend policies for the United States to adopt in the United Nations on a wide variety of topics. At the other end, U.S. spokesmen in international forums are expected to state these policies with clarity and authority. This presents the government with a formidable task of coordination.

The stages at which the coordination process comes to light are the instruction of U.S. delegates and representatives and the expression by them of the official policies and views of the United States at meetings of international organizations. In addition to the permanent mission in New York, the United States has permanent missions at the International Civil Aviation Organization in Montreal, at the International Atomic Energy Agency in Vienna, and in Geneva for liaison with the U.N. European Office and the several specialized agencies located there. There are also U.S. liaison officers for F.A.O. at Rome, for U.N.E.S.C.O. at Paris, for the Economic Commission for Latin America (E.C.L.A.) at Santiago, and for the Economic Commission for Asia and the Far East (E.C.A.F.E.) at Bangkok.

The central point for the coordination necessary in this funneling process is the Bureau of International Organization Affairs, which through its offices of U.N. Political and Security Affairs, International Economic and Social Affairs, International Administration, and International Conferences furnishes staff support to the U.S. Representative to the United Nations and to U.S. delegates to other U.N. agencies and some non-U.N. bodies. It performs a number of functions requiring special expertise, on which the rest of the Department relies:

(1) It coordinates the policy views and technical requirements originating in other parts of the Department and other agencies, so that the U.S. representatives in international organizations can be sure they are always stating consistent and unified U.S. positions.

(2) It develops U.S. policy on questions that are peculiarly multilateral in nature, that cut across the bilateral functions of the geographic units and the specialized subject units in other agencies, and that no other office is staffed to handle. Examples of these questions are peacekeeping preparations, parliamentary tactics that have been proved best by experience in specific U.N. agencies, international secretariat problems, problems of non-self-governing territories, world health, social welfare, narcotics, human rights, interpretation of the articles of the U.N. Charter, international budgets, and the U.N. aspects of disarmament and arms control, outer space, and other new concerns.

(3) It assembles in one unit the knowledge and experience the United States has built up in the field of multilateral diplomacy so that the government can most efficiently prepare itself to uphold its interests in international organizations. This means chiefly the political and organizational work of the U.N. bodies — questions of constitutions, credentials, elections, budgets; secretariat organization and practices, agenda and procedural problems, and the relation of other multilateral bodies to the United Nations.

A considerable part of the coordinating is done through informal day-to-day contacts between the Bureau's desk officers and "subject specialists" elsewhere in the Department or other government agencies. Often this is the only way in which deadlines can be met at U.N. meetings or prompt action taken to deal with imminent votes or sudden shifts in position by other countries. In this way also the countless routine matters that arise in international organization operations can be resolved with a minimum of formal clearance.

The Office of International Conferences screens invitations to international conferences, recommends as to U.S. participation, negotiates throughout the government the makeup of the U.S. delegations, assists (when appropriate) with preparations of U.S. positions, allocates funds, makes travel and housing arrangements, and (in meetings away from the U.N. headquarters) furnishes the service staff of the delegation, and (after the meeting) makes sure that responsibilities for official reports, documents, and other items are properly discharged.

In the political field, when there are indications that a political problem will come before the United Nations, a team is formed. The director of the Office of U.N. Political and Security Affairs usually chairs the group, prepares papers for its consideration, and drafts instructions for the U.S. Representative. His responsibility is to ensure that the views of all interested offices are secured and that any information required is obtained from Department and overseas files. He furnishes the knowledge of the U.N. Charter considerations, precedents in U.N. bodies, past performances of delegations and delegates, voting probabilities, and the operation of regional and special-interest blocs in the United Nations. Frequently senior officers of the Bureau will serve as principal advisers to the U.S. Representative during U.N. meetings when the political problem is considered.

Also on the team are U.S. representatives from the affected geographic areas, who furnish information as to the general U.S. policies toward the countries in question. These policies, however, must be reconciled where, for example, one desk officer is speaking of U.S. interests with respect to Portugal and Britain, another regarding our interests in Zambia and another speaking for the Bureau of Economic Affairs, as in the Rhodesian case in the General Assembly. In addition, they furnish knowledge of geographic factors, national idiosyncrasies, and official personalities; often they participate in General Assembly or Security Council sessions as political liaison officers with delegates from countries in their areas. To harmonize the work of the geographic and economic bureaus with that of the Bureau of International Organization Affairs, each normally has a full-time adviser on U.N. affairs, who collaborates with officers of the Bureau on relevant problems affecting the region.

These teams often also include representatives of the legal adviser's office as well as the public affairs, economic, and research officers. The member from the Office of U.N. Political and Security Affairs often consults informally on military aspects of the cases with officers in the Defense Department. The team members turn to their respective assistant secretaries, and these in turn consult higher echelons, as required, before approving U.S. positions. Many political issues in the United Nations require decisions by the Secretary of State to reconcile differing opinions among assistant secretaries, and in some cases the President to reconcile differing opinion among cabinet members. Either the Bureau of International Organization Affairs or the geographic offices undertake consultation with appropriate U.S. missions abroad and foreign envoys in Washington.

A similar process takes place within the Department on economic and social questions before the United Nations and specialized agencies. Since the clearance process here involves not only many different units within the State Department but also other government agencies, a group of interdepartmental committees furnishes the chief means of coordination. Unless another agency clearly has a predominant interest (for example, the Department of Agriculture, for F.A.O.), the State Department furnishes the chairman or secretary of the committees. Within the State Department, the Bureau usually provides either or both.

Coordination of foreign policy activities by the Department was importantly formalized by President Johnson's announcement on March 4, 1966 to the effect that the Secretary of State, as his agent, would assume responsibility to the full extent permitted by law for the overall direction, coordination and supervision of interdepartmental activities of the United States Government overseas.[5] Up to then, the Secretary of State had been in theory the supreme coordinator of the United States Government departments and agencies. This supplied him with specific and formal overall directive authority from the President. This authority has been put into effect by making the Under Secretary chief of a new committee called the "Senior Interdepartmental Group." The State Department's geographic bureaus are all represented on this Senior Interdepartmental Group. For some inexplicable reason, I.O. was not specifically mentioned, but in practice this has not reduced I.O.'s effectiveness as a coordinator of U.S. Governmental positions vis-à-vis the United Nations. Its role was bolstered on March 15, 1966 by a Presidential Memorandum emphasizing the importance of the United Nations and its agencies to the United States.[6]

[5] Foreign Affairs Manual Circular #385, March 4, 1966.

[6] *Department of State Bulletin,* Vol. LIV, No. 1398, April 11, 1966, pp. 576–578.

Index